HISTORY AS MYSTERY

BOOKS BY MICHAEL PARENTI

America Besieged (1998)
Blackshirts and Reds: Rational Fascism and the Overthrow of
    Communism (1997)
Dirty Truths (1996)
Against Empire (1995)
Democracy for the Few (1974, 1977, 1980, 1983, 1988, 1995)
Land of Idols: Political Mythology in America (1994)
Inventing Reality: The Politics of News Media (1986, 1993)
Make-Believe Media: The Politics of Entertainment (1992)
The Sword and the Dollar (1989)
Power and the Powerless (1978)
Ethnic and Political Attitudes (1975)
Trends and Tragedies in American Foreign Policy (1971)
The Anti-Communist Impulse (1969)

HISTORY AS MYSTERY

MICHAEL PARENTI

CITY LIGHTS BOOKS
SAN FRANCISCO

Copyright © 1999 by Michael Parenti
All Rights Reserved
10 9 8 7 6 5 4

Cover design: John Miller, Big Fish
Book design: Nancy J. Peters
Typography: Harvest Graphics

Library of Congress Cataloging-in-Publication Data

Parenti, Michael, 1933–
    History as mystery / by Michael Parenti.
       p.   cm.
    Includes bibliographical references.
    ISBN 0-87286-357-3 (pbk.). — ISBN 0-87286-364-6 (cloth)
    1. Historiography.   2. History—Errors, inventions, etc.
  I. Title.
  D13.P35   1999
  907'.2—dc21   99-34698
                                                CIP

Visit our website: www.citylights.com

CITY LIGHTS BOOKS are edited by Lawrence Ferlinghetti and Nancy
J. Peters and published at the City Lights Bookstore, 261 Columbus
Avenue, San Francisco, CA 94133.

ACKNOWLEDGMENTS

Gary Aguilar, Charles Briody, Lauren Coodley, Charlotte Dennett, Elazar Friedman, Leonard Pitt, Sally Soriano, Vincent Sauvé, and my son Christian Parenti furnished me with pertinent materials, as did the reference staff at the Berkeley (California) Public Library.

Peggy Karp critiqued the manuscript and also provided valuable research assistance for chapter six. Nancy J. Peters also did a critical reading of these pages. And Beth Garber and Holly Earl rendered additional valuable service. June Felter took the photograph of me that appears on the book cover (as part of her Men In Hats series). I owe all these fine people an expression of gratitude.

To the memory of Judi Bari

Quia induit me vestimentis salutis
et indumento justitiae circumdedit me

For he has adorned me in salvation
And wrapped me in a mantle of Justice

In my own country
amnesia is the norm,
the schools teach us
to unremember from birth,
the slave taking, the risings up,
the songs of resistance,
the first May first,
our martyrs from Haymarket
to Attica to the redwoods of California
ripped whole from our hearts,
erased from official memory . . .

—John Ross, "Against Amnesia"

CONTENTS

PROLOGUE:
AGAINST THE MAINSTREAM

The writing of history, Voltaire believed, should be one form
of battle in the age-old war for our intellectual emancipation. Too often, however, history is written and marketed in
such a way as to be anything but liberating. The effect is not to
enlighten but to enforce the existing political orthodoxy. Those
who control the present take great pains to control our understanding of the past. What J. H. Plum calls "the acquisition of
the past by ruling and possessing classes" and the exclusion of
working people "is a widespread phenomenon through
recorded time."[1] Little room is left for an honest picture of how
the common people of history have struggled for a better life, or
how politico-economic elites have ruthlessly pursued a contrary
course, doing whatever necessary to maintain and expand their
wealth and privileges.

Much written history is an ideologically safe commodity. It
might best be called "mainstream history," "orthodox history,"
"conventional history," and even "ruling-class history" because
it presents the dominant perspective of the affluent and influential people who preside over the major institutions of society.
It is the kind of history dished up by textbook authors, mainstream academicians, political leaders, government officials,
and news and entertainment media, a mass miseducation that

begins in childhood and continues throughout life. What we usually are taught "is not 'reality' but a particular version of it,"[2] a version that must pass muster with the powers that be.

"Our sense of the past," writes John Gager, "is created for us largely by history's winners. The voices of the losers, when heard at all, are transmitted through a carefully tuned network of filters."[3] Here I endeavor to deconstruct some of the filters, to show that much of the mainstream history we are commonly taught, the popular version of events that enjoys maximum circulation, is seriously distorted in ways that serve or certainly reflect dominant socio-economic interests.

To challenge all the major misrepresentations of history is an impossible feat for any single book or person. But as Ninon de L'Enclos said when asked if she believed that the martyred St. Denys had walked two miles carrying his head under his arm, "*La distance ne vaut rien. Ce n'est que le premier pas qui coute*" ("The distance means nothing. It is only the first step that counts").[4] By saying this book is a first step, I don't mean to imply that I am the first ever to have striven for a truer rendering of history. Indeed, there are many historians, not all of them dissident revisionists, whose contributions I gratefully draw upon.

Andrew Johnson believed history would set all things right, surely an extraordinary leap of faith even for a U.S. president.[5] On the pages ahead, I attempt to set at least a few things right. This book does *not* offer a popularized version of history. If anything, it does battle against a number of mass-marketed historical misinterpretations that enjoy wide currency today. I try to address the class biases of the history that has been propagated in the wider society and sometimes within academe itself. On these pages the reader will find the *un*popular, marginalized view that violates the acceptable mainstream orthodoxy.

There are inescapable limitations to my effort. For one thing, I am concerned essentially with political history rather than cultural, military, or other specialized varieties, though the boundaries between these subdisciplines are not always clearly fixed, and I do trespass now and then.

Furthermore, I focus mostly on the United States and Europe, both modern and ancient, areas of particular interest to me. Relatively little is offered herein on the histories of Asia, Africa, and Latin America. There is some treatment of women's history and less on the history of people of color in the United States. Earlier works of mine have given substantial attention to both subjects.[6] It is encouraging to note that in recent decades, women's studies and African American studies have burgeoned.[7] Still, we must keep in mind the comment by Dominican sociologist Magaly Pineda: "We women have been the great missing subject of history. We do not have the reference points of our past."[8] The same could be said of Third World peoples in general and—as I try to show on the pages ahead—of all common folk, female and male, at the bottom of the social pyramid.

That I focus on European and U.S. history is not itself indicative of a Eurocentric or American chauvinist perspective. I do not think Europe and the United States are the only regions worthy of serious study; they are just the ones in which I have done the most work. Eurocentrism is a supremacist approach; it applies to those who are invincibly ignorant of non-European history and "less developed" civilizations, and who think that little of note ever happened anywhere outside Europe—until the Europeans got there. Eurocentric history distorts the non-European history it *does* offer, making all sorts of patronizing presumptions about the levels of cultural and political development of Asia, Africa, and the pre-European Western Hemisphere. So eminent a historian as Trevor-Roper offers a perfectly repugnant example:

> It is fashionable to speak today as if . . . historians in the past have paid too much attention to [European history]; as if, nowadays, we should pay less. Undergraduates, seduced as always, by

the changing breath of journalistic fashion, demand that they should be taught the history of black Africa. Perhaps in the future there will be some African history to teach. But at present there is none, or very little: there is only the history of the Europeans in Africa. The rest is largely darkness.

If all history is equal, as some now believe, there is no reason why we should study one section rather than another; for certainly we cannot study it all. Then indeed we may neglect our own history and amuse ourselves with the unrewarding gyrations of barbarous tribes in picturesque but irrelevant corners of the globe.[9]

As for my failure to deal with the rich and complex histories of Asia, Africa, and Latin America, I must plead, along with Ranke, for a division of labor: "For who could apply learned research . . . to the mass of materials already collected without being lost in its immensity?"[10] Ranke wrote that in 1859. Imagine what he might say today. Nonetheless, in the preface to his *Universal History,* he grandiosely claimed to treat "the events of all times and nations." In fact, Ranke's "universal" history is nothing more than a history of the West—which to him was indeed the entire universe. So while he was aware of his limits in handling research materials, he remained predictably unaware of his Eurocentric bias in defining subject areas.[11]

Eurocentrism is as old as antiquity. Some two thousand years before Ranke, historians treated the Mediterranean region, along with parts of central Europe and Asia Minor, as "the world." Thus, in the second century B.C., in his *Histories*—sometimes also entitled *Universal History*—Polybius marveled at how "the Romans succeeded in less than fifty-three years in bringing under their rule almost the whole of the inhabited world."[12]

Many history and political science programs offered in middle and higher education rest on a Eurocentric bias. In the mid-1950s, I taught college-level Comparative Politics courses that dealt exclusively with the modern history of the British, French, and West German political systems, these being considered the only countries besides the United States worthy of consideration. Nearly a half-century later, college courses on World History and World Politics continue to deal almost exclusively with Europe and the United States, with only passing mention of China and Japan, and hardly a word about Africa, the Middle East, Southeast Asia, Central and South America, or Canada, except as objects of European exploration and settlement. Even then, scant attention is alloted to the outrages perpetrated by colonizers over the last five centuries.[13]

Within the confines of European and U.S. history, I pursue themes that range far and wide, from antiquity to modern times, forgoing any attempt at being strictly chronological. When dealing with aspects of the past that are downplayed or distorted by the manufacturers of mainstream history, do I not unavoidably introduce biases of my own? To be sure, there is always that possibility. But the danger of dissident bias is probably nowhere as great as the danger posed by conventional history because readers who approach the dissenting viewpoint after a steady diet of mainstream myths will be alerted to what is different and questionable. Far more insidious and less visible are the notions that fit the dominant ideology so well as to appear unchallengeable.

Heterodoxy always offers a better learning experience than orthodoxy. A dissenting view invites us to test the prevailing explanations and open ourselves to neglected ones. Through this clash of viewpoints we have a better chance of moving toward a closer approximation of historical truth.

Dissidents (or revisionists, as they have been called) are not drifting with the mainstream but swimming against it, struggling against the prevailing range of respectable opinion. They are deprived of what Alvin Gouldner called "the background assumptions," the implicit, unexamined, but commonly embraced notions that invite self-confirming acceptance because of their conformity to what is already accepted as properly true.[14] This established familiarity and unanimity of bias is frequently treated as "objectivity." For this reason, dissidents are constantly having to defend themselves and argue closely from the evidence.

In contrast, orthodoxy can rest on its own unstated axioms and mystifications, remaining heedless of marginalized critics who are denied a means of reaching mass audiences. Orthodoxy promotes its views through the unexamined repetition that comes with monopoly control of the major communication and educational systems. In sum, while dissidents can make mistakes of their own, they are less likely to go unchallenged for it. Not so with orthodoxy. It remains the most insidious form of ideology for it parades the dominant view as the objective one, the only plausible and credible one.

Having noted what this book attempts to do, let me also mention what it does not do. *History as Mystery* is not of the genre that deals with the esoteric mysteries of prehistoric times: unexplained sacred sites, symbolic landscapes, near-forgotten realms, lost civilizations, mysterious ancient monuments, and the like. Such explorations are serious and interesting undertakings, but they are beyond my present effort.[15]

Nor does this book attempt to debunk the more gossipy anecdotes of history. Elsewhere one can read that Paul Revere never made it to Concord but was captured by the British, that George Washington was not a cold prude but liked to drink and dance and fell in love with his best friend's wife, and that Eli Whitney did not really invent the cotton gin. Such revelations are sometimes diverting but they commonly add little to our understanding of politically important historical questions. In any case, they are not the subject of this volume.[16]

On these pages the reader is offered what I call "real history." Rather than debating whether it was Christopher Columbus, Lief Ericson, or Amerigo Vespucci who discovered America, real history argues that the Western Hemisphere was not "discovered" but forcibly invaded in a series of brutal conquests that brought destruction to millions of indigenous inhabitants and hundreds of cultures. Real history deems the "New World" a Eurocentric misnomer, connoting a largely uninhabited place. Well before Columbus's arrival, the Western Hemisphere was home to tens of millions of people in age-old civilizations that were in many respects further advanced and more humane than the Europe of 1492.[17] Such a realization, in turn, invites us to rethink the many dubious claims made about the civilizing impact of European colonization upon the world.

Besides criticizing orthodox history, I attempt some historical investigations of my own. The critic should not only *tell* but *show* how it ought to be done—or at least try to put his or her own critical perceptions to the test of praxis. This I do in chapter six, which at first glance seems to deal with one of those minor and gossipy "who dunnit" questions: Was President Zachary Taylor poisoned? I embarked on that odd inquiry because there was something inherently intriguing about the problems of evidence and investigation raised by the case. Sometimes an event in history wins our attention not solely because of its generalizable significance but because of its inviting singularity. In addition, the Taylor case is a perfect example of how pack journalists and pack historians can settle a controversy by fiat, manufacturing orthodox conclusions out of thin air. The case demonstrates the sloppy and superficial investigative methods of both pathologists and mainstream historians. It also demonstrates how ideological gatekeepers close ranks against any issue that challenges their expertise, or challenges the legitimacy and virtue of our political institutions by suggesting the possibility of foul play in high places.

Other subjects treated herein include the class biases of history textbooks, the way common people have been misrepresented throughout history, and the way the recording of history has been monopolized by the privileged few. I make no attempt at being comprehensive in my coverage. Two whole chapters treat the darker side of Christianity, a subject that usually receives little attention. Additional attention is given to how history is marketed, the systems of suppression and distribution, and how historians are influenced by the class environment in which they work. A final chapter deals with the fallacies of psychopolitics and psychohistory. I treat these somewhat offbeat subjects because I found myself so interested in them and because I found them significant for understanding what history and historiography are about.

This book is written in accordance with scholarly standards but without adherence to the tedious evasions and pretensions of mainstream academia, for my intent is to enlist rather than discourage the interest of lay readers without underestimating their capacity to enjoy informative investigations. From past endeavors I have discovered that it is possible and often most desirable to educate and gratify at the same time. I hope my efforts will help spice the pabulum while demystifying the prevailing orthodoxy.

I also hope that a better understanding of the past will offer revelatory insights into the present—just as our understanding of the present helps us to understand the past. There are those who maintain that past and present cannot inform each other because historic events are so fixed to a specific time and place that they can be understood only in their idiosyncratic context, without reference to larger parallels drawn across different eras. But if every event were unique in every respect—as every event certainly is in *some* respects—then all events would be incomprehensible. Our perceptions would be overwhelmed and exhausted if we were unable to organize reality into identifiable patterns.

It was Lord Acton who once noted that it is not factuality, but the emphasis on the essential, that makes an account historical. Unless we can seek out the essential, in part by exposing the disinformingly unessential, we gain no insight into past or present. Those who say we "cannot make comparisons" seem to forget that comparison is one of the major means by which human understanding develops. If the past cannot be pondered in a comparative way, then there are no lessons to be learned from history. And if so, then there are no lessons to be learned from any human experience, past or present. I hope the pages ahead will demonstrate something to the contrary.

NOTES:

1. J. H. Plumb, *The Death of the Past* (Boston: Houghton Mifflin, 1970), 30.
2. Kenneth Teitelbaum, "Critical Lessons from Our Past: Curricula of Socialist Sunday Schools in the United States," in Michael Apple and Linda Christian-Smith (eds.), *The Politics of the Textbook* (New York and London: Routledge, 1991), 137.
3. John G. Gager, *The Origins of Anti-Semitism: Attitudes Toward Judaism in Pagan and Christian Antiquity* (Oxford: Oxford University Press, 1983), 265.
4. Quoted in George Zabiskie Gray, *The Children's Crusade* (New York: William Morrow, 1972), 44.
5. Gene Smith, *High Crimes and Misdemeanors, The Impeachment and Trial of Andrew Johnson* (New York: McGraw-Hill, 1976), 295.
6. I deal with imperialism's mistreatment of Latin America, Asia, and Africa in *Against Empire* (San Francisco: City Lights Books, 1995); and *The Sword and the Dollar* (New York: St. Martin's Press, 1989). And I treat ethnic and gender oppression in *Land of Idols: Political Mythology in America* (New York: St. Martin's Press, 1994), chapters 9, 10, and 11; *Make-Believe Media: The Politics of Entertainment* (New York: St. Martin's Press, 1992), chapter 8 and passim; and *Democracy for the Few*, 6th edition (New York: St. Martin's Press, 1995), chapters 4, 8, and passim.
7. On women's history, interested readers might consider Meredith Tax, *The Rising of the Women* (New York: Monthly Review Press, 1980); Sheila Rowbotham, *Hidden from History: Rediscovering Women in History from the 17th Century to the Present* (London: Pluto Press, 1973); Elise Boulding, *The Underside of History: A View of Women Through Time*, vol. 2, rev. ed. (Newbury Park: Sage Publications, 1992); Gerda Lerner, *Women and History*, 2 vols. (New York: Oxford University Press, 1986, 1993); Antonia Fraser, *The Weaker Vessel* (New

York: Vintage Books, 1985); Linda Kerber, Alice Kessler-Harris, Kathryn Kish (eds.), *U.S. History as Women's History* (Chapel Hill: University of North Carolina Press, 1995); Claire Goldberg Moses and Heidi Hartmann (eds.), *U.S. Women in Struggle: A Feminist Anthology* (Urbana: University of Illinois, 1995); Rosalind Miles, *The Women's History of the World* (New York: HarperPerennial, 1990); Pauline Schmitt Pantel (ed.), *A History of Women in the West, I. From Ancient Goddesses to Christian Saints* (Cambridge, Mass.: Belknap Press, 1992); Linda Grant DePauw, *Founding Mothers: Women in the Revolutionary Era* (Boston: Houghton Mifflin, 1975); Susan Ware, *Beyond Suffrage: Women in the New Deal* (Cambridge, Mass.: Harvard University Press, 1981); Eleanor Flexner, *Century of Struggle: The Woman's Rights Movement in the United States* (New York: Atheneum, 1971).

On African American women in particular, see Gerda Lerner, *Black Women in White America: A Documentary History* (New York: Vintage, 1973); Angela Davis, *Women, Race and Class* (New York: Random House, 1981); Darlene Clark Hine, Wilma King, Linda Reed, *"We Specialize in the Wholly Impossible": A Reader in Black Women's History* (Brooklyn, N.Y.: Carlson Publishing, 1995); and Shirley Yee, *Black Women Abolitionists, A Study in Activism 1828–1860* (Knoxville: University of Tennessee Press, 1992).

On African American history in general, see Lerone Bennett Jr., *Before the Mayflower: A History of the Negro in America* (Baltimore: Penguin Books, 1966); John Hope Franklin, *From Slavery to Freedom* (New York: Alfred Knopf, 1967); Staughton Lynd, *Class Conflict, Slavery and the United States Constitution* (Indianapolis: Bobbs-Merrill, 1976); Nell Irvin Painter, *The Narrative of Hosea Hudson, His Life as a Negro Communist in the South* (Cambridge, Mass.: Harvard University Press, 1979); William Loren Katz, *Eyewitness: The Negro in American History* (New York: Pitman, 1967); Richard P. Young (ed.), *Roots of Rebellion: The Evolution of Black Politics and Protest Since World War II* (New York: Harper & Row, 1970); John White, *Black Leadership in America 1895–1968* (London and New York: Longman, 1985); Herbert Aptheker (ed.), *A Documentary History of the Negro People in the United States*, 7 vols. (Secaucus, N.J.: Citadel Press, 1989–94 reprint edition); and numerous other works by Herbert Aptheker, James McPherson, W. E. B. Du Bois, Benjamin Quarles, Herbert Gutman, Philip Foner, and Eric Foner.

8. As quoted in Mirta Rodriguez Calderon, "Recovering the History of Women," *CUBA Update*, April/June 1995, 13.

9. Hugh Trevor-Roper, *The Rise of Christian Europe* (New York: Harcourt Brace Jovanovich, 1974), 9.

10. Leopold von Ranke, *History of England, Principally in the Seventeeth Century* (Oxford: Clarendon Press, 1875), I, v.

11. Leopold von Ranke, *Universal History* (New York: Charles Scribner's Sons, 1884).

12. Polybius, *Histories* I.1. This work is available in a 1979 Penguin Classics edition entitled *The Rise of the Roman Empire*. For a discussion of Eurocentrism and imperialism, see Samir Amin, *Eurocentrism* (New York: Monthly Review Press, 1989).

13. I have dealt with the colonization and forced maldevelopment of the Third World in my book *The Sword and the Dollar* and to some extent in *Against Empire*. For other works on that subject, see L. S. Stavrianos, *Global Rift: The Third World Comes of Age* (New York: William Morrow, 1981); William Blum, *Killing Hope: U.S. Global Interventions Since World War II* (Monroe, Me.: Common Courage Press, 1995).

14. Alvin Gouldner, *The Coming Crisis of Western Sociology* (New York: Basic Books, 1970), 29–30 and passim.

15. For such works, the reader might start with Jennifer Westwood (ed.), *The Atlas of Mysterious Places* (New York: Weidenfeld & Nicolson, 1987); and Lionel Casson et al., *Mysteries of the Past* (New York: American Heritage Publishing Co. 1997).

16. The above examples are taken from Richard Shenkman, *Legends, Lies & Cherished Myths of American History* (New York: Harper & Row, 1988); see also Richard Shenkman and Kurt Reiger, *One Night Stands with American History* (New York: Morrow, 1980). To be fair, I should note that along with many lighter topics, Shenkman does treat some important controversies: the use of the atomic bomb against Japan, the warfare perpetrated against Native Americans, and misrepresentions about the role of African Americans in the Reconstruction era.

17. Francis Jennings, *The Invasion of America* (New York: W. W. Norton, 1976); Pierre Clastres, *Society Against the State* (New York: Urizen Books, 1977).

1

HISTORY AS MISEDUCATION

The term "history" refers both to past happenings and to the study of them, both the experiencing of a social process and the recording of it.[1] However, the distinction is not an absolute one. For those who write history help influence the course of events by shaping our understanding of things past and present. Conversely, those who actively participate in a historical event, especially if they occupy elite policy positions, often manipulate the materials needed for documenting that event. In addition, there are some individuals who both make history and write it.

Mainstream Orthodoxy

Among those involved in manufacturing history are political leaders, military commanders, journalists, television producers, government and corporate scribes, clergy, amateur investigators, textbook editors, schoolteachers, retooled fiction writers, and academics. An individual can be both a historian and an active participant in historic events. In antiquity, among those who both engaged in events and recorded them were Polybius, Cicero, Caesar, Sallust, and Dio Cassius. Polybius believed that experience in public affairs was an essential qualification for the historian: "Until that day comes, there will be no respite from the errors that historians will commit."[2] Even if we agree with him that political experience is a necessary qualification, it is hardly a sufficient guarantee against error—and it often invites distortions of its own.[3]

In the first century A.D. Josephus wrote his history of the Jewish uprising against Rome after playing a prominent political and military role in that struggle. And centuries before, there was Thucydides, a military leader who wrote a monumental history of the very Peloponnesian War in which he had participated. The nineteenth century gave us Guizot, Macaulay, Mommsen, Rotteck, and Thiers.[4] It was Thiers who presided over the bloody suppression and mass executions of thousands of revolutionary Parisian Communards.

To any list of historian-cum-political officeholders, or political officeholder-cum-historians, we could add Gibbon, Tocqueville, Theodore Roosevelt, Henry Cabot Lodge, populist leader Tom Watson, and French socialist leader Jean Jaurès, who took time to write a history of the French Revolution.[5] Later on, there were antifascist scholar-politicians like Herman Rauschning and Gaetano Salvemini. In our own day, alas, we must make do with Arthur Schlesinger Jr., Henry Kissinger, and Zbigniew Brzezinski.

Winston Churchill was supposed to have assured his Tory associates, "History will be kind to us, gentlemen, for I plan to write it." With a concern that history be kind to them and with the additional inducement of munificent advances from their publishers, political leaders regularly produce self-serving memoirs whose contributions to historical truth are often parsimonious.

Perhaps the premier example of the politician/historian is Churchill himself. Gordon Lewis sees Churchill as someone who could never quite make up his mind whether he was a historian writing about politics or a politician writing about history.[6] My understanding of Churchill is that he strongly preferred *vita activa* to *vita quieta;* he was above all a political animal whose historiography served to justify his leadership and his worldview.

How his history supported his politics and, more generally, British ruling-class ideology would itself be the subject of an interesting study. Clive Ponting relates how impressed he was by Churchill's study of World War II with its wonderful language and dramatic narrative. But years later, reading through war documents in the Public Record Office, he realized that much of the account had been oversimplified or omitted, and that Churchill's history "despite all its virtues . . . is a politician's memoir designed to relate his version of events and to present the story as he wanted."[7] Churchill portrayed his country as a lonely citadel of freedom valiantly holding out against Hitler, determined to fight to the bitter end on the beaches and in the towns. Without slighting the heroic dedication of the many Britons who sacrificed so much to help defeat Nazism, we should note that as early as 1940 Great Britain was financially depleted with few military or industrial assets at hand, yet expending much of its scarce and precious resources to keep the restive peoples of its vast empire forcibly subjugated.[8] For the Tory government, maintaining the empire was at least as great an imperative as defeating the Nazis.

British leaders seriously considered coming to peace terms with Berlin so that they might make common cause with the Nazis against their real bête noir, Russian Bolshevism. Most members of the British ruling class did not merely seek to appease Hitler but admired him and his anti-Soviet crusade.[9] While ostensibly at war with Germany, Britain's Tory leaders sought passage of Allied forces through Scandinavia and Finland in order to launch an attack against the Soviet Union — an action Churchill supported even after the Finns had signed a peace treaty with Moscow in March 1940 and at a time when the Nazis were overrunning Europe.[10] All this fits poorly with the image of a British government single-mindedly dedicated to resisting Nazism at all costs.

As with most British and American accounts of the war, Churchill's history ignores the major role played by the Soviet Union in Nazism's defeat, and the horrendous losses in life and property sustained by the Soviets fighting on a scale that was many times greater than anything on the Western front.[11]

Much of the distortion within mainstream history is neither willful nor conscious, one may presume, since it is an outgrowth of the overall political ideology and culture.[12] If there is no conscious intent to miseducate, it is because many historians who claim to be disciples of impartial scholarship have little sense of how they are wedded to ideological respectability and inhospitable to counterhegemonic views. This synchronicity between their individual beliefs and the dominant belief system is treated as "objectivity." Departures from this ideological orthodoxy are themselves dismissed as ideological.

Let me add that much of the distortion *is* willful, perpetrated by those who are consciously dedicated to burying the past or shaping our understanding of it to suit their interests. In a moment of candor Churchill himself told William Deakin, who had helped him write *The Second World War,* "This is not history, this is my case."[13]

Few mainstream historians seem willing to reflect upon how the power structure of their society influences their discipline.[14] Many, including some who claim to be on the left, are discomforted by such Marxist-sounding terms as "ruling class history." They consider the label undeserved because history is written by professionally trained academics and other independent investigators who are not members of any ruling class. But such history can still be heavily influenced by the ruling ideology. Nor do you have to be a member of the ruling class to serve its interests. That a religious belief is propagated by its lower clergy and ordinary adherents does not make it any less the hierarchy's dictum. Indeed, such lower echelon transmission is an essential factor in maintaining the belief's hegemony.

It is also argued that there is no ruling class history because there is no ruling class in a pluralistic democratic country like the United States. In fact, it is a matter of public record that a tiny portion of the population controls the lion's share of the wealth and most of the command positions of state, manufacturing, banking, investment, publishing, higher education, philanthropy, and media. And while not totally immune to popular pressures, these individuals exercise a preponderant influence over what is passed off as public information and democratic discourse.

The ruling class is the politically active component of the owning class, the top captains of finance and policy who set the standards for investment and concentration of capital at home and abroad. They play a dominant role in determining the wage scales and working conditions of millions. They strip away employee benefits and downsize whole workforces, while warring tirelessly against organized labor. They set rates of interest and they control the money supply, including the national currency itself. They enjoy oligarchic control of the principal technologies of industrial production and mass communication. They and their adjuncts populate the boards of directors (or trustees or regents) of corporations, universities, and foundations. They repeatedly commit serious corporate crimes but almost never go to prison. They raid the public treasury for corporate welfare subsidies, for risk capital, bailout capital, export capital, research and development capital, promotional capital, and equity capital. They plunder the public domain, dominating the airwaves, destroying ancient forests, polluting lands and waters with industrial effluent, depleting the ozone layer, and putting the planet's entire ecology at risk for the sake of quick profits. At home and abroad, they are faithfully served by the national security state with all its covert and repressive apparatus. Their faithful acolytes occupy the more powerful security agency positions and cabinet posts regardless of what party or personality controls the White House. They create international agreements like NAFTA and GATT that circumvent the democratic protections of sovereign states and undermine the ability of popular government to develop public-sector services for anyone other than these powerful interests. Their overall economic domination and their campaign contributions, media monopoly, high-paid lobbyists, and public relations experts regularly predetermine who will be treated as major political candidates and which policy parameters will prevail. These ruling elites are neither omnipotent nor infallible. They suffer confusions and setbacks, and have differences among themselves. They sometimes grope for ways to secure and advance their interests in the face of changing circumstances, learning by trial and error. Through all this, their capital accumulation continues unabated. Though relatively few in number they get the most of what there is to get. Their wealth serves their power, and their power serves their wealth.[15]

The Hunt for Real History
    The most comprehensive federal survey, released by the U.S. Department of Education, finds that nearly six in ten high school seniors lack even a rudimentary knowledge of American history. A survey conducted by the Gallup Organization shows that 25 percent of college seniors cannot come within a half-century of locating the date of Columbus's voyage. About 40 percent do not know when the Civil War occurred. Most cannot describe the differences between World War I and World War II (though they suspect that World War II came after World War I). Another Gallup poll finds that 60 percent of adult Americans are unable to name the president who ordered the atomic bomb

to be dropped on Japan, and 22 percent have no idea that such an attack ever occurred.[16] A 1995 survey in the *New York Times* reports that only 49 percent of U.S. adults knew that the Soviet Union had been an ally of the United States during World War II, with the rest either having no opinion or thinking that the Soviets were noncombatants or on the enemy side.[17]

The picture is no better in regard to current affairs. A survey by the National Assessment of Educational Programs reveals that 47 percent of the nation's high school juniors do not know that each state has two U.S. senators.[18] A 1998 survey reports that nearly 95 percent of U.S. teenagers can name the lead actor in *Fresh Prince of Bel Air,* a television show, but less than 2 percent know the name of the chief justice of the Supreme Court. And while only 41 percent of teenagers can name the three branches of government, 59 percent can name the Three Stooges — demonstrating once again that television is a more commanding teacher than school.[19]

Almost all these surveys focus on U.S. history. Were questions asked about the history of other nations and pre-U.S. epochs, the figures would be even more dismal. This historical and political illiteracy should come as no surprise. Most states require not more than a year of history in high school, and some states — like Alaska, Michigan, and Pennsylvania — require no history of any kind. According to the National Center for Education Standards, as of 1994, fewer than 19 percent of high-school and middle-school social studies teachers had majored or minored in history.[20]

But something else is operating besides mass ignorance and mass media. The important question is, what is so desirable about knowing most of these facts in the first place, especially if they remain unconnected to any meaningful socio-historic explanation and often mask more than they reveal? To be sure, we cannot grasp the significance of an event or epoch if we do not even know it existed. But if all we know are a few bare facts, we comprehend little of importance. Contrary to the popular adage, it is seldom the case that the facts speak for themselves. While factual data are a prerequisite for understanding social realities, we must find ways of making sense of them, of appreciating their import and showing their relevance to larger developments. As Lord Acton put it: "History exhibits truths as well as facts—when [the facts] are seen not merely as they follow, but as they correspond; not merely as they have happened but as they are paralleled."[21]

Instead of just wishing more students knew that the Monroe Doctrine was issued in 1823 and that it attempted to discourage European colonization in the Western Hemisphere, we might want to ask *why* U.S. leaders felt compelled to introduce this "doctrine." Was it an altruistic gesture to protect Latin countries from European despotism, as some claimed at that time and many textbooks have maintained ever since? Was it to assure the peace and safety of the United States, as the doctrine itself declares? Or could a major consideration have been to guarantee a free hand for U.S. investors in the Western Hemisphere? Secretary of State John Quincy Adams (a principal shaper of the Monroe Doctrine) understood that even the British were aware that "the new Spanish-American markets simply had to be kept open" for U.S. commercial interests, and free from colonization by the continental powers.[22]

Such considerations could lead to others: Does U.S. foreign policy, as embodied in declarations such as the Monroe Doctrine, represent the interests of the American people? How so, or why not? Why would U.S. policy be so considerate of investor interests abroad? Why do U.S. corporate interests pursue overseas investments in the first place? What effects do these investments have on the people who inhabit these other lands and on our own people at home?

Historical parallels could be entertained. Thus, how does the Monroe Doctrine compare to the Truman Doctrine, the

Eisenhower Doctrine, the Nixon Doctrine, the Carter Doctrine, and other assertions of U.S. primacy in various regions of the world? Why do so many U.S. presidents feel compelled to promulgate such "doctrines"? Is there a common pattern behind these various proclamations? By linking the Monroe Doctrine to a broader set of questions about past and present events, we make it a more relevant and more interesting topic of study. The important thing is not just to identify specific historical events — as might a quiz show contestant — but to think intelligently and critically about them, and be able to relate them to broader social relations.

If people know little about standard history, they know even less about the silenced, hidden parts of history. More meaningful than remembering the date of Columbus's voyage is knowing about the cold-blooded slaughter and plunder he perpetrated against Native Americans, a homicidal rapacity that was reenacted and surpassed by many who came after him, many whose crimes also are whitewashed in mainstream narratives.

Other underplayed parts of North American history would include the early agrarian rebellions, the industrial class struggles of the last two centuries, the suppression of radical political dissent, the private plunder and spoliation of public resources, the bloody expansionism inflicted on indigenous peoples in North America and throughout the world, U.S. global expansionism, and U.S.-sponsored atrocities against revolutionaries and reformers throughout the Third World.[23]

Despite the miseducation they may have endured — or *because* of it — many people are hungry for real history. Far from being bored, they start paying attention when history offers an analysis that advances their understanding of events. They enjoy history when it is written in an accessible way (but not necessarily in a facile, light-handed manner), when it presents interesting narrative and provocative observations that relate to broader questions of social conflict and development, when it offers revealing parallels to what is going on now, suggesting that current events are not merely the result of particular personalities and passing phenomena but have compelling analogues in times long past.

Real history is interesting also when it deconstructs the pap we learned in school or from the media, when it demonstrates how we have been misled. More exciting than learning history is *un*learning the disinformational history we have been taught. Real history goes the extra step and challenges existing icons, offering interpretations that have a healthy subverting effect on mainstream ideology.

Attempts at real history are dismissed by conservatives as "revisionism." To use "revisionism" as an epithet is to say that there is no room for historical reinterpretation, that the standard version is objective and factual, and that any departure from it can only be ideological and faddish. Revisionism's real sin is that it challenges many time-honored bourgeois beliefs about the world, including the happy-faced image of America the Beautiful, the image "to which most Americans particularly those raised on 'consensus history' textbooks, [have] become accustomed."[24]

Revisionism also opens up new areas of inquiry. It is remarkable the things that most of us never learn in school about our own history, the topics and inquiries we are never introduced to. Consider this incomplete listing:

§ Why were human beings held in slavery through a good part of U.S. history? Why were they not given any land to till after their emancipation? Why were Native American Indians systematically massacred time and again?

§ What is property in the context of American civilization? What is wealth? How have large concentrations of capital been accumulated? Is there a causal relationship between wealth for the few and poverty for the many?

§ What role has government played in the formation of great

10

fortunes and giant corporations? What effect has this had on the democratic process?

§ Why in past generations did people work twelve hours a day or longer, six and seven days a week? Where did the weekend and the eight-hour day come from? Why were labor unions considered unconstitutional through much of the nineteenth century and into the early twentieth century?

§ Who were the Wobblies, the Knights of Labor, the Populists, and the Progressives? Why did tens of thousands of Americans consider themselves anarchists, socialists, or communists? Why did hundreds of thousands vote for radical candidates?

§ How did poor children get to go to public schools? How did communities get public libraries? What role has social class played in education and in American life in general?

§ How did we get laws on behalf of occupational safety, minimum wage, environmental protection, and retirement and disability benefits? How effective have they been? Who still opposes them and why?

§ What historic role has corporate America played in advancing or retarding the conditions of workers, women, African Americans, Native Americans, and various other ethnic groups? Why are most corporate decisions regarding investments, jobs, use of resources, and markets considered to be private?

§ Why have U.S. military forces intervened directly or indirectly in so many countries over the last century?

§ Why have U.S. leaders opposed revolutionary and even reformist governments, and supported right-wing autocracies around the world?

Questions of this sort are seldom asked in our media, schools, or textbooks.

Textbooks: America the Beautiful

In failing to teach us about class conflict and class domination, mainstream history shows itself to be an extension of that domination in cultural form. This can be seen in the history packaged for classroom use. The history textbook is a crucial instrument for advancing our miseducation. Among elementary and secondary school students, most classroom time and almost all homework time is spent with textbook materials.[25]

People complain that the history they encountered in school was just a mind-numbing compilation of a lot of names, dates, and facts. But is that really the problem? After all, names, dates, and facts can be intriguing and eye-opening, depending on what is being considered. In any case, history textbooks offer much more than that. Current editions are filled with stories, character profiles, vignettes, anecdotes, and colorful graphics and illustrations. Why then are they—and much of the rest of mainstream history—so unsatisfying? Why did a Harris poll find that high school students ranked history as the "most irrelevant" of twenty-one subjects?[26]

It was Catherine Morland who thought it odd that history "should be so dull, since a great deal of it must be invention."[27] In fact, such invention itself may contribute to the dullness. In a well-received critique of U.S. history textbooks, James Loewen notes how the books tell predictably constructed stories and "exclude conflict and real suspense." "Every problem has already been solved or is about to be solved." While textbooks sometimes try for drama, "they achieve only melodrama, because readers know that everything will turn out fine in the end." As one textbook put it: "Despite setbacks, the United States overcame these challenges." Furthermore, most textbook authors "write in a tone that if heard aloud might be described as 'mumbling lecturer.' No wonder students lose interest."[28] Tyson-Bernstein makes a similar point: While there are some good textbooks on the market, most "confuse students with non sequiturs . . . mislead them with misinformation, and . . . profoundly bore them with pointlessly arid writing."[29]

The lack of drama, a mumbling style, and arid writing are

not the only problems with textbooks. Boredom is bad enough but miseducation is worse. It is the dilution and flattening of *content* that turns fascinating history into tedious pabulum. Rather than being dense compendiums of facts and dates, textbooks often suffer from a shallow comprehensiveness, the superficiality that comes when attempting to cover too much too meekly. Textbooks—and many other mainstream history books—also suffer from a lack of critical perspective and a need to avoid any scrapes with the U.S. capitalist belief system. Loewen notes that textbooks "leave out anything that might reflect badly upon our national character."[30] In addition, they leave out anything that might reflect badly on the world's dominant politico-economic power circles. There is scant mention of the endless succession of injustices and atrocities perpetrated by potentates, patriarchs, princes, popes, prime ministers, presidents, and plutocrats. Instead, they offer what Christopher Hitchens calls "a story of uplift or . . . a chronicle of obstacles overcome."[31]

On most subjects, textbooks dilute controversy, preferring to be ideologically safe, offering a highly processed product that contains little flavor and few nutrients. More than just a stylistic problem, this is an informational and ideological bias reflective of larger power arrangements within society.[32]

Not just textbooks but much of mainstream history offers only passing murmurs about the great labor struggles of the last two centuries. In his history of the American people, a 1,122-page tome to be seriously avoided, Samuel Eliot Morison touches only lightly on labor struggles, with not a word about popular champions such as John Swinton, Charles Steinmetz, Albert Parsons, Jacob Coxey, W. E. B. Du Bois, Big Bill Haywood, Clarence Darrow, Mother Jones, Joe Hill, William Z. Foster, Elizabeth Gurley Flynn, and Emma Goldman. Morison offers a representative example of the kind of U.S. history that would not cause a moment's discomfort to persons of influence and fortune.[33] Nor was it much different in earlier times, as Ruth Miller Elson found in her study of some one thousand history, geography, and civics textbooks used during the nineteenth century. In no book published before the 1870s are labor combinations mentioned. In later decades the schoolbooks are virtually unanimous regarding the evil effects of labor unions. "Strike," "riot," and "labor disturbances" are often used interchangeably. Strikers include "the idle and vicious," the "dangerous classes," "restless agitators," and "foreigners." "Property destruction is always carefully detailed while grievances of the workmen are not. . . . [N]ot only is labor identified with violence, but this is the only context in which the organization of labor appears."[34]

Elson's nineteenth-century authors consider poverty to be symptomatic of "indolence and vice" and other "degenerate morals." Since America is the land of opportunity, the indigent have only themselves to blame. Wealth is accumulated through diligent work and good character. As one book put it, "Riches are the baggage of virtue," a sign of God's approval — never the result of having the good fortune to be born into a good fortune. No mention is made of the often unsavory ways that riches have been accumulated: by plundering public resources, pilfering the public treasury, violating public safety and antitrust laws, engaging in criminal undertakings, paying starvation wages, and using force and violence to maintain exploitative labor relations. The business tycoons of that day are hailed as American heroes.[35] In fact, none of them were heroes, and many were not even American. The Vanderbilts were Dutch, the first DuPont was French, Carnegie was a native Scot, the first Guggenheim was a Swiss Jew, and the first Astor was German born.[36]

Anarchism, communism, and socialism, Elson observes, are repeatedly linked to subversion and violence — an association still made today. The books make much of how Americans are blessed with liberty, but of a kind not intended for labor leaders and radicals.[37] Nothing is said about how the moneyed class bitterly opposed extending the vote and other basic democratic rights to propertyless working people. The American Revolution is lauded for bringing about the birth of a great nation but all the rebellions that followed, writes Elson, "are always the work of unscrupulous agitators arbitrarily fomenting trouble." While all the books agree that Shays's Rebellion demonstrated the need for a stronger national government, none mention that it revealed a need for helping the tax-ridden, debt-ridden farmers of Massachusetts whose desperate straits drove them to take up arms. The Whiskey Rebellion is treated in similar fashion, being termed a "criminal resistance" in one book.[38] In sum, the nation's history is viewed from the top down, to be deeply revered, not critically examined.

A study by Frances Fitzgerald of nineteenth- and twentieth-century history textbooks found that few of them admit the existence of economic or political inequality. Many of them boost "the American Way of Life" and the glories of free enterprise, though never using the word "capitalism" and never explaining how the American economy actually works. With only one or two exceptions, class conflict remains an inadmissable subject, as does economic history in general. "American history texts are remarkable for their lack of economic analysis."[39] Instead of conflicts between interests and social classes, the textbooks refer to "problems": there were problems during Reconstruction; also problems of poverty, pollution, and racial unrest—all of unstated origin.[40]

Equally mysterious problems arise around the globe, for which "we" are "taking up our responsibilities," exercising world leadership for the benefit of all peoples, notes Fitzgerald. The texts of the 1950s make estimates about Soviet power and "the threat of world communism" that are far more fearsome than anything written in the earlier wartime texts about Nazi aggression and the threat of World War II. The textbooks have titles like *The Free and the Brave: The Story of the American People; History of a Free People;* and *America: Land of Freedom.* The implication is that the reader must identify positively with just about everything that has happened in U.S. history.[41]

Fitzgerald detects a number of facelifts in the textbooks published in the early seventies, in the wake of the social activism of the 1960s. Portraits of Dolly Madison are replaced with photographs of Susan B. Anthony. The ubiquitous George Washington Carver gives way to Booker T. Washington and even W. E. B. Du Bois. Mention is made of Frederick Douglass, Martin Luther King Jr., Nat Turner, and Caesar Chavez, though little actual history is provided. The seventies texts offer not a profound recasting but mostly a tacking on of fragmentary information about some protests and protest leaders. Thus the books may note that Thomas Paine's *Common Sense* was an influential pamphlet but they do not discuss what it says.[42] In the seventies texts, the Chicano farmworkers are "struggling," but no hint is given about what they are struggling against, namely, the economic power of agribusiness. Native Americans also struggle in a void, with no word about the historic collusion between big corporations and the Bureau of Indian Affairs in expropriating the lucrative natural resources of tribal lands. And racism is treated as an attitudinal problem having no link to institutional or class interests. "The principle that lies behind textbook history," concludes Fitzgerald, "is that the inclusion of nasty information constitutes bias even if the information is true."[43]

The Council on Interracial Books for Children studied thirteen widely used U.S. history texts published in the seventies and found them to be an improvement over earlier ones that had "presented a picture of our society that was virtually all-white and all-male." But the newer ones remain seriously deficient and inaccurate in their treatment of ethnic peoples and women.[44] In regard to African American history, for instance, the books (a) ignore the enormous wealth that was accumulated from unpaid slave labor and was the prime impetus behind slavery; (b) minimize the brutality of the chattel system and the extent of slave resistance; (c) make no mention that for seventy-eight years the Constitution contained protective provisions for the slaveholding class; (d) describe the Reconstruction governments as corrupt and incompetent (a still common image) and failed to note that they were less corrupt and more progressive and democratic than the all-white Southern governments that both preceded and replaced them; (e) the texts also fail to recognize that the lack of land reform was a major factor in the continued economic oppression of the former slaves—who proved to be efficient farmers on the relatively rare occasions they were given land. Instead, the texts portray the former slaves as helpless, unable to live without the guidance of their former masters.[45]

Textbooks generally have little to say about the violent rapacity that ushered in the capitalist system. There is no mystification more fundamental to capitalism than the silence maintained about its own origins. A social order divided into boss and worker, landlord and farm laborer, is treated as the natural order. Never is it asked how the peasants were dispossessed of their land, artisans of their tools, and cottagers of their plots and gardens. It was a "primitive accumulation" achieved with sword, gun, hangman, and prison.[46] In the face of such silence, Marx felt compelled to write his own history of what he called "the secret of primitive accumulation," the massive and coercive theft of the common lands and smallholdings by big landowners.[47] Primitive accumulation, as Michael Ignatieff points out, was not a Marxist invention but a historic reality, its dynamic of "enclosure, eviction, and expropriation" was being experienced two generations before Marx's work appeared.[48]

For Business, Against Labor

A study by Jean Anyon of seventeen high school U.S. history texts widely used in the late 1970s, covering the period from the

Civil War to World War I, finds that the books present a consistently probusiness, antilabor slant, covering many of the same persons and events with much the same vocabulary and strikingly similar judgments. All seventeen devote substantial space to the presumed benefits of industrial development for the general public, while ignoring or glossing over the staggering human costs inflicted upon millions of working women, men, and children. Low wages are attributed to the willingness of unskilled immigrants to work for subsistence pay rather than to the owners' determination to impose poverty-level pay scales.[49]

Twelve of the books in Anyon's sample take no notice of the Socialist Party of America or its platform, nor the existence of any other radical organization. Four of the five remaining texts disparage the intentions of the socialists and assert that they had only a small number of adherents.[50] In fact, during the early twentieth century, 1,200 socialists were elected to office in U.S. cities, including seventy-nine mayors in twenty-four states. In 1912, socialist labor leader Eugene Victor Debs received nearly 900,000 votes for president in a contest that saw Woodrow Wilson elected with a plurality of only 6,293,152 votes. Runner-up Theodore Roosevelt received 4,119,207, and William Howard Taft 3,486,333. These figures suggest that, while Debs was a minority candidate in popular votes, as were all three of his opponents, he was more than an insignificant contender.[51] Not surprisingly, mainstream history textbooks, if they mention Debs at all, have little to say about his leadership of railway employees, his valiant confrontation against the plutocracy, his belief in socialism and international worker solidarity, and his years in jail for his opposition to the First World War.[52]

Radical historians have pointed out that almost all financiers and industrialists of the late nineteenth century launched themselves in business either with inherited wealth or access to large loans and corrupt deals, or by profiteering during the Civil War, or in other ways acquiring funds and land from the government.[53] The textbooks Anyon studied either avoid this subject or present a historically false view of how wealth was accumulated, crediting a financial mogul like Andrew Carnegie with having started on a weekly wage of only $1.20, from which he supposedly saved enough to invest and make a fortune.[54]

In fact, Carnegie earned that meager sum when he was thirteen years old, and saved not a penny of it. Over the years, benefiting from a network of fellow-immigrant Scots, he procured jobs as a telegraph operator, then manager and railroad superintendent. But all his hard work still left him a relatively poor man. Things changed only when his wealthy boss and mentor lent him a tidy sum to invest in some promising stocks. Thus did Carnegie launch his career as a financier, eventually becoming a multimillionaire. He never again worked hard in the usual sense, preferring to concentrate on frequent and luxurious vacations, world tours, and extended stays in his native Scotland.[55]

Although there were more than thirty thousand strikes between the Civil War and World War I, the textbooks Anyon studied give only brief and usually negative mention to labor struggles and labor unions. Some of the books claim inaccurately that radical leaders were feared and hated by the public.[56] Workers are never treated as belonging to a social class with common interests that are contrary to those of owners.[57] Anyon concludes that these textbooks serve more as promoters of the existing corporate order than as independent sources of information.

William Griffen and John Marciano studied how the Vietnam War was treated in twenty-eight high school textbooks widely used throughout the United States.[58] They found that the books said almost nothing about the anticolonial nature of the Vietnamese struggle, the ecological destruction and massive casualties caused by U.S. forces, the widespread torture and execution of prisoners, and other U.S. war crimes including CIA-sponsored political assassination campaigns (Operation

Phoenix). Nor did the texts mention the politico-economic considerations behind U.S. interventionism, the significance of the antiwar movement at home and U.S. government attempts to suppress it, and the unconstitutional exercise of executive power in waging such a war.

The textbooks embraced the official justification for U.S. involvement in Indochina ("containing Communist aggression" and "protecting democracy"). The judgment they invited on the war invariably concerned tactics rather than purposes. Through their pretensions of neutrality and suppression of crucial facts and alternative viewpoints, the textbooks fortify the official rendition of a benign, well-intentioned U.S. foreign policy, conclude Griffen and Marciano.[59]

After studying world history textbooks used in several high schools in New Jersey, Charlotte Kates concludes that they lionize the United States and demonize "socialist states, and socialism in general." "The class nature of history is completely denied." National liberation movements, especially those of Latin America, are derided as "Communistic" and "Soviet-aided," the assumption being that anything linked to Communism is evil. Imperialism, a dominant force in world history, is afforded scant treatment. The two bitterly opposed social systems of fascism and Communism are lumped together. Attempts by the Soviet Union to form a collective security pact against fascism during the 1930s, Moscow's support of antifascist forces in the Spanish civil war, and the Soviet people's heroic contribution in World War II all go unmentioned.[60]

Kates also looked at U.S. history textbooks and found that the horrors of slavery are treated but not the underlying class exploitation of African labor or, for that matter, the exploitation of any labor. The role played by Communists during the Great Depression in the fight for industrial unionism, unemployment insurance, and public assistance goes unnoted. The struggle for African American rights is depicted as having been settled with the civil rights acts of the late 1950s. There are some "wonderful teachers who take the time to depart from textbooks" and teach a more revealing version of history, Kates writes. But many more need to be educated so they can "present the other side and go further than the textbooks." And finally, the "publishing of textbooks must be taken from the corporations."[61]

Indeed, textbooks are marketed by a publishing industry increasingly dominated by giant corporate conglomerates with combined annual textbook sales of several billion dollars. The bulk of the textbook market is controlled by only ten publishers.[62] With concentration has come greater homogenization and standardization. As a result, progressive teachers find it increasingly difficult to include more critically oriented materials in their course readings.[63]

Along with textbook history we now have at least one CD-ROM disk that provides hours of video clips and audio narration under the lofty title, "The History of the United States for Young People." While no worse than many textbooks, the disk can be more insidious: A grisly image of human skulls appears on the screen and we are told of a North Vietnamese Communist advance into South Vietnam. The unproven association is clear. But the skulls quickly disappear when it is announced that President Nixon bombed Communist bases in Cambodia. With slick visuals and slanted text, the CD reassures its youthful audiences that Washington warmakers during the Vietnam era were champions of peace and democracy. "Ironically," writes Norman Solomon, "kids who use the glitzy history disk to learn about the war in Vietnam are encountering the same distortions that many of their parents and grandparents rejected three decades ago."[64] The disk is marketed by *American Heritage* magazine, owned by Forbes. Simon & Schuster, a subsidiary of the media giant Viacom, also had a hand in producing it.

The School as a Tool

To say that schools fail to produce an informed, critically minded, democratic citizenry is to overlook the fact that schools were never intended for that purpose.[65] Their mission is to turn out loyal subjects who do not challenge the existing corporate-dominated social order. That the school has pretty much fulfilled its system-sustaining role is no accident. The educational system is both a purveyor of the dominant political culture and a product of it.

Throughout their existence, schools and universities have been objects of concern to conservatives who seek to control what is taught in them. Consider what happened to one of the few progressive textbook series used during the 1930s, *Man and His Changing World* by Harold Rugg and his associates. The American Legion, the National Association of Manufacturers, and other such business and "patriotic" groups launched a concerted campaign to get Rugg's books removed from classrooms and libraries, charging that they were antibusiness, anti-American, and socialistic. In fact, Rugg wrote virtually nothing about the industrial warfare of the late nineteenth and early twentieth centuries, but he did have the temerity to point out the markedly uneven distribution of national income. This was more than conservative groups could tolerate. Their campaign against Rugg's books proved successful enough to cause a drop in sales from nearly 300,000 copies in 1938 to a mere 20,000 by 1944.[66]

During the 1980s, when some U.S. universities began revamping their Western Civilization courses to allow for a more diverse and less Eurocentric approach, cries of alarm arose from conservatives who accused radicals, feminists, "cultural elites," and ethnic minorities of trying to politicize scholarly subjects and devalue educational standards. Such critics failed to mention that the Western Civilization curriculum—which they sought to preserve as a sacrosanct cultural construct free of "politically correct" multicultural diversity—was actually the progeny of government-sponsored propaganda courses initiated during World War I at Columbia University and hundreds of other institutions of higher jingoism. Fashioned by white Christian gentlemen who used heavy doses of standardized Western history, politics, and philosophy, the War Issues course was designed, according to one of its directors, to instill male students—who were soon to be inducted into the army—with "an understanding of what the war is about and of the supreme importance to civilization of the cause for which we are fighting."[67]

During World War I, university officials across the nation attempted to impose ideologically correct views upon their faculty. Nicholas Murray Butler, president of Columbia University, explicitly forbade faculty from criticizing the war, arguing that such heresy was no longer tolerable, for in times of war, wrongheadedness was sedition and folly was treason. This was the same Butler who said that "an educated proletariat is a constant source of disturbance and danger to any nation."[68] At Columbia, one of the nation's leading historians, Charles Beard, was interrogated and, as he tells it, ordered "to warn all other men in my department against teachings 'likely to inculcate disrespect for American institutions.'" Beard described the trustees and Columbia's president Butler as "reactionary and visionless in politics, narrow and medieval in religion," who sought "to drive out or humiliate or terrorize every man who held progressive, liberal, or unconventional views on political matters."[69]

After World War I, many universities and colleges took the War Issues course as the model for a new offering called Contemporary Civilization, which now was intended to immunize students from communism and other radical contaminants. The Hun was replaced by the Bolshevik as the great menace to democracy.[70] During the cold war years of the 1950s and early 1960s, millions of U.S. schoolchildren were treated to regular infusions of *My Weekly Reader* and *Current Events,* neither of which ever alluded to the civil rights movement that was challenging and transforming race relations across the nation.[71] The two publications projected a Manichean world: on one side, the Soviet Union, a totalitarian evil intent upon bringing the entire world under its heel, propelled by a dangerously aggrandizing ideology, armed with weapons of mass destruction; on the other side, the United States, champion of human freedom, prosperity, peace, and national self-determination, the purveyor of all that was virtuous and admirable among nations. Twenty years later, the editors of *My Weekly Reader* did concede that with the benefit of hindsight they could see that their publication "does not seem to have adhered to its platform of fair and unbiased reporting." But such a shortcoming, they claimed, merely reflected the "prevailing bias of the age."[72]

Today, right-wing campaigns attempt to get textbooks and curriculums to commit themselves to a totally celebratory view of American history, placing still greater emphasis on patriotism, the free market, family values, creationism, and other fundamentalist religious verities.[73] During a struggle in Kanawha County, West Virginia, that won national attention when it became violent, the county board of education adopted guidelines demanding, among other things, that textbooks "must encourage loyalty to the United States and the several states . . . shall teach the true history and heritage of the United States," and "must not defame our nation's founders or misrepresent the ideals and causes for which they struggled and sacrificed."[74] Strict adherence to such guidelines conceivably could prohibit future history books from giving a true account of the winning of the West, slavery, racism, Watergate, and other topics that might cause students to cast a critical eye upon our heritage.[75]

Controversies regarding grade school curricula percolate up to the national level. Beginning in 1992, the National Endowment for the Humanities (NEH) and the Department of

Education enlisted a broad range of historical and teaching associations to put together a report on "national history standards" that offered voluntary guidelines—and illustrative materials and lessons—to help school districts upgrade their history curricula and improve student performance.[76] The first draft of the national standards project, a volume entitled *Lessons from History,* was attacked by Lynne Cheney, the Bush-appointed NEH chairperson who initially had approved the project, for having slighted "traditional history" in favor of "political correctness." This was followed by attacks from right-wing radio talk-show hosts, a 99-to-1 condemnatory vote in the U.S. Senate, and much unsympathetic coverage in the major media.

Far from ignoring the Constitution, as rightist critics charged, the report provides a whole section on the Constitution and the Bill of Rights and numerous other constitutional references. Rather than pushing a "politically correct" line, it goes out of its way to accommodate "differing pedagogical and interpretive approaches."[77] If the report had a serious defect, it was not its radical perspective but its lack of a radical perspective. It did attend to the subjects of racial oppression and gender discrimination, but its treatment of the realities of class power, labor struggles, and the U.S. radical tradition were markedly inadequate.

What bothers the conservatives, though they do not say it, is not that liberal historians are imposing their politically correct monopoly but that they are departing in mild and tentative ways from the ongoing conservative ideological monopoly. *Lessons from History* was attacked not because it boosted the supposedly doctrinaire standards of leftist "cultural elites," but because it strayed occasionally from the doctrinaire standards of right-wing superpatriots. What really upset critics like Cheney was the report's unwillingness to devote itself exclusively to bolstering the kind of "traditional history" that rhapsodizes about national virtues and glories.

Rightist campaigns against school curricula and textbooks are not unlike rightist attacks against the mainstream media. Schools and media both pretty much reflect a conservative centrist view of the world. But such a view is not conservative enough for the rightists, who consider anything to the left of themselves as "liberal," and anything liberal as ideologically contaminated. Curriculum disputes, as with media disputes, are between the "moderate" center and the far right, with the entire critical left portion of the spectrum consigned to oblivion.

Those who preside over our educational institutions generally are fully cognizant of their ideological responsibilities, though they may never describe them as ideological. Bored, uninformed students are a small price to pay in order to better secure cultural orthodoxy and politico-economic hegemony. Under such arrangements, real history is among the first casualties.

NOTES:

1. For a discussion of the distinction between history as a social process and the recording of history, see Michel-Rolph Trouillot, *Silencing the Past* (Boston: Beacon Press, 1995), chapter one. Ranke makes a distinction between *Geschichte,* which is more the actual happening that forms the objective subject matter, and *Historie,* which is the more subjective process, "the science that admits the subject matter *(Gegenstand)* into itself": Leopold von Ranke, *The Theory and Practice of History,* edited with an introduction by Georg Iggers and Konrad von Moltke (Indianapolis/New York: Bobbs-Merrill, 1973), 50. A distinction between the writing of history and gathering of historical evidence, the editing of sources, and related activities is made by J. H. Hexter, *Doing History* (Bloomington: Indiana University Press, 1971), 15. For the present discussion, research and writing can be treated as part of the same process.
2. Polybius, *Histories,* XII.28.
3. One historian, for example, speculates that Caesar's *Gallic War* "was rushed out in order to catch votes for his intended candidature for the consulship of 49 B.C.": Jane F. Gardner, introduction to Caesar, *The Civil War* (London: Penguin Books, 1967), 27.

4. On the nineteenth-century historian/politician, see Felix Gilbert, *History: Politics or Culture? Reflections on Ranke and Burckhardt* (Princeton, N.J.: Princeton University Press, 1990), 9.

5. Gibbon, of course, is best known for his monumental work on the decline of the Roman Empire, referenced herein in more detail in chapters 2 and 3. Tocqueville's major historical effort dealt with the fall of the ancien régime; Roosevelt wrote a biography of Gouverneur Morris in 1888 and a number of lesser works; Lodge edited the works of Alexander Hamilton in twelve volumes published in 1904, reissued by Haskell House in 1971; Watson wrote a history of France, contracted with Macmillan in 1898 and discussed sympathetically in C. Vann Woodward, *Tom Watson, Agrarian Rebel* (London, Oxford, and New York: Oxford University Press, 1975 [1938]), 335–339; Jaurès's work is still available in French, edited by Albert Mathiez: Jean Leon Jaurès, *Historie Socialiste de la Révolution Française* (New York: AMS Press, 1922–1927).

6. Gordon K. Lewis, *Slavery, Imperialism, and Freedom* (New York: Monthly Review Press, 1978), 273.

7. Clive Ponting, *1940: Myth and Reality* (Chicago: Ivan R. Dee, 1991), 1. Not everyone is of this opinion. John Keegan for one, being nowhere as critical of Tory leaders as he is of popular revolutionaries, accepts Churchill's six-volume account of the war as having succeeded "as both history and memoir": John Keegan, *The Battle for History* (New York: Vintage, 1996), 50. But even he allows that Churchill's history is "triumphalist."

8. John Newsinger, "Churchill: Myth and Imperialist History," *Monthly Review*, January 1995: 56–64; Ponting, *1940: Myth and Reality*, passim.

9. Well demonstrated by Clement Leibovitz, *The Chamberlain-Hitler Deal* (Edmonton, Alberta: Les Editions Duval, 1993).

10. Ponting, *1940: Myth and Reality*, 50. The British elites were not the only bourgeois leaders obsessed with Communism. Shortly before his country would be overrun by German forces, French premier Paul Reynaud was proposing an Anglo-French invasion of the Caucasus, targeting the Russian oil fields: Maurice Cowling, *The Impact of Hitler: British Politics and British Policy 1933–1940* (Chicago: University of Chicago Press, 1977), 363–364.

11. John Newsinger, "Churchill: Myth and Imperialist History," 56–57; and Clive Ponting, *Churchill* (London: Sinclair Stevenson, 1994). More than 80 percent of all German casualties were sustained on what was called "the Russian front."

12. Of course, the political culture is itself not free of the effects of class power. Much of what is thought to be our common culture is the "selective transmission of class culture" or class-dominated culture: Philip Wexler, "Structure, Text, and Subject: A Critical Sociology of

School Knowledge," in Michael Apple (ed.), *Culture and Economic Reproduction in Education: Essays in Class Ideology and the State* (London: Routledge and Kegan Paul, 1982), 279.

13. As quoted by Kenneth Harris in *New York Times Book Review,* April 27, 1997, 30.

14. Harvey Kaye wrote an essay directed at the subject of how and why ruling interests in society try to control the production of history, but he makes only passing mention of capitalist societies and Nazi Germany, and focuses mostly on the Soviet Union and, to a lesser degree, Communist China. Like some others on the Left, Kaye seems more interested in pursuing his preoccupation with what he calls "Stalinism" than in criticizing the hegemonic capitalist power under which the entire world actually lives; see his *Why Do Ruling Classes Fear History? and Other Questions* (New York: St. Martin's Griffin, 1996), 7–28.

15. For a fuller discussion and documentation of the ruling class, see my *Democracy for the Few,* 6th edition (New York: St. Martin's Press, 1995), especially chapters 2, 3, 6, and 12; also my *America Besieged* (San Francisco: City Lights Books, 1998), passim.

16. The results of these three surveys were reported respectively in *Washington Post,* November 1, 1995; *Commentary,* October 1994, 24; *New York Times,* March 1, 1995.

17. The poll published in the *Times* is discussed in Christopher Hitchens, "Goodby to All That," *Harper's Magazine,* November 1998, 39.

18. *New York Times,* January 2, 1977.

19. Survey by the National Constitutional Center: *UAW Washington Report,* October 9, 1998.

20. Hitchens, "Goodby to All That," 39–40. Hitchens notes that when the British play *The Madness of George III* was released as a motion picture, its title was changed to *The Madness of King George* because Hollywood's marketers feared that U.S. audiences might think they had missed parts I and II: ibid., 40.

21. Acton, *History of Freedom and Other Essays* quoted in Ernest Scott, *History and Historical Problems* (London: Oxford University Press, 1925), 200.

22. As Bailey observes, "The [U.S.] commercial world was especially gratified by this assurance that the Spanish-American markets would not be slammed shut": Thomas A. Bailey, *A Diplomatic History of the American People,* 10th edition (Englewood Cliffs, N.J.: Prentice-Hall, 1970), 184–185.

23. For an extended treatment of U.S. global expansionism, see my *Against Empire* (San Francisco: City Lights Books, 1995). Much of what is called "people's history" is really the history of people's rebellions. Equally important is the history of how power and wealth

have been used, by what interests for what purposes. Among the radical historians who have provided us with accounts of people's resistance are: Howard Zinn, *A People's History of the United States* (New York: Harper & Row, 1980); Herbert Aptheker, *American Negro Slave Revolts* (New York: International Publishers, 1987, originally 1943); Richard Boyer and Herbert Morais, *Labor's Untold Story* (New York: United Electrical, Radio, and Machine Workers, 1971); Sidney Lens, *Radicalism in America* (New York: Thomas Y. Crowell, 1969); and Franklin Folsom, *America Before Welfare* (New York: New York University Press, 1996).

24. Mark H. Leff, "Revisioning U.S. Political History," *American Historical Review* 100 (June 1995): 843 and passim; also Gary B. Nash, "The History Children Should Study," *Chronicle of Higher Education,* April 21, 1995: A60.
25. Paul Goldstein, *Changing the American Schoolbook* (Lexington, Mass.: D.C. Heath, 1978), 1.
26. *New York Times,* July 3, 1971.
27. Catherine Morland in *Northanger Abbey,* chapter 16, front page quotation in Edward Hallett Carr, *What Is History?* (New York: Random House, 1961).
28. James W. Loewen, *Lies My Teacher Told Me: Everything Your American History Textbook Got Wrong* (New York: New Press, 1995), 2.
29. Harriet Tyson-Bernstein, *A Conspiracy of Good Intentions: America's Textbook Fiasco* (Washington, D.C.: The Council for Basic Education, 1988), 3.
30. Loewen, *Lies My Teacher Told Me,* 2.
31. Hitchens, "Goodby to All That," 42; see also Alexander Stille, "The Betrayal of History," *New York Review of Books,* June 11, 1998, 15–20.
32. This is not to imply that textbook authors just wish to avoid unpleasantness, for they readily make much of what they consider to be the crimes perpetrated by anarchists, communists, and other revolutionaries.
33. Samuel Eliot Morison, *The Oxford History of the American People* (New York: Oxford University Press, 1965). See the critical remarks in Sender Garlin, *Three American Radicals* (Boulder, Colo.: Westview, 1991), xvii–xviii.
34. Ruth Miller Elson, *Guardians of Tradition* (Lincoln, Neb.: University of Nebraska Press, 1964), 248–250.
35. Elson, *Guardians of Tradition,* 252–256.
36. Stewart Holbrook, *The Age of the Moguls* (Garden City, N.Y.: Doubleday, 1953), viii.
37. Elson, *Guardians of Tradition,* 287–288.
38. Elson, *Guardians of Tradition,* 291.
39. Frances Fitzgerald, *America Revised: History Schoolbooks in the*

Twentieth Century (Boston: Little, Brown, 1979), 105, 109.

40. Fitzgerald, *America Revised*, 109, 155–157. Fitzgerald notes that New Left history was never incorporated into seventies textbooks. It might be added that neither was any Old Left history.

41. Fitzgerald, *America Revised*, 55–57, 121.

42. Fitzgerald, *America Revised*, 8–12, 85–89, 150–155.

43. Fitzgerald, *America Revised*, 96, 101–102.

44. Council on Interracial Books for Children, *Stereotypes, Distortions and Omissions in U.S. History Textbooks* (New York: Racism and Sexism Resource Center for Educators, 1977), 11 and passim. For earlier commentaries, see R. Costo and J. Henry, *Textbooks and the American Indian* (San Francisco: Indian Historical Press, 1970); and Jesus Garcia and D. C. Tanner, "The Portrayal of Black Americans in U.S. History Textbooks," *Social Studies,* 76 (September 1985): 200–204.

45. Council on Interracial Books for Children, *Stereotypes, Distortions and Omissions*, 18–26; the textbook quoted is *The Pageant of American History* (Rockleigh, N.J.: Allyn and Bacon, 1975), 281–282. The council also notes, "Our specific concern with third world people and women is not meant to imply that we feel textbooks accurately portray the experiences of the average, white workingman. Indeed, similar content analysis of labor history and its treatment in textbooks is critically needed": ibid., 12–13.

46. Michael Ignatieff, "Primitive Accumulation Revisited," in Raphael Samuel, ed., *People's History and Socialist Theory* (London: Routledge & Keegan Paul, 1981), 130; see also Roxanne Dunbar Ortiz, "The Responsibility of Historians," *Monthly Review*, July/August 1994: 60–65.

47. Karl Marx, *Capital*, I, chapters 26–33.

48. Ignatieff, "Primitive Accumulation Revisited," 130.

49. Jean Anyon, "Ideology and United States History Textbooks," *Harvard Educational Review* 49 (August 1979): 361–364.

50. Anyon, "Ideology and United States History Textbooks," 365–371.

51. *Congressional Quarterly's Guide to U.S. Elections,* 2nd edition (Washington, D.C.: Congressional Quarterly Inc., 1985), 348.

52. See Ray Ginger, *The Bending Cross* (New Brunswick, N.J.: Rutgers University Press, 1949); and Nick Salvatore, *Eugene V. Debs, Citizen and Socialist* (Urbana/Chicago: University of Illinois Press, 1982).

53. For critical treatments of capitalist class power in nineteenth century United States, see Gustavus Meyers, *History of the Great American Fortunes* (Chicago: Charles Kerr, 1911); Matthew Josephson, *The Robber Barons* (New York: Harcourt Brace Jovanovitch, 1962, originally 1934); Gabriel Kolko, *The Triumph of Conservatism* (Chicago: Quadrangle Books, 1967, originally 1963); Richard DuBoff, *Accumulation & Power: An Economic History of the United States* (Armonk, N.Y.: M. E. Sharpe, 1989).

54. Anyon, "Ideology and United States History Books," 372. Carnegie amassed a fortune of $400 million.

55. Harold Livesay, *Andrew Carnegie and the Rise of Big Business* (New York: HarperCollins, 1975), 16–46.

56. Anyon, "Ideology and United States History Textbooks," 372–376.

57. Jean Anyon, "Workers, Labor and Economic History, and Textbook Content," in Michael Apple and Lois Weis (eds.), *Ideology and Practice in Schooling* (Philadelphia: Temple University Press, 1983), 51.

58. William Griffen and John Marciano, *Lessons of the Vietnam War* (Totowa, N.J.: Rowman & Allanheld, 1979). This book includes a concise, well- documented history of the Vietnam War, with attention given to the origins of U.S. involvement.

59. Griffen and Marciano, *Lessons of the Vietnam War*, 163–165, 167; see also John Marciano, *Civic Illiteracy and Education* (New York: Peter Lang, 1997).

60. Charlotte Kates, "The Secret History," *Collingswood Chronicle* (New Jersey), June 1995: 7. For a detailed study of how the history of socialism in the United States is misrepresented in textbooks used in New Paltz, N.Y., see Robert Weil, "'A Communist named Salvador Allende . . .' The Teaching and Unteaching of Socialism in U.S. High School and Middle School Texts," *Socialism and Democracy*, spring/summer 1989: 89–117.

61. Kates, "The Secret History," 7. Even more one-sided interpretations of history can be found in ROTC courses in high school and college, including a blatant boosting of the U.S. military, as Catherine Lutz of the University of North Carolina is finding in her study of ROTC textbooks. One ROTC text teaches that the use of the army to "settle labor disputes" was widely respected, as "when the army put an end to the national railroad strike of 1894," by serving as strikebreakers: Ken Cunningham, "High Schools Target of Military Invasion," *On Guard*, vol. 4, no.3, 1994 (publication of *Citizen Soldier*, New York, N.Y.).

62. Lewis Coser, Charles Kadushin, and Walter Powell, *Books: The Culture and Commerce of Publishing* (New York: Basic Books, 1982), 3; and "The Media Nation: Publishing," *Nation*, March 17, 1997, 23–26. The rate of concentration within publishing in general continues unabated, with the top conglomerates reaping estimated revenues of $52.8 billion in 1995. Textbook publishing is like any other corporate industry with its speedups and downsizing. Thus, while posting record profits, McGraw-Hill forced more than one hundred editorial employees to become Kelly Girl temporary workers in September 1997. Less than a month later, the company fired them and denied them severance pay and other compensations guaranteed under their contract as temporary workers. A week before the firings, McGraw-Hill's management announced that the division

had made more money on school texts than anyone else in the industry: Rob Neuwirth, "Quick-draw McGraw: Text Publisher Pulls Trigger on Writers," *American Writer*, winter 1997–98: 7, 13.

63. Kenneth Teitelbaum, "Critical Lessons from Our Past," in Michael Apple and Lina Christian-Smith, eds., *The Politics of the Textbook* (New York and London: Routledge, 1991), 135.

64. Norman Solomon, "Virtual Mendacity," *Z Magazine*, July/August 1997, 27.

65. "The notion that schools were developed as institutions designed to foster scholarship or the life of the mind has no basis in historical fact": Yehudi Cohen, "The State System, Schooling, and Cognitive and Motivational Patterns," in N. K. Shimahara and A. Scrupski (eds.), *Social Forces and Schooling* (New York: David McKay, 1975), 110.

66. Apple and Christian-Smith, *The Politics of the Textbook*, 4; Miriam Schipper, "Textbook Controversy: Past and Present," *New York University Education Quarterly* 14 (Spring/Summer 1983), 31–36; and Gary B. Nash, Charlotte Crabtree, and Ross E. Dunn, *History on Trial: Culture Wars and the Teaching of the Past* (New York: Knopf, 1998), 40–45.

67. Cyrus Veeser, correspondence, *New York Times*, June 23, 1988; also Carol Gruber, *Mars and Minerva: World War I and the Uses of the Higher Learning in America* (Baton Rouge: Louisiana State University Press, 1975); and William Summerscales, *Affirmation and Dissent: Columbia's Response to the Crisis of World War I* (New York: Teachers College Press, 1970).

68. Arnold Petersen, *Daniel De Leon: Social Architect* (New York: New York Labor News Co. 1941), II, 168. For other comments on and by Butler, see Scott Nearing, *The Making of an American Radical: A Political Autobiography* (New York: Harper & Row, 1972).

69. On the mistreatment of Beard, see Richard Hofstadter and Wilson Smith, *American Higher Education*, vol. 2 (Chicago: University of Chicago Press, 1961), 883–892.

70. Gruber, *Mars and Minerva*, 241–242.

71. Marc Richards, "The Cold War World According to *My Weekly Reader*," *Monthly Review*, October 1998: 36.

72. Richards, "The Cold War World According to *My Weekly Reader*," 34.

73. Many disputes revolve around what conservative religionists consider unacceptable values and profanity found in fictional writings used in high school courses. Fewer controversies focus on history curricula because most of the history taught is already of the conventional, celebratory kind. See Joan DelFattore, *What Johnny Shouldn't Read* (New Haven: Yale University Press, 1992); and Edward Jenkinson, *Censors in the Classroom* (Carbondale and Edwardsville, Ill.: Southern Illinois University Press, 1979).

74. Jenkinson, *Censors in the Classroom,* 23–24. Preparing students to be good citizens, however, seldom seems to include teaching them community organizing and lobbying skills, how to petition and pressure officialdom, and how to build political protest movements.
75. See the comments by an investigative panel of the National Educational Association: Jenkinson, *Censors in the Classroom,* 25.
76. The professional groups included the American Historical Association, the Organization of American Historians, the National Council for History Education, and the Organization of History Teachers. Their report: National Center for History in the Schools, *National Standards for United States History: Exploring the American Experience, Grades 5–12* (Los Angeles, 1994).
77. Mark H. Leff, "Revisioning U.S. Political History," *American Historical Review,* 100 (June 1995): 841. For a full account of this controversy, see Gary B. Nash, Charlotte Crabtree, and Ross E. Dunn, *History on Trial* (New York: Alfred A. Knopf, 1998), 149–277.

2

PRIESTS AND PAGANS,
SAINTS AND SLAVES

History is largely a one-sided record composed by the victors. This is well demonstrated by the sanitized history of the origins and triumph of Christianity. While acknowledging such aberrations as the Inquisition and the church's suppression of scientific investigators like Galileo, the popularized account depicts Christianity as having been a civilizing force in late antiquity, a beacon of light in the Dark Ages, and a citadel of faith and learning throughout medieval times.

The reality is something else. For more than a thousand years, the higher clergy presided as rich and powerful ecclesiastical lords over vast satrapies, owners of slaves, and masters of serfs, exercising a regressive influence upon every area of culture and learning.

Triumph of the One True Faith

In ancient Rome, pagan rule generally was more tolerant of Christianity than Christianity was of paganism once the Christians gained the upper hand.[1] The polytheistic pagans welcomed all manner of gods at the pantheon, with new deities being added over time. What discomforted them about Christianity was its unyielding monotheism and its readiness to regard every other form of worship as impious and idolatrous. Here was an obscure sect that proffered a fantastical cosmic scenario of everlasting salvation for proselytes, and eternal flames for heathens and their ancestors.[2]

To the extent that it existed, pagan repression of Christianity seemed propelled more by political than theological considerations. The pagan side had its zealots, those who deeply believed in the old order and who blamed the Christian sect for all of Rome's maladies. Ever wary of private societies, the empire kept a mistrusting eye on the recalcitrant Jesus worshippers who might be induced to pray *for* the emperor, but never *to* him. With their unlicensed, secretive, international associations and militant messianic belief in the *Christos* god-king, the Christians did not fit comfortably into the polytheistic pantheon over which the deified Roman emperor presided.[3] Disloyalty to the polity's gods was seen as being not far from disloyalty to the polity itself.

In his well-known correspondence with Emperor Trajan late in the first century A.D., the younger Pliny made clear that official concern was more political than religious. He informed the emperor that Christians in Bithynia had discontinued their practice of secretly meeting "since my edict, issued on your instructions, which banned all *political* societies" [my italics]. Those who persisted under interrogation in avowing their membership in "this wretched cult," were sent away to be executed for their disloyalty.[4]

Trajan supported Pliny's measures but counseled against an excess of inquisitional zeal: "These people must not be hunted out," and if they repent they must be pardoned no matter how suspect their past conduct may have been. "But pamphlets circulated anonymously must play no part in any accusation. They create the worst sort of precedent and are quite out of keeping with the spirit of our age."[5]

During the first three centuries A.D., though an illegal institution, the Christian church was usually left to itself as long as it did not foment disturbances. In the schools of Rome and Athens, religion was not a prejudicial factor for either teachers or students. One could confess faith in either Jupiter or Jesus. "This was no concern to the authorities in charge of the schools."[6] Generally, out of concern for peace and stability, the pagan emperors discouraged any heated outcry against the Jesus followers. Unlike the eager Pliny, the average Roman governor was averse to coming down hard on the Christians brought before him, preferring to reclaim rather than punish the deluded enthusiasts, urging them to make a minimal obeisance to the emperor or just take some simple oath that might serve as an excuse to release them. To the governors,

> it all sounded so odd, this doctrine of Resurrection, body and all, and this trust in books by St. Paul. "Was he not a common sort of chap who spoke Aramaic?" a governor of Egypt was said to have asked Bishop Phileas in c. 305. "Surely he was not in the same class as Plato?" "Well, then," another despairing governor had asked in Smyrna, in March 250, "do you pay attention to the air? If so, sacrifice to the air instead." "I do not pay attention to the air," replied his prisoner, "but to him who made the air, the heaven and everything in it." "Tell me, then, who did make it?" "It is not right for me to tell." This childlike obstinacy was very irritating. "Do you want to wait a few days to think it over?" asked the governor who tried Colluthus, also in Egypt in the early fourth century. . . . "Don't you see the beauty of this pleasant weather?" asked his hopeful judge. "No pleasure will come your way if you kill yourself. But listen to me and you will be saved." "The death which is coming to me," Colluthus was said to have answered, "is more pleasant than the life which you would give."[7]

"Christianity," writes Mattingly, "was a religion of peace, with the peace of God in its heart."[8] One would never know it from the way Christians attacked other Christians whose views deviated somewhat from their own. Over and above their clashes with pagan authorities, Christ believers waged uncompromising fratricidal war, often over doctrinal esoterica that might seem oddly frivolous to modern readers. Christianity's early history "was more plagued by splits within the church than by threats from without," notes Joyce Salisbury.[9] According to Edward Gibbon, the Christians inflicted far greater casualties on each other in the course of their internecine conflicts than ever was visited upon them by the infidels. This bloodletting continued well beyond the Reformation era. Relying on Grotius, Gibbon notes that the number of Christians executed by other Christians in a single province during the reign of Charles V far exceeded that of all the martyrs who perished at the hands of pagans throughout the entire Roman Empire in the space of three centuries.[10]

Almost from Christianity's inception, charges of criminal misconduct were regularly hurled by one Christian sect against leaders of another. Paul himself putatively was a victim of such factional strife in Rome. Early in its existence, the church did its utmost to suppress Gnosticism, Marcionism, and Montanism, followed with campaigns against various other heretical offshoots. Strife between Christian sects in Rome was violent enough to necessitate intervention by the emperor and city prefect.[11]

In 317, in cities throughout northern Africa, riots between Donatist Christians and Catholic Christians cost numerous lives.[12] There was a dimension of class struggle in some of these conflicts. Donatism found its strongest following among the lower orders, whose rejection of the church of Carthage was part of their hostility toward the rich. Donatist social rebels led what Joseph Vogt calls "undisciplined mobs" to "drive out Roman proprietors and compel hated slave-owners to perform servile tasks."[13] Not until well into the fourth century, when the dominant sect was established as the empire's preferred religion, was Christianity's doctrinal orthodoxy firmly secured.

It is usually taught that Christianity won the hearts and minds of antiquity in part because of the inspirational examples set by its martyrs. Perowne writes that "the heroism of the Christians who faced death calmly, confidently, and with prayers of forgiveness on their lips, deeply impressed their pagan brethren."[14] And Gibbon claims that many Gentile spectators were converted by the enthusiasm of the condemned proselytes; "the blood of the martyrs . . . became the seed of the church."[15]

What evidence we have would seem to indicate something less inspirational. While kept vividly alive in the modern imagination by popular novels like *Ben Hur* and Hollywood films of Christians being thrown to the lions, persecution "remained an exceptional occasion," according to Michael Grant.[16] Between Nero's cruel campaign in A.D. 64–68 and the limited one launched during the reign of Diocletian in A.D. 303–304, there were long periods of toleration, marred by sporadic incidents of harassment and repression.[17] Regarding the Diocletian "Great Persecution," a leading Catholic historian, Monseigneur Duchesne, found only a score of proved cases of martyrdom in the entire empire.[18] In the brief interlude of 361–363, after Christianity had become the established religion, a cautious and largely ineffectual pagan restoration was attempted by Emperor Julian (Julian the Apostate), a campaign "not pressed to the point of shedding blood," notes one Catholic writer.[19]

Origen, a church leader writing in the third century, candidly admits that those who had died for their faith were "few" and "easily numbered."[20] Despite his assertion that martyrdom was "the seed of the church," even Gibbon judges the actual victims to be an "inconsiderable number." He speculates that their ranks may have been misleadingly magnified by the custom of bestowing the title of martyr on all confessors of the faith.[21] W. H. C. Frend remarks that only "hundreds not thousands" of Christians were ever martyred.[22] And Rodney Stark concludes that "the Roman government seems to have cared very little about the 'Christian menace.' There was surprisingly little effort to persecute Christians. . . . [Persecutions] were infrequent and involved very few people. The early Christians may have faced some degree of social stigma but little actual repression."[23]

If so, how prevalent could martyrdom have been as a proselytizing tool? To be sure, some individuals like Justin Martyr converted to Christianity after witnessing Christians bravely facing death. But whether the martyrs' heroism explains Christianity's triumph is another matter. Even by Christian accounts, those most impressed by such sacrifices were other believers who convinced themselves that the Holy Spirit abetted their comrades in the final ordeal. The number of pagans who actually saw Christians die in the arena could not have been a substantial portion of the empire's population, and the number who thereby experienced a religious conversion would have been fewer by far.

From the accounts we have, the arena crowds usually threw stones and heaped abuse upon the aspiring martyrs, offended by what the pagans perceived as their moral and spiritual arrogance. It was the pagan populace who demanded that Cyprian, bishop of Carthage, be thrown to the lions. "The impatient clamor of the multitude denounced the Christians as the enemies of gods and men."[24] And there is no evidence of a public outcry of any sort to stop the execution of Christians. Had there been, we would have heard of it through Christian sources. That some Christian clergy strongly opposed the enthusiasms of martyrs further suggests that martyrdom was not a bountiful source of recruitment.[25]

Bearing witness to martyrdom sometimes actually had a chilling effect. Far from inspiring emulation among the unconverted, Vibia Perpetua's insistence on going to her death in the arena visited dismay and sorrow upon her heathen kin and acquaintances.[26] Furthermore, there were many examples of backsliding Christians, including the earliest group of bishops who lacked the fortitude to persevere in their convictions when faced with the threat of extinction. Just as the martyrs may have inspired brethren to keep the faith, so the terrified retractions of less resolute believers bred hesitation and even apostasy among co-religionists.[27]

In the final analysis, Christianity's triumph owed more to Constantine's state power than to the exemplary inspiration of martyrdom or to mass enthusiasms. To be sure, Christianity presented a more gratifying belief system than paganism, with promises of a blissful hereafter and the solicitude of a loving providential God. It also offered earthly rewards, notably a close community of worshippers and some limited measure of care for widows, children, and elderly. Not all donations were pocketed by the clergy; some portion went for charity, unlike contributions to pagan temples, which were expended on feasts and drinking bouts. Paganism generated little sense of connection to a loving, all-wise godhead, offering instead an ever increasing number of parochial gods, themselves of sometimes imperfect morality.[28]

Stark explains that Christianity's early growth was due to (a) the communal social care that Christians provided for their brethren which allowed for a higher survival rate among Christians than pagans during epidemics (the evidence he gives for this is at best scanty); (b) the church's prohibition against the common practices of infanticide, abortion, and birth control, endowing Christians with a faster population growth; and (c) the high conversion rate of pagan husbands who were married to Christian women.[29] Still, the early growth of Christianity could not have been all that dramatic. Early in the third century, Origen observed that the number of faithful was quite inconsiderable. Extrapolating from what he knew about Antioch and Rome, Gibbon guesses that not more than 5 percent of the empire's population enlisted themselves under Christ's banner in the pre-Constantine era.[30]

To be sure, the Christian church was a widely tolerated and viable organization by the early fourth century even before Constantine elevated it to official status. Its well-knit structure and often prestigious membership were probably the very things that convinced the emperor to incorporate it into his political base. But none of these considerations lessen the importance of the immense material support afforded the church by Constantine and the Christian emperors who came after him.

Constantine's edict of 313 withdrew state recognition of the traditional gods but with an appearance of tolerance that initially placed all faiths on an equal footing. Facing a large pagan majority in the Senate and throughout the empire, the emperor moved cautiously at times. He granted permission for pagan temples to be built in Constantinople and, as late as 331, erected several himself in areas where pagan sentiment must have been especially strong. Most other times, he vigorously promoted Christianity as his personal religion with rescripts and other public communications. Constantine restored property and meeting houses taken from Christians during the Diocletian persecution of the previous decade. He provided the church with regular state revenues mostly in landed property and crop shares, and granted it the right to accept legacies. In a matter of years, the emperor's rulings helped to transform the Christian sect into a state-chartered Church Universal, with majestic edifices and imposing rituals.[31]

Under Constantine, bishops were made privileged dignitaries and entrusted with official duties, enjoying jurisdiction over civil cases within Christian communities and over capital crimes involving other bishops, who were granted the aristocratic privilege of being tried by their peers. Christian clergy were exempted from imposts and granted immunity from municipal tributes. Such favored treatment induced a sudden spate of conversions by various wealthy individuals who sought to secure tax-free episcopal posts. Constantine built a chain of lavish churches from Rome to the Holy Land. And in 321 the state officially accepted the Lord's Day, declaring Sunday a public holiday.[32]

At the same time, the first Christian emperor made sure to tighten his grip on secular power. Constantine murdered his son, his wife, and the eleven-year-old son of a vanquished rival, while plunging into wars that caused the death of hundreds of thousands,[33] setting an example that was to be emulated by other Christian rulers over the centuries. Burckhardt notes that church leaders "uttered no word of displeasure against the murderous egoist." Enjoying every guarantee of favor from Constantine, the well-organized clergy became "the most devoted agents for spreading his power," completely disregarding the fact that he stood with one foot in paganism and hands drenched in blood.[34]

Whether Constantine's conversion to Christianity was sincere is still debated. More important is the impact it had upon the religious landscape. Under his rule, the church gained a measure of political power and material wealth that opened the way for its temporal triumph. Just as Christianity waxed upon being granted official sanction, so did paganism wane. In the fourth century, paganism was far from moribund. But once Constantine defunded its shrines and diverted its treasures to Christian coffers, and once the ancient temples lost their claim over local taxes, estate donations, and festivals, paganism began to decline precipitously.[35] Mindful of the power of the newly installed Christian magistrates, substantial numbers of the empire's subjects took to the reigning faith. In one year alone, twelve thousand men were baptised in Rome, along with a proportional number of women and children.[36]

As the church's earthly power flourished, so did its enmity toward any kind of theological deviation. Generally, a willingness to tolerate dissent does not increase with a group's sense of empowerment. In the years after Constantine, the practices of holy communion and baptism were enforced by police, while the bishops prevailed upon secular rulers to suppress all competing beliefs. In April 356, Constantius II, Constantine's successor, issued an edict that sanctioned death for persons convicted of worshipping idols.[37] The true believers of Christ deprived pagans of their houses of worship, destroyed their literature and sacred icons, and tortured them "in authority in the city," to get them to admit to religious fraud.[38] Riots incited by the closing of pagan temples only spurred the bishops to demand more severely repressive measures. The determination to increase the "opportunities for faith" was a euphemism for suppressing any credo that departed from the One True Faith. As Augustine and others argued, coercion against pagans and against Christians who reverted to paganism was a virtue, for Christ was like a general who must use military means to retrieve deserters.[39]

In his famous debate with St. Ambrose, the learned pagan aristocrat, Symmachus, made a last-ditch plea for religious tolerance and freedom of conscience: "Since I do not repent, permit me to continue in the practice of my ancient rites. Since I am born free, allow me to enjoy my domestic institutions." Predictably, Ambrose, archbishop of Milan, responded that Christianity alone was the doctrine of truth and that every form of polytheism led only to the abyss of eternal perdition. Ambrose's friend, Emperor Theodosius, drove home the archbishop's argument by arbitrarily forcing Symmachus into exile. Theodosius then propelled the hasty conversion of the Roman Senate, which, keenly aware of the dangers of opposing a determined monarch, voted by a lopsided majority for Jesus and against Jupiter.[40]

As Burckhardt notes, the pagans "did not know, or they forgot, that Christianity, once tolerated, must inevitably become the predominant religion."[41] Indeed, its determined intent was to become the *only* religion. By January 395, paganism was completely banished from public life and largely suppressed as a faith. With "the one true Church universal apostolic and Roman" established by law, heresy was now likened to subversion.[42] The pagan rites of animal sacrifice and divination were declared a crime of high treason against the state. The use of garlands, frankincense and libations of wine, and other harmless ceremonies subjected the offender to forfeiture of his home and estate or a heavy fine in gold and silver. Those who failed to report or punish such deeds faced equally severe sanctions.[43]

Silencing the Pagans

Anyone attempting to investigate pagan critiques of early Christianity discovers that such literature no longer exists. It was systematically destroyed by church authorities after Christianity became the approved religion early in the fourth century. To determine what pagan writers thought about Christianity, modern researchers must forage for comments in letters and writings dealing with other topics. Other fragments survive, ironically, because they are quoted by Christian polemicists who are bent on refuting them.

One tireless critic was the third-century philosopher Porphyry, a neoplatonist theist and student of Plotinus. The surviving remnants of his fifteen-volume work, *Against the Christians,* contained many surprisingly modern-sounding arguments, and evoked critical responses from several generations of Christian writers, including church fathers like Jerome and Augustine.[44] To their credit, Porphyry and other pagan philosophers gave no currency to widely circulated accusations that Christians practiced ritual murder, incest, cannabilism, and group sex.[45] Instead, they concentrated on what was to them Christianity's highly improbable history and theology, posing such questions as:

§ Why would God select such a backwater as Galilee to send his son? And why such a laborious and haphazard method of propagating the faith across the entire world?

§ Why would an omnipotent, omniscient God need to descend to earth in human form to bring about a moral reformation?

§ Why would God so heartlessly deny an opportunity for salvation to the countless generations born before the advent of Jesus? Was it only then, after such a long period, that he remembered to judge the human race?

§ How does it happen that Christians take their origins from Judaism yet despise some of the very things that Jewish Scriptures teach? Why did God give contradictory laws to Moses and Jesus?

§ If the Gospels are eyewitness reports, why do they all give such widely conflicting accounts of Christ's suffering and crucifixion?

§ Why do the miraculous events described in the Gospels seem so fraught with deceit and trickery, as when the tiny placid lake of Galilee is described as a tumultuous sea that Jesus calms and walks upon?

§ Why did Peter (Acts 5.1–12) preside over the deaths of two devoted believers who handed over all their land and possessions to the Christ sect but committed the "sin" of keeping a little for themselves?

§ Why would Jesus reappear after his death only to an obscure few rather than to the multitude or to his enemies who never believed he was the Messiah? What evidence do we have that the dead can be resurrected?[46]

Emperor Constantine sought to silence Porphyry's voice by destroying his treatises. Later pro-Christian emperors also burned pagan critiques of Christianity. A century after Constantine, in 448, all surviving copies of Porphyry's work were condemned to the flames by church authorities. Other notable pagans whose anti-Christian polemics were torched include Celsus, Galen, Lucian, and Julian the Apostate.[47]

One of today's historians who looks favorably upon the early Christians, Stewart Perowne, makes no mention of how they relentlessly eradicated critical pagan literature. Of Celsus's book, *The True Word,* Perowne comments laconically "this we do not possess," without explaining *why* we do not possess it. He assures us that Celsus puts forth "the usual appeal" and "all the familiar arguments" against the Christian faith, though he offers not a hint as to what these familiar arguments might be. Perowne then refers to the eight volumes of Origen's "learned" and "great apologetic work," *Against Celsus,* "all of which have come down to us."[48] The reader is left with the impression that it was just by happenstance that Origen's writings survived intact while Celsus's work is entirely lost to us. We know of Celsus's critique only as much as Origen chooses to tell us.

Some of the Christian texts that incorporated sections of Porphyry's polemic solely for purposes of rebuttal were themselves burned in order to eradicate what the bishop of Apollinarius called the "poison of his thought."[49] In sum, a rich corpus of critical literature, one whole side of a monumental debate that lasted over two centuries, is mostly lost to history because the ascendent side chose to silence its opponents by force when it could not do so by reasoned argument.

Accepting the Powers that Be

Christianity is sometimes credited with cleansing Western society of pagan decadence, and with standing against class power and privilege. "By renouncing all that the pagan world had coveted and striven for," writes Lewis Mumford, "the Christian took the first steps toward building up a new fabric out of the wreckage."[50] It is a dubious hypothesis. Far from renouncing the values and institutions of antiquity, the early church embraced Roman notions of law and property, and offered no resistance to the emperor's autocratic rule or to the corruption and venality of the royal entourage, no opposition to aristocratic wealth and entitlement, no objection to the merciless tax machine and harsh criminal law, and no noticeable protest against poverty, slavery, female subjugation, and most other social abuses.[51] "What is certain," remarks Aram Vartanian, "is that the Christianization of the Roman Empire did nothing to democratize or liberalize its laws. Rome continued to be what we would now call a military dictatorship, even under the best of its emperors." The church accommodated itself to the existing imperial absolutism "and even set up the bishops of Rome as 'spiritual emperors' in their own domain."[52]

Writing in the *Wall Street Journal,* conservative historian Elizabeth Fox-Genovese gives credence to another specious, time-worn notion: "[I]t was in Christianity that the concept of individual freedom originated."[53] In fact, long before Christ, during the Roman Republic and before that in ancient Athens and other Greek city-states, there existed pagan jurists and democratic leaders who expressed concern for the rights of citizens against privilege and arbitrary state power.[54] Fox-Genovese notwithstanding, one is hard put to locate in the entire corpus of early Christian thought an advocacy of individual freedom against secular or ecclesiastical power. Such a concept is not to be found in Paul, Jerome, Ambrose, or Augustine. If anything, we repeatedly encounter a ready acceptance of autocratic secular power and an eagerness to enlist it to hunt down heretics, free thinkers, reformers, and other purveyors of heterodoxy.

In Europe, both before and after the Reformation, whether in Protestant or Catholic countries, the established ecclesiastics usually sided with the princes against the peasants, showing little sympathy for the democratic rights of commoners. Even as late as the French Revolution and the uprisings of 1848 which raised the banner of individual rights against monarchist rule throughout Europe, Catholic and Protestant churchmen sided overwhelmingly with the antidemocrats.[55] Through the Middle Ages, the church hierarchy opposed workers guilds, and through the eighteenth and nineteenth centuries and even into much of the twentieth century, Catholic and Protestant churches were more likely to oppose than support labor unions.[56]

Not long after Jesus' death, the apostle Paul counseled total obedience to the state (the very Roman state that had crucified his savior), claiming in Romans 13.1 that "The powers that be are ordained by God." Since there exists no authority save by act of God, it follows that those who do not submit to earthly rulers are in effect resisting celestial authority "and shall receive to themselves damnation." Preaching while that homicidal autocrat, Nero, was sitting on the throne, Paul assures his followers that the ruler is both virtuous and benign, working for the good of all and ready to punish evildoers. He deserves obedience not only out of fear "but also for conscience sake" "for he is the minister of God." So should people "render tribute" (taxes) to the authorities, for they do God's service.[57] Soon after this, at the instigation of a rival Christian faction, Paul himself is said to have been arrested and executed by the divinely ordained secular authorities.[58]

Did Christianity ameliorate the plight of the poor, as is often supposed? In fact, once the Roman Empire became Christianized, the chasm between the prosperous and the impoverished, especially in the West, reached new extremes "with enormous riches concentrating in the hands of the senatorial class."[59] "Distinctions of rank and degree multiplied and the inequalities of property widened."[60] The year 332 saw the promulgation of a law binding all *coloni* and their progeny to the estates upon which they labored. Henceforth, they could neither flee nor be released by their masters. By reducing free peasants to the legal status of serfs, ecclesiastical and secular landholders secured a permanently cheap labor supply. Similarly in the towns, membership in crafts and trades were unalterably fixed with no possiblity of transfer. Two privileged groups exempted from these onerous laws were the landowners and high officials. "As for the role of the Christian Church in all this," even Vogt grudgingly allows, "it cannot be said to have voiced any protest against the subjugation of the middle and lower orders."[61]

In sum, contrary to conventional belief, Christianity launched no great challenge against the dominant socio-economic order. The church raised no outcry against the inequitable social relations that bred poverty, slavery, and wars of conquest—as well as patriarchal domination, homophobia, cruelty to animals, and the like. Under the Christianized Roman Empire, taxation became still more oppressive, and the criminal law grew increasingly severe. Crucifixion was abolished but burning people alive at the stake became a favored mode of execution, a way of killing someone without technically violating the stricture against shedding blood.

During the "post-classical era," writes Joseph Vogt, pagan jurists were "partially responsible for an increasing brutality in the criminal law and in forms of punishment. . . . Numerous crimes were subject to the death penalty, often carried out in hideous fashion." Vogt avoids mentioning that the "post-classical era" was the Christian era, and that the increasing brutality of the Roman law occurred during a time of Christian ascendancy.[62] The practice of torture and mutilation—applied by the Romans in their judicial proceedings under severely limited circumstances—now became more common and was sanctioned by law. Ordeal by torture replaced the trial. The rack, the wheel, the stake, the spiked collar, spiked bed, spiked box, thumbscrews, branding irons, scalding vats, and hot pincers became part of Christianity's hideous new arsenal in the war against heretics and infidels. Punishment by ordeal—involving everything from branding and whipping to stocks and ducking stools—carried into Protestant regions centuries later, including newly settled communities in North America.[63]

Some things did change for the better. By the fifth century, an end was put to the bloody extravaganzas of the amphitheater. Never one to mince words, Augustine referred to the Roman games as "the filths of the Circensian pastimes."[64] Christian leaders generally opposed the arena not so much for its bloodletting and brutality but for the pagan rites and processions and the cultlike homage paid to the emperor at such events.[65] ~ ꝗꝙ

There were other Christian reforms. The church abolished human sacrifice and denounced infanticide. Certain prison conditions were made less harsh, at least on paper. Unilateral divorce, an exclusively male prerogative, was made more difficult as was the keeping of concubines by married men. The bishops ruled that the prohibition against adultery applied to husbands as well as wives, which had not been so among the Roman pagans. But under early Christian codes, the husband of an adultress could compensate for his injury by remarrying, while the wife of an adulterer could not.[66]

Those who celebrate Christianity's contributions to Western civilization might want to remind themselves of one of the church's most appalling gifts to human tyranny, the Inquisition, a heresy hunt ordained by the papacy that wreaked misery upon Europe from the early thirteenth century until well into the eighteenth. Endowed with nearly limitless authority, shrouded in secrecy, and freed from all accountability, the inquisitors indulged in unfettered butchery and rapacity, taking lives and confiscating property, growing rich in the process, treating the accused as having no rights, and treating everyone, from the meanest to the highest, as potentially suspect.

The victim's guilt was assumed in advance and confession was to be extracted by guile or ordeal. One's regular church attendance and generous oblations, one's verbal professions of strict devotion to orthodox doctrine, one's willingness to subscribe to whatever was demanded by the tribune — all were as naught. For the accused might still be nursing a secret heresy. The Inquisition had to uncover the impossible: the unspoken thoughts in a person's head. But luckily, the task was made easier by the procedure itself. The victim need not be proven guilty; suspicion alone was enough to bring on the fatal judgment. The inquiry almost always ended in execution or, less frequently, life incarceration in a dark dungeon.

Along with its judges, the Inquisition had its armed retainers, extortionists, spies, and of course, torturers and executioners. Lea writes that, except among the Visigoths, torture had been "unknown among the barbarians who founded the commonwealths of Europe, and their system of jurisprudence had grown up free from its contamination." Not until the thirteenth century did it begin to be employed "sparingly and hesitatingly" in judicial proceedings, after which it rapidly won its way into the Inquisition, administered at first only by secular authorities— on command from the Inquisitional tribune. In 1252, church canons prohibited ecclesiastics from being present when torture was administered, perhaps an implicit admission that the procedure was morally tainted. Yet within a few years, inquisitors and their servitors were absolving each other of "irregularities" under the papal bull so that they might directly supervise torture sessions.[67]

Those who confessed were burned as admitted heretics. Those who withstood all pain and mutilation and did not confess were burned as unrepentant heretics. Heresy itself retained a conveniently vague and elastic meaning. Prisoners who confessed under torture were tortured again to gain information about other evil-doers among their own family and friends, then tortured again if they subsequently recanted any of the coerced testimony—after which they were burned at the stake. Witnesses too were sometimes tortured in order to extract properly damning testimony. Anyone who showed sympathy or support for the accused, who dared to question the relentlessly self-confirming process, was doomed to meet the same fate.[68]

In 1484 German princes were reluctant to give the Roman

Inquisition entry into Germany. The Inquisition loomed as a rival authority, one inclined to go into business for itself, condemning not only the poor but some of the rich and well born and expropriating their estates. But the grave anxiety occasioned by peasant insurrections made the princes more tractable. The Inquisition opportunely arrived upon the scene, in Michelet's words, "to terrorize the country and break down rebellious spirits, burning as Sorcerers today the very men who would likely enough tomorrow have been insurgents," channeling popular restiveness away from the ruling interests and against witches and demons.[69]

One immortal character whom Christian mythology let loose upon the world with renewed vigor for the better part of two thousand years was Satan. Endowed with an unflagging potency excelled by no one save God himself, the devil exuded an evil presence that inspired churchmen to evils of their own. Sometimes Satan displayed a ubiquity that even the Almighty did not seem able to emulate. The more the "Evil One" was hunted down, the more he surfaced everywhere, until God's world seemed to be his. Indeed, among his various titles were the "Prince of Darkness" and "Prince of the World." Beheld in the depths of night or in broad daylight, on shadowy lanes or by well-lit hearths, in bedrooms and even church pews, Satan incarnate was a protean genius who could assume the form of any creature or object, able to occupy any space including the bodies of ordinary mortals. Thus did Inquisitional judges sometimes tremble when the bedraggled widow or frightened shepherd was hauled before them, for these "simple-minded devils of shepherds and sorceresses might be taken with the ambition to enter an Inquisitor."[70]

Some historians actually have apologetic words for the Inquisition. Ignoring all evidence to the contrary, Carlton Hayes and his associates claim that the Inquisition's most frequent penalty was a mere fine and confiscation of property, with imprisonment reserved only for the "more severe cases." And some suspects were required to undertake expensive pilgrimages, or "wear distinctive markings on their clothes." Hayes makes no mention of torture, and claims that the death penalty was applied only to the "relatively few" who refused to recant their heresy or who relapsed after recantation. The inquisitors, it seems, did not burn heretics but conscientiously strove to save their immortal souls through conversion.[71]

A different summation of the Inquisition is offered by Lea, who has done the monumental study of this subject: "Fanatic zeal, arbitrary cruelty, and insatiable cupidity . . . it was a system which might well seem the invention of demons."[72] In fact, it was the invention of the Christian church of that day. A religion is not something entirely apart from the crimes committed in its name. The church's war against heresy began in the first generation of its existence and continued without stint for more than sixteen hundred years. Centuries of Christianity's mean-spirited, violent propagation of a monopoly faith created the fertile soil upon which the Inquisition took root and flourished.

Affluent Believers

A popularly accepted view, as one writer puts it, is that Christianity's "converts were drawn in an overwhelming majority from the lowest classes of society."[73] Another writer maintains that Christian proselytizers made their earliest inroads "chiefly, if not exclusively, among the obscurer and poorer classes."[74] Another claims that Christianity was busy "planting itself among the poor and ignorant and deriving its support for centuries from the laboring man."[75]

Certainly, numbers of Jesus worshippers were drawn from the lower ranks since the vast majority of people were of modest means. But the early Christ sects were not primarily vehicles of the downtrodden and misbegotten. They took root within settled communities, among rich merchants as well as poor

canve seen differently

workers, prosperous slaveholders as well as slaves, attracting a disproportionate number of middle- and upper-class people, including such contemporaries of Jesus as Joseph of Arimathea; Sergius Paulus, governor of Cyprus; and Publius, the head citizen of Malta.[76] Jesus himself appears not too troubled with the plight of the poor. When his apostles criticize a woman who poured precious ointment on his head, "for this ointment might have been sold for much, and given to the poor," he praises the woman for having "wrought a good work upon me," and advises his disciples not to worry themselves, "For ye have the poor always with you; but me you have not always."[77]

The Acts of the Apostles reveal that Paul—himself an educated upper-class Roman citizen—converted a number of propertied persons such as Erastus, "steward of the city" at Corinth; Crispus, the chief ruler of the synagogue in Corinth; Felix, a noble Roman official and his wife; King Agrippa; Phoebe, the "patroness" of many; Lydia, a wealthy "trader in purple," a luxury product; and Greeks and Jews in the city of Ephesus, who responded to Paul's preaching by destroying their books valued at fifty thousand pieces of silver.[78]

As with any sect, the Jesus proselytizers were not indifferent to converting persons whose wealth and rank would lend prestige and material assistance to their cause. "Mindful of their precarious status in Roman society," notes Torjesen, "Christian communities looked to members with social status and wealth to be patrons and to function as their protectors."[79] During Christianity's earliest decades, various apostles were dependent on persons of means for their expenses, including the costs of their many voyages. Paul and Barnabas journeyed to distant Pisidian Antioch less because they were moved by the Holy Spirit and more because the Cypriot governor "directed them to the area where his family had land, power and influence."[80] In time, the Christian clergy came to live completely off the offerings of their parishioners.

By the third century, aristocratic converts were being moved quickly into leadership positions within the church.[81] Cyprian of Carthage, a pecunious landowner and aristocrat, became a benefactor of the church after his conversion and was easily elected bishop although he was still only a catechumen and had not even been baptized.[82] Luise Schottrof maintains that the early church was populated mostly by persons of modest means, yet she observes that "rich women and educated men" made invisible the gospel of the poor and came to play a predominant role in church organization.[83] From I Timothy (written probably in the early second century and falsely ascribed to Paul) and I Peter to the treatises of Tertullian (c. A.D. 155–220), church leaders felt it necessary to urge Christian women to eschew elaborate adornment, jewels, gold, finery, and cosmetics.[84] Such admonitions were so persistent, we might infer, because enough female church members could afford elaborate attire.

There was a notable presence of moneyed women in the early church.[85] A Christian lady of wealthy social status was Egeria, who in Jerome's time revealed herself as "well-read in Scripture and worthy of the hospitality of great bishops and monks."[86] There was also Melania the Younger, born into a wealthy Roman family at the end of the fourth century, who taught Emperor Theodosius and polemicized against heresy.[87]

Elevation in the church hierarchy came not only to those of affluent background but to those who won the patronage of rich backers. In the middle of the third century, for instance, the wealthy matron, Lucilla, bought the bishopric of Carthage for her servant Majorinus with a large amount of silver.[88] An unidentified Christian woman of wealth financed Origen's education and launched his career as the foremost theologian of the Greek-speaking churches.[89] Origen's vision was of a church led by upper-class males who gave guidance to those elements in society who needed it: workers, women, the poor, and the uneducated.[90]

In 212, Tertullian informed the governor of his province that Christians permeated every stratum of Carthaginian society, "men of your own rank among them, noble ladies and all the outstanding persons of the city. . . ."[91] In the eastern cities, likewise, affluent Christians were already serving on town and city councils, funding civic games, and working as magistrates, lawyers, and other professionals in provincial cities. During the first few years of Valerian's reign (A.D. 260–267), the emperor's secretariat was staffed mostly by Jesus worshippers.[92] Valerian himself evidently believed that Roman knights, senators, and ladies of quality were involved in the Christ sect.[93]

If early church fathers like Augustine, Ambrose, and Jerome championed a church of the indigent and oppressed, of slaves and penniless peasants, they gave remarkably little evidence of it. Descended from an aristocratic Roman family, Ambrose (339–397) acquired a liberal education, hobnobbed with Roman nobility, and served as consular of Liguria. At age thirty-four, before he had received the sacrament of baptism, Ambrose was transformed from governor to archbishop of Milan.[94]

Jerome maintained a literary correspondence with cultivated persons all over the world, and socialized with prosperous parishioners, one of his students being the wealthy Pammachius.[95] Another of Jerome's close acquaintances was Paula, a Roman matron of considerable wealth and social standing who founded monasteries.[96] While living in Rome from 382 to 385, Jerome "taught asceticism to a circle of wealthy women,"[97] for whom the instruction must have been an uplifting divertimento.

As befitting the devotees of Jesus, affluent church leaders sometimes downplayed their own prosperous origins. While serving as bishop of Hippo, Augustine announced (Sermon 356), "A gift of costly raiment . . . may sometimes be presented to me as becoming apparel for a bishop to wear; but it is not becoming for Augustine, who is poor, and who is the son of poor parents. . . ." The bishop was seriously misleading his congregation. He and his parents were anything but poor. Never in his life did he suffer material want. As a youth, Augustine frequented the baths and was sent to Carthage to pursue his studies. Like other upper-class young men, he supported a concubine, a woman whom he could not marry because of her lower social rank but with whom he lived for fifteen years and raised a son. Early in his career, Augustine was appointed to the prestigious chair of rhetoric in Milan, where members of the imperial court were in residence. And for a number of his adult years he resided on his portion of the family estate in Thagaste.[98]

On one occasion, Bishop Augustine admonished his congregation for failing to take up a clothing collection for the poor. This suggests that the congregation itself was not poor, just not very charitable.[99] Augustine himself associated mainly with well-appointed Christians. There was Nebridius, a close friend who had "an excellent family estate and house"; Dioscorus, a young Greek, and Alypius, a Carthagenian youth, both of whom could afford to study abroad; Romanianus, a man of great riches whose wealthy male companions also associated with Augustine; Pontitianus, who occupied a high office in the emperor's court; Innocentia, whom Augustine describes as "a very devout woman of the highest rank in the state"; Hesperius, a large property owner; Verecundus, to whose sumptuous estate Augustine retreated for a time; Largus, proconsul in Africa; Count Darius, imperial agent sent to Africa; Boniface, military commander of the Roman army; Classicianus, described by Augustine as "a man of high rank"; Proba, widow of a man who was said to have been the wealthiest individual in the Roman Empire; and Paulinus, who acquired great wealth by the two quickest means, inheritance and marriage, and who as bishop of Nola erected a majestic basilica for the congregation and a lavish dwelling for himself and his rich wife.[100]

Not without reason does one modern-day Catholic scholar, Abbot Ricciotti, conclude that the Christians were "not inferior to the pagans and often superior" in social status. Many "were cultured and learned," "held high offices in the state and were leaders of their communities."[101]

Vogt would have us believe that the wealthy church of the post-Constantine era had the resources and dedication "to relieve poverty and distress . . . shouldering the task of relieving misery wherever it was found."[102] But how could the church muster sufficient resources to alleviate "misery wherever it was found" when poverty and misery were so widespread? How could the church attend so generously to the impoverished multitude while not draining its own coffers and, indeed, while continuing to amass more and more wealth for itself? Individuals and organizations become rich not by giving away treasure but by accumulating it. Rather than sharing the wealth, the upper clergy busily shared *in* the wealth. So, by the 250s, there were men like Paul of Samosata who, while occupying the metropolitan see of Antioch, accumulated a vast personal fortune by extorting "frequent contributions from the most opulent of the faithful."[103]

The church proved less than immune to temporal blandishments. As early as the fourth century, corruption, luxury, and declining morals had become a serious problem among clergy and vagabond monks who "wandered about in search of legacies and inheritances."[104] In July 370, Emperor Valentinian instructed the pope that male clerics and unmarried ascetics must stop lurking about the homes of affluent women and widows with a mind to insinuating themselves or their churches into the ladies' bequests. Twenty years later, his successor deplored these "despoilers of the weaker sex," while conceding that the law had not stopped them.[105] Apparently, neither had the pope.

By the reign of Constantine, "most of the bishops, many of the priests and deacons and some of the minor clergy and monks were or had been wealthy men, who had never done any productive work."[106] In the centuries to follow, the higher clergy became the special province of the sons of moneyed and pedigreed families, men who invested their energies wholly in maintaining their landed estates and increasing their revenues.[107] In time, priests were appointed by the nobility, while church offices were sold outright to the highest bidder.[108]

As of the late sixth century, the church owned hundreds of thousands of slaves, who worked its immense holdings in Gaul, Italy, Greece, Syria, Egypt, and other parts of northern Africa, with bishops enjoying incomes considerably larger than those of any provincial governor. In Italy alone, the church possessed 1,600 square miles of the best land.[109] The papacy was the pre-eminent feudal overlord, claiming among its fiefs not only a number of towns and principalities but the kingdoms of Portugal, Aragon, Poland, Sicily, Hungary, and, for a time, England.[110]

Rather than relieving misery wherever it was found, the church through most of its early history performed no concerted missionary outreach to impoverished rustics and latifundia slaves. With Christianity a predominantly urban movement, the great mass of rural poor remained largely inaccessible to itinerate preachers like St. Paul who traveled from city to city. "The peasantry and persons in slavery on the land were the most underprivileged classes. Christianity left them largely untouched."[111] The downtrodden seldom had the leisure to indulge in pursuits relating to their immortal souls. The relatively few Christian clergy who ventured into rural areas thought none too well of the impecunious inhabitants, in some cases considering them little better than clodhoppers and savages.[112] A remark by Origen reveals a class bigotry that one might expect from a high-ranking churchman: "Not even a stupid man would praise the poor indiscriminately; most of them have very bad characters."[113]

Beginning with Paul, Christianity focused attention on personal piety and individual salvation, offering no opposition to the unjust economic conditions of the day. This approach allowed the church to appeal to persons of high rank, including eventually the emperor himself, who would have been decidedly put off by any kind of egalitarian religio- economic agenda.

The collusion with temporal authority and wealth continued well into the Reformation. Martin Luther championed the cause of his rich and powerful patrons, the German princes, and vehemently denounced the half-starved, overtaxed peasants who dared to rebel.[114] The supposedly austere John Calvin was not immune to the blandishments of royalty, entertaining a thirty-year friendship with the Duchess of Ferrara to whom he presented the first copy of his *Institutes*.[115]

Christianity is not the only new religion to have attracted— and been attracted to— affluent followers at its inception. The earliest converts to Islam were mostly young men of considerable privilege. Studies of the Mormon Church, Christian Science, the Unification Church (Moonies), Hare Krishna, and various Hindu sects in North America show that followers are drawn predominantly from the relatively affluent and better educated classes.[116] My impression of Buddhist groups in California, Colorado, New York, and Massachusetts is that the participants are overwhelmingly college educated and middle or upper class. The Buddha himself was born Siddharta Gautama (c. 560 B.C.) into a wealthy and privileged family in northern India. It seems that lower-income working people, while not immune to evangelical enthusiasms, generally have neither the time nor inclination to pursue newly packaged esoteric belief systems.

In the final analysis, contrary to the widely received view, Christianity prospered and triumphed because it aligned itself with the prosperous and the triumphant. The blood of the martyrs measured less than the commanding collaboration of secu-

lar authorities, the threat of the sword, the fires of the stake, and
the worldly puissance of the bishops.

Saints for Slavery

Enjoying wide currency is the notion that Christianity challenged "the whole institution of slavery" with "the idea of broth-
erly love," as one historian puts it.[117] Another claims that the
post-Constantine church obeyed the Christian command to "set
the captives free."[118] In fact, the church did no such thing.
Sacred Christian texts have nothing critical to say about slavery.
The Old Testament, incorporated as part of the Christian Bible,
repeatedly condones the taking of slaves in war. In Numbers
31.17–18, after killing all the men of Midian, Moses instructs his
soldiers to murder every male child and every mature woman.
But "all the women children," the child virgins, "keep alive for
yourselves." So through much of the Old Testament: mass murder, pillage, rape, and the enslavement of foreigners are acceptable practices, sometimes mandated by the Almighty himself.[119]

The New Testament either keeps its silence or actually
endorses slavery. St. Paul's claim in Galatians 3.28 that "there
is neither bond nor free, there is neither male nor female: for
ye are all one in Christ Jesus" is sometimes mistakenly treated
as an egalitarian avowal. In fact, he is simply dismissing
worldly inequities as being of no great moment, urging his
followers to focus on the higher—if less tangible—equality we
presumably enjoy in God's eyes. One's station in life matters
not, for God loves all, but with a love that leaves earthly
inequalities much intact.

Paul makes clear where lie his sympathies. He tells his followers to "cast out the bondwoman and her son; for the son of
the bondwoman shall not be heir with the son of the free-
woman." He instructs servants to "be obedient to them that are
your masters . . . with fear and trembling, in singleness of your
heart, as unto Christ." He admonishes "servants" to "obey in all

things your masters," and "count [your] own masters worthy of all honor, that the name of God and his doctrine be not blasphemed."[120] Since all authority comes from God, the master's command must be obeyed.

When a runaway slave (identified only as a "servant"), joins Paul's entourage and becomes a Christian, the apostle is faced with a problem. He is personally acquainted with the slave's master Philemon, who is also a Christian and who hosts a church at his residence where Paul himself had been active. As a Christian, the runaway supposedly is now like Paul "a prisoner of Jesus Christ," and in Christ everyone is equal. Yet the apostle, ever mindful of the master's earthly interests, sends him back to Philemon, with a letter urging that he be treated "not now as a servant, but above a servant, a brother beloved."[121] Paul has not a critical word about Philemon's presumed right to treat another human being as his property. We have no record of why the slave had felt compelled to flee a presumably good Christian such as Philemon, nor how he was received upon being returned to his overlord.

It should be noted that in most English translations of the New Testament and in the writings of post-apostolic church fathers such as Augustine, we repeatedly encounter the misleading term "servant"—which in contemporary English denotes a free employee—to describe those who were actually slaves. Paul was not admonishing and reproaching servants, as we understand the term, but slaves. The Greek *doule* and *doulos* are translated as maidservant and servant, when in fact the references usually are to slaves. In Latin, *servus* means servant or slave, with no real distinction between the two terms and no suggestion of free labor; just as in modern English, "servitude" does not refer to service but is synonymous with slavery. Such euphemistic translations conceal the truly oppressive nature of social relations during early Christianity and their ready acceptance by certain apostles.

In keeping with their own class backgrounds, the post-apostolic saints and bishops are all drearily supportive of the ruling-class crime of slavery. St. John Chrysostom advises affluent Christian widows not to remarry since they themselves are perfectly capable of disciplining their slaves without need of a husband.[122] St. Augustine considers slavery divinely ordained, a needed corrective for some. He observes that even Daniel, "that man of God," confessed to the Almighty that the sins of his people were the cause of their captivity. "The prime cause, then, of slavery is sin," that is, the sins of the enslaved not the enslaver. Servitude "does not happen save by the judgment of God, with whom there is no unrighteousness, and who knows how to award fit punishments to every variety of offense."[123] No slaveholder could have fashioned a more serviceable ideology.

Regarding those "exceptional instances" when virtuous believers find themselves in bondage to wicked slavemasters, Augustine offers this feeble reassurance: "[T]he lowly position does as much good to the servant as the proud position does harm to the master." Echoing Paul, he urges slaves to serve their masters "heartily and with good-will . . . not in crafty fear, but in faithful love." He concedes that God created none of us by nature to be slaves, but the present penal servitude "is appointed by the law" to preserve "the natural order and forbids its disturbance."[124]

Another illustrious saint-for-slavery is Ambrose. For him, enslavement is a path to rectitude, for "the lower the station in life, the more exalted the virtue."[125] Needless to say, the aristocratic Ambrose never thought to exalt his own virtue by placing himself in servitude. For St. Ignatius, slaves should "bear their slavery for the glory of God, that they may win from Him thereby a better liberty" in the next life. When Christian slaves proposed that their freedom be bought by funds from an Asian church community, Ignatius opposed the move. He feared that once free to indulge themselves, they would become "the slaves of desire."[126]

Early church authorities cautioned ordinary Christians against sheltering fugitive slaves. In the 340s, the Council of Gangra threatened to excommunicate and anathematize anyone who provoked slaves to insubordination. Slaves who took refuge in church were returned to their owners after an inquiry, with a rebuke to whichever party was thought to deserve it, a procedure whose aftermath likely bore more heavily upon the slave than the slaveholder. The church did little to evangelize slaves, even those owned by the worshippers of Christ. In time, the monastaries, being among the biggest landowners, numbered among the biggest slaveholders. Many Christian owners considered pagan slaves of better value than Christian slaves, for they would not have to be excused from work on the Sabbath. Slaves were regularly denied baptism unless given a good testimonial by their Christian masters, and they were accepted into the church only with reluctance.[127]

Persons held in servitude were debarred from ordination into holy orders, for as an early pope and saint, Leo I, noted, "[T]he sacred ministry is polluted by such vile company, and the rights of owners are violated."[128] An early church council in Spain ruled that Christian women who beat their maidservants (slaves) to death were to be punished by being denied holy communion for several years.[129] The relatively mild sanction bespeaks the slight value placed on a slave's life by ecclesiastical authorities.

It is easier to find pagan writers who were critical of slavery than Christian ones. The pagan Roman jurist, Florentinus, condemned servitude as "contrary to nature." And the younger Seneca vigorously denounced the inhumane treatment of slaves — but stopped short of advocating their emancipation.[130] Occasionally, Christian writers deplored the enslavement of Christians, but they accepted the enslavement of heathens, a practice that became especially praiseworthy in later times if it led to forced conversion. Indeed, from the fifteenth to the eighteenth centuries, Christian missionaries in search of forced conversions became actively connected to slave traffickers.[131]

In sum, there was nothing in early Christian teaching and practice that rejected slavery and much that supported it. So it was for over a thousand years, throughout the entire Middle Ages. There were a few minor exceptions such as Pope Gregory the Great (540–604) who, upon freeing two of the church's many slaves, talked of the "men whom nature from the beginning produced free" and who should be reinstated to their birthright. Yet Gregory ordered no widespread manumission, except of Christian slaves owned by Jews. Ste. Croix was able to find "no general, outright condemnation of slavery, inspired by a Christian outlook, before the petition of the Mennonites of Germantown in Pennsylvania in 1668."[132]

But there were individual Christian dissidents more than a century before the Mennonites. In the early 1500s in Santo Domingo, Bartolomé de Las Casas and a few other clergy (including the Dominican Antonio de Montesinos, probably the earliest champion of Indian rights) preached against the enslavement of native West Indians. Las Casas prevailed upon Pope Paul III to issue a papal bull declaring that the indigenous peoples had reason and souls and were therefore entitled to freedom. Las Casas eventually came out against the use of African slaves as well.

Such voices were the rare exceptions that should not distract us from the many Christian friars who not only supported but profited from the cruel vassalage imposed upon native populations—be it in Mexico, Peru, Española, California, or the Philippines.[133] Regarding the Philippines, under Spanish rule, the priests and friars took possession of the lands without benefit of legal title, "until they were in a position of absolute dictatorship in their respective parishes," writes Charles Olcott. "Enormous rents were charged and the people were taxed without mercy, while the friars, who held the land, escaped all taxation and accumulated fortunes. . . . Many stories were circulated, and not denied, of gross immorality on the part of the priests, besides rapacity and cruelty."[134]

In California and the Caribbean, the missions were centers for enslaving indigenous populations, forcing the natives to work under conditions that amounted to slave labor. Normally healthy and vigorous people, the Indians sickened and died in great numbers once they were confined to mission compounds.[135]

For centuries, the church was itself the largest slaveholder in Europe. As late as the sixteenth century in Spain, Christians were still debating whether African slaves had souls or were subhuman animal creations.[136] Well into the nineteenth century, in the United States, while some clergy joined the abolitionist ranks, many more remained vigorous apologists for slavery, writing almost half of all defenses on its behalf, often citing the Bible as their authority. Prominent proslavery clergy could be found in the North as well as the South.[137]

It cannot be held that Christians preached one thing on Sunday and practiced another the rest of the week. In respect to slavery, preachment and practice coincided all too well. Whether during the late Roman Empire or in the antebellum United States, Christian teaching offered an ideological justification for the worldly interests of a ruthless slaveholding class, and Christians themselves were among the leading slaveowners. Few of us were taught such things in Sunday school or any other school.

NOTES:

1. Elaine Pagels, *The Gnostic Gospels* (New York: Random House, 1979), xviii; also Robert Wilken, *The Christians as the Romans Saw Them* (New Haven, Conn.: Yale University Press, 1984), xii; and John H. Smith, *The Death of Classical Paganism* (New York: Charles Scribner's Sons, 1976), passim.

2. G. E. M. de Ste. Croix, "Why Were the Early Christians Persecuted?" *Past and Present* 26 (1963): 16–24; and Edward Gibbon, *The Decline and Fall of the Roman Empire,* edited by D. M. Low (New York: Harcourt, Brace, 1960), chapter 16, 193 and passim. I have consulted several different editions of Gibbon's book while writing this one, so notations will vary accordingly. I cite chapter and page but not volume, since the various editions have been published in one, three, six, or more volumes.
3. Hugh J. Schonfield, *The Passover Plot: New Light on the History of Jesus* (New York: Bantam Books, 1967), 190–191; Harold Mattingly, *Christianity in the Roman Empire* (New York: W. W. Norton, 1967), 33 and 57; Stewart Perowne, *Caesars and Saints* (New York: W. W. Norton, 1962), 58.
4. Pliny, *The Letters of the Younger Pliny* (London: Penguin Books, 1969), X.96.
5. Pliny, *Letters* X.97.
6. Giuseppe Ricciotti, *Julian the Apostate* (Milwaukee: Bruce Publishing, 1960), 197.
7. Robin Lane Fox, *Pagans and Christians* (New York: Alfred A. Knopf, 1987), 421. On the early Christian readiness to embrace martyrdom, see A. J. Dodge and James D. Tabor, *A Noble Death: Suicide and Martyrdom among Christians and Jews in Antiquity* (New York: Harper, 1992).
8. Mattingly, *Christianity in the Roman Empire,* 49.
9. Joyce E. Salisbury, *Perpetua's Passion: The Death and Memory of a Young Roman Woman* (New York: Routledge, 1997), 173; also Gregory J. Riley, *One Jesus, Many Christs: How Jesus Inspired Not One True Christianity But Many* (New York: Harper, 1997).
10. Gibbon, *The Decline and Fall of the Roman Empire,* chapter 16, 238.
11. Perowne, *Caesars and Saints,* 64–68; Joseph Vogt, *The Decline of Rome* (New York: New American Library, 1965), 161.
12. Fox, *Pagans and Christians,* 625, 664.
13. Joseph Vogt, *The Decline of Rome* (New York: New American Library, 1965), 92, 112.
14. Perowne, *Caesars and Saints,* 171.
15. Gibbon, *The Decline and Fall of the Roman Empire,* chapter 16, 215.
16. Michael Grant, *History of Rome* (New York: Charles Scribner, 1978), 403–404. Yet Grant claims that Diocletian's persecution produced "perhaps three thousand martyrs," which strikes me as a rather high estimate: ibid, 405.
17. Gibbon notes that "the afflicted church enjoyed many intervals of peace and tranquility": *The Decline and Fall of the Roman Empire,* chapter 16, 200.
18. Joseph McCabe, *History's Greatest Liars* (Girard, Kansas: Haldeman-Julius, 1951), 10–11. See also Ricciotti, *Julian the Apostate,* 49 and

passim, for another Catholic historian who puts the "Great Persecution" in skeptical quotation marks.

19. Ricciotti, *Julian the Apostate,* 203. For extended treatments of Julian, see Paul Allard, *Julien L'Apostat,* vols. 1 and 2, troisieme édition (Paris: Librairie Victor Lecoffre, 1906, 1910); G. W. Bowersock, *Julian the Apostate* (Cambridge, Mass.: Harvard University Press, 1978); and Gibbon, *The Decline and Fall of the Roman Empire,* chapters 22 and 23.

20. Robin Lane Fox, *Pagans and Christians* (New York: Alfred A. Knopf, 1987), 434. Origen's minimal assessment is all the more impressive in that his own father was martyred in Alexandria: Salisbury, *Perpetua's Passion,* 22.

21. Gibbon, *The Decline and Fall of the Roman Empire,* chapter 16, 214 and 214fn. Gibbon notes that Eusebius's history offers small numbers of martyrs: ibid., 237. And we should keep in mind that Eusebius was not wont to underplay the sacrifices made by the faithful.

22. W. H. C. Frend, *Martyrdom and Persecution in the Early Church* (Oxford: Basil Blackwell, 1965), 413.

23. Rodney Stark, *The Rise of Christianity: A Sociologist Reconsiders History* (Princeton, N.J.: Princeton University Press, 1996), 192.

24. Gibbon, *The Decline and Fall of the Roman Empire,* chapter 16, 208, 211.

25. Salisbury, *Perpetua's Passion,* 139–145; and Karen Jo Torjesen, *When Women Were Priests: Women's Leadership in the Early Church and the Scandal of Their Subordination in the Rise of Christianity* (San Francisco: HarperCollins, 1995), 90, 207.

26. "The Martyrdom of Saints Perpetua and Felicitas," in Herbert Musurillo (ed.), *The Acts of the Christian Martyrs* (Oxford: Clarendon Press, 1972), 109–119.

27. Salisbury, *Perpetua's Passion,* 135; also Eusebius's comments on those who recanted in Stark, *The Rise of Christianity,* 179; and Gibbon, *The Decline and Fall of the Roman Empire,* chapter 16, 216.

28. Stark, *The Rise of Christianity,* 189, 211–212. Gibbon offers primary causes for the triumph of Christianity: "the convincing evidence of the doctrine itself," and "the ruling providence of its great Author"; and secondary causes: the inflexible uncompromising zeal of its adherents, the promise of a blissful afterlife, the miraculous powers of Jesus and his disciples, and "the pure and austere morals of the Christians and their unity and organizational discipline": *The Decline and Fall of the Roman Empire,* chapter 15, 143–144.

29. Stark, *The Rise of Christianity,* 73–128; also Michael J. Gorman, *Abortion and the Early Church* (Downers Grove, Ill.: Intervarsity Press, 1982), passim.

30. Gibbon, *The Decline and Fall of the Roman Empire,* chapter 15, 187.

31. Jacob Burckhardt, *The Age of Constantine the Great* (New York: Pantheon Books, 1949 [1852]), 310 and passim; Gibbon, *The Decline and Fall of the Roman Empire*, chapter 20, 304–307.

32. Lane Fox, *Pagans and Christians*, 610, 623–668; Grant, *History of Rome*, 410; Vogt, *The Decline of Rome*, 91–94, 97–8, 117; Burckhardt, *The Age of Constantine the Great*, 304–309; Gibbon, *The Decline and Fall of the Roman Empire*, chapter 20, 301.

33. For an account of Constantine's reign that emphasizes his ambition and pursuit of power, see the classic work by Burckhardt, *The Age of Constantine the Great*, 285–286 and passim.

34. Burckhardt, *The Age of Constantine the Great*, 293, 306.

35. For further readings on the decline of paganism and the ascendancy of Christianity, see Henry Chadwick, *The Early Church* (Harmondsworth, Middlesex: Penguin Books, 1967); E. R. Dodds, *Pagan and Christian in an Age of Anxiety* (New York: Norton, 1970); and Ramsay MacMullen, *Christianizing the Roman Empire* (New Haven: Yale University Press, 1984).

36. Gibbon, *The Decline and Fall of the Roman Empire*, chapter 20, 299 and 420; and Vogt, *The Decline of Rome*, 118.

37. Ricciotti, *Julian the Apostate*, 82; Burckhardt, *The Age of Constantine the Great*, 319.

38. Lane Fox, *Pagans and Christians*, 666; see also George Mylonas, *Eleusis and the Eleusinian Mysteries* (Princeton: Princeton University Press, 1961).

39. Grant, *History of Rome*, 453–458.

40. Gibbon, *The Decline and Fall of the Roman Empire*, chapter 28, 411–412; and Vogt, *The Decline of Rome*, 162–3. By that time, some pagans had moved from an anthropomorphic polytheism to a platonistic monotheism, as was true of Roman philosophers such as Plotinus and Porphyry. While he sometimes spoke of "Providence," Symmachus seems to have remained polytheistic, contrary to what Cantor says: Norman F. Cantor, *The Civilization of the Middle Ages* (New York: HarperCollins, 1993), 73–74. Symmachus urged his compatriots not to abandon the old rituals directed to numerous deities, and he pleaded for the preservation of pagan temples in the face of Christian opposition: Salisbury, *Perpetua's Passion*, 10.

41. Burckhardt, *The Age of Constantine the Great*, 295.

42. Vogt, *The Decline of Rome*, 165; Jean Bacon, *The Greater Glory* (Bridport, Dorset: Prism Press, 1986), 10.

43. Gibbon, *The Decline and Fall of the Roman Empire*, chapter 28, 419.

44. See Saint Augustine, *The City of God* X.9–32, XIX.23, XXII.26–28.

45. No charges of cannibalism or incest were brought against any Christian—if we are to judge from the trial records of the martyrs: Salisbury, *Perpetua's Passion*, 78.

46. For surviving fragments of Porphyry, see *Porphyry's Against the*

Christians: The Literary Remains, with an introduction and epilogue by R. Joseph Hoffman (Amherst, N.Y.: Prometheus Books, 1994). Hoffman also includes a discussion of the second-century pagan philosopher Celsus, whose work we know only through Origen, his ardent Christian opponent: ibid, 147–151. For additional information on Celsus, see Robert L. Wilken, *The Christians as the Romans Saw Them* (New Haven, Conn.: Yale University Press, 1984), 94–125. For commentaries on Origen's work, see Charles Kannengiesser and William L. Petersen (eds.), *Origen of Alexandria: His World and His Legacy* (Notre Dame, Indiana: University of Notre Dame, 1988). For modern-day quests of the historical Jesus that offer critical treatment of the Gospels, how they came into being, how they blend history and legend, and how they were elevated to the status of Holy Scripture, see Burton L. Mack, *Who Wrote the New Testament: The Making of the Christian Myth* (New York: HarperCollins, 1995); and Schonfield, *The Passover Plot.*

47. Wilken, *The Christians as the Romans Saw Them,* 126ff; and Hoffman's comments in *Porphyry's Against the Christians: The Literary Remains,* passim.

48. Perowne, *Caesars and Saints,* 121–122.

49. Hoffman, *Porphyry's Against the Christians,* 164–165.

50. Lewis Mumford, *The City in History* (New York: Harcourt, Brace & World, 1961), 243.

51. Mattingly, *Christianity in the Roman Empire,* 63–64.

52. Aram Vartanian, "Democracy, Religion, and the Enlightenment" *Humanist,* November/December 1991, 11. On how Christianity incorporated Roman attitudes about law, property, and governance, see Richard Fletcher, *The Barbarian Conversion* (New York: Holt, 1998).

53. *Wall Street Journal* Op-Ed, December 30, 1994.

54. I discuss Rome in more detail in a forthcoming book.

55. Joseph McCabe, *Rome's Syllabus of Condemned Opinion* (Girard, Kansas: Haldeman-Julius, 1950).

56. For a significant example of the Protestant clergy's conservative anti-labor role in the American South, see Liston Pope, *Millhands and Preachers* (New Haven: Yale University, 1942).

57. All the quotations from Paul in that paragraph are from Romans 13.1–6.

58. The year was A.D. 64 or perhaps a year or two later: Michael Grant, *History of Rome* (New York: Charles Scribner, 1978), 345. As Tacitus tells it, the Roman populace had bitterly accused the emperor of having started the great fire that destroyed most of Rome in July 64, as part of a plan to build a new city named after himself. In order to divert suspicion from himself, Nero fingered the newly emerging secretive Christian sect as the perpetrators. He threw Christians to the beasts in the amphitheater, used some as living torches to light

the night games held in the imperial gardens, and crucified others: Tacitus, *Annals* XV, 38–44; also the discussion in Harold Mattingly, *Christianity in the Roman Empire* (New York: W. W. Norton, 1967), 31; and H. H. Scullard, *From Gracchi to Nero* (London: Methuen, 1959), 319–320. Tradition has it that Nero's victims included both St. Peter and St. Paul. Some historians say there is little evidence that Christians were persecuted outside the capital. Others say the persecution was not confined to Rome. Suetonius gives the matter only one sentence: "Punishments were also inflicted on the Christians, a sect professing a new and mischievous religious belief": Suetonius, *Nero* 16.

59. G. E. M. de Ste. Croix, *The Class Struggle in the Ancient Greek World* (Ithaca, N.Y.: Cornell University Press, 1981), 439. Despite its title, a large portion of this book is devoted to ancient Rome.

60. Lane Fox, *Pagans and Christians,* 21.

61. Vogt, *The Decline of Rome,* 98.

62. Vogt, *The Decline of Rome,* 203.

63. Alice Morse Earle, *Curious Punishments of Bygone Days* (Rutland, Vermont: Charles E. Tuttle, 1972).

64. Augustine, *Confessions* VI, 106. Constantine ruled against the gladiator games and eventually they died out: Lane Fox, *Pagans and Christians,* 669.

65. See Tertullian's comments in Salisbury, *Perpetua's Passion,* 127–128.

66. Vogt, *The Decline of Rome,* 105; Lane Fox, *Pagans and Christians,* 354.

67. Henry Charles Lea, *The Inquisition of the Middle Ages: Its Organization and Operation* (New York: Citadel Press, 1961), 117–118. This is a single-volume edition drawn from Lea's classic *A History of the Inquisition of the Middle Ages* (1887).

68. Lea, *The Inquisition of the Middle Ages,* 96–97 and passim.

69. Jules Michelet, *Satanism and Witchcraft* (New York: Citadel Press, 1939), 131–132.

70. Michelet, *Satanism and Witchcraft,* 136 and passim. For a study of the identity of the devil in early Christianity, see Elaine Pagels, *The Origin of Satan* (New York: Random House, 1996). On how the idea of Satan was used as a tool by the powerful for political and religous purposes, see Gerald Messadie, *A History of the Devil* (New York: Kodansha, 1997).

71. Carlton J. H. Hayes, Marshall Whithed Baldwin, and Charles Woolsey Cole, *History of Europe,* rev. ed. (New York: Macmillan, 1956), 306.

72. Lea, *The Inquisition of the Middle Ages,* 257.

73. Erwin R. Goodenough, *The Church in the Roman Empire* (New York: Henry Hold, 1931), 37.

74. Cyril E. Robinson, *History of the Roman Republic* (New York: Thomas Y. Crowell/Apollo edition, 1965), 429.

75. C. Osborne Ward, *The Ancient Lowly,* vol. 2 (Chicago: Charles H. Kerr, 1900), 651.

76. Perowne, *Caesars and Saints,* 83; Jean Danielou and Henri Marrou, *The First Six Hundred Years* (New York: Paulist Press, 1964), 240; Robert M. Grant, *Early Christianity and Society* (San Francisco: Harper and Row, 1977), 11.

77. Matthew 26.7–11.

78. See Acts 13.7, 16.14, 18.8, 19.17–19 and 31, 20.33–34, 24.24–26, and 26.28. Peter also preached to affluent people such as the ultimately unfortunate Ananias and Sapphira; and Philip preached to a "eunuch of great authority under Candace queen of the Ethiopeans": Acts 5.1–2 and 8.27–31.

79. Torjesen, *When Women Were Priests,* 12. Even some heretical leaders were well off. Thus Marcion, an early Christian convert who broke away and started his own movement, was a rich shipbuilder.

80. Lane Fox, *Pagans and Christians,* 294.

81. Torjesen, *When Women Were Priests,* 91–92, 155ff.

82. Torjesen, *When Women Were Priests,* 99–100.

83. Luise Schottroff, *Lydia's Impatient Sisters: A Feminist Social History of Early Christianity* (Louisville, Kentucky: Westminister John Knox Press, 1995), 150 and passim.

84. I Timothy 2.9 admonishes women to "adorn themselves in modest apparel, with shamefacedness and sobriety; not with broided hair, or gold, or pearls, or costly array." See also I Peter 3.3 and Tertullian, "On the Apparel of Women," in MacHaffie, *Readings in Her Story,* 27–33. Tertullian's main concern was that women not use alluring attire to tempt men and give license to their own innately impure female inclinations.

85. Lane Fox, *Pagans and Christians,* 311.

86. MacHaffie's comment in Barbara J. MacHaffie (ed.), *Readings in Her Story: Women in Christian Tradition* (Minneapolis: Fortress Press, 1992), 40.

87. Elizabeth Clark, *The Life of Melania the Younger* (New York: Edwin Mellen, 1984).

88. Gibbon, *The Decline and Fall of the Roman Empire,* chapter 16, 221fn.

89. Torjesen, *When Women Were Priests,* 91–92 and 100.

90. Origen, *Against Celsus,* 3.49, 51, 56, 59.

91. Salisbury, *Perpetua's Passion,* 61. From 260 and thereafter, the church was "attracting more upper-class converts than ever before": Vogt, *The Decline of Rome,* 70.

92. Perowne, *Caesars and Saints,* 145; Lane Fox, *Pagans and Christians,* 268–269, 294–295, 311.

93. Gibbon, *The Decline and Fall of the Roman Empire,* chapter 15, 188.

94. See Boniface Ramsey, *Ambrose* (New York: Routledge, 1997); also Gibbon, *The Decline and Fall of the Roman Empire,* chapter 27.

95. Vogt, *The Decline of Rome*, 202, 208.

96. Jerome, "To Eustachium, Memorials of Her Mother Paula," in MacHaffie, *Readings in Her Story: Women in Christian Tradition*, 33–40.

97. Leinenweber's notation: John Leinenweber (ed.), *Letters of Saint Augustine* (Tarrytown, N.Y.: Triumph Books, 1992), 39.

98. Leinenweber, *Letters of Saint Augustine*, 17; also Augustine, *Confessions*, passim. When he was sixteen, "compelled by no hunger, nor poverty," Augustine stole pears from a tree adjacent to his family's vineyard, an act for which he offers six pages of mea culpas. The point is, he admits to not being driven by poverty and to coming from a family that owned a vineyard: *Confessions*, II, 29.

99. "To the Clergy and People of Hippo," in Leinenweber, *Letters of Saint Augustine*, 109–110.

100. Augustine, *Confessions*, VI, VIII, and passim; Leinenweber, *Letters of Saint Augustine*, passim; Augustine, *The City of God*, I.10, XXII.8; Vogt, *The Decline of Rome*, 170, 176, 202.

101. Ricciotti, *Julian the Apostate*, 31 and 194.

102. Vogt, *The Decline of Rome*, 118.

103. Gibbon, *The Decline and Fall of the Roman Empire*, chapter 16, 221.

104. Ricciotti, *Julian the Apostate*, 51.

105. Lane Fox, *Pagans and Christians*, 310. Gibbon writes of the monks in A.D. 381–389 who engaged in "holy plunder" and indulged themselves with food and drink "at the expense of the people." Libanius's denunciation of the Christian monks for eating "more than elephants" was considered by Gibbon to be an unfair comparison: "Poor elephants! *they* are temperate animals": *The Decline and Fall of the Roman Empire*, chapter 28, 415.

106. Ste. Croix, *The Class Struggle in the Ancient Greek World*, 495.

107. Lea, *The Inquisition of the Middle Ages*, 9.

108. Torjesen, *When Women Were Priests*, 225, and Malcolm Hay, *Europe and the Jews* (Boston: Beacon Press, 1950), 158–159.

109. Ste. Croix, *The Class Struggle in the Ancient Greek World*, 495–496.

110. Hayes, Baldwin, and Cole, *History of Europe*, 307.

111. E. A. Judge, *The Social Patterns of Christian Groups in the First Century* (London: Tyndale, 1960), 60; and Wayne A. Meeks, *The First Urban Christians* (New Haven: Yale University Press, 1983), passim.

112. Consider the coercive and disregarding manner in which Symeon treats illiterate shepherds during his mission to Claudius: Lane Fox, *Pagans and Christians*, 289–291.

113. Lane Fox, *Pagans and Christians*, 301.

114. In his frothy tract, *Against the Robbing and Murdering Hordes of Peasants*, Luther writes: "Let everyone who can, smite, slay, and stab [the peasants], secretly or openly, remembering that nothing

can be more poisonous, hurtful, or devilish than a rebel. It is just as when one must kill a mad dog. . . ."

115. F. Whitfield Barton, *Calvin and the Duchess* (Louisville, Kentucky: Westminister John Knox, 1989).
116. Stark, *The Rise of Christianity*, 39–45, 54.
117. Harold Mattingly, *Christianity in the Roman Empire* (New York: W. W. Norton, 1967), 13. But Mattingly concedes that there was "no immediate movement for wholesale enfranchisement" of slaves after Christianity became the established creed.
118. Vogt, *The Decline of Rome*, 118.
119. Gibbon refers to "the sanguinary list" of murders, executions, and massacres that "stain every page" of the Old Testament annals: *The Decline and Fall of the Roman Empire*, chapter 15, 150.
120. The above quotations of Paul are found respectively in Galatians 4.30, Ephesian 6.5, Colossians 3.22, and I Timothy 6.1.
121. Philemon 1–16.
122. John Chrysostom, "Against Remarriage" in Sally Rieger Shore (ed.), *Studies on Women in Religion*, vol. 9 (New York: Edwin Mellen Press, 1983).
123. Augustine, *The City of God* XIX.15; see also Daniel 9.4–13.
124. Augustine, *The City of God* XIX.15.
125. Ste. Croix, *The Class Struggle in the Ancient Greek World*, 421.
126. David Brion Davis, *The Problem of Slavery in Western Culture* (Ithaca, N.Y.: Cornell University Press, 1966), 87.
127. Lane Fox, *Pagans and Christians*, 298–311; Burckhardt, *The Age of Constantine the Great*, 320.
128. Ste. Croix, *The Class Struggle in the Ancient Greek World*, 421–422.
129. Lane Fox, *Pagans and Christians*, 323.
130. M. I. Finley, *Aspects of Antiquity*, 2nd ed. (New York: Penguin, 1968), 15 and 158; Jérôme Carcopino, *Daily Life in Ancient Rome* (New Haven: Yale University Press, 1940, 1968), 57. On the protections and "rights" extended to Roman slaves in pagan times, see Carcopino, 56–61.
131. Ste. Croix, *The Class Struggle in the Ancient Greek World*, 424.
132. Ste. Croix, *The Class Struggle in the Ancient Greek World*, 423. The information on Gregory is from this same citation.
133. Bartolomé de Las Casas, *In Defense of the Indians* (De Kalb: Northern Illinois University Press, 1992); and Daniel Fogel, *Junípero Serra, the Vatican, and Enslavement Theology* (San Francisco: Ism Press, 1988), 18–25 and passim.
134. Charles S. Olcott, *William McKinley*, vol. I (Boston: New York, Houghton Mifflin, 1916), 157–158.
135. Fogel, *Junípero Serra, the Vatican, and Enslavement Theology*, 129.
136. Norman F. Cantor, *The Civilization of the Middle Ages* (New York: HarperCollins, 1993), 38.

137. On the prominent proslavery role played by Christian clergy in the United States, including many from elite colleges, see Larry Hise, *Pro-Slavery: A History of the Defense of Slavery in America, 1701–1840* (Athens, Ga.: University of Georgia Press, 1987), 261–285 and passim.

3

BISHOPS AND BARBARIANS, JEZEBELS AND JEWS

Christianity is credited with having saved Western civiliza-tion from barbarism. In truth, for more than a thousand years, during what some call "the Age of Faith," church leaders persecuted heretics and Jews, championed the subjugation of women, propagated homophobic intolerance, and collaborated with secular overlords in the oppression of the peasantry. Our schoolbooks and Sunday school classes have scarcely a word to say about such things. The church also warred against scientific exploration and exercised a censorial grip on learning, enjoying a monopoly control over written records, a control that still influences the popular understanding of the role of Christianity in history.

The Myth of the Devout Peasant
For an example of how Christian hegemony monopolizes the historical record, consider the prevailing image of medieval peasants and their relationship to the church. Many of us have been taught that during the Middle Ages, Europe's peasants enjoyed a symbiotic system of vassalage with their secular and

ecclesiastical lords. Furthermore, they were sustained in their daily toil by their deeply held religious convictions. As one noted textbook on European history put it, the peasant's "simple piety was proverbial."[1] Regarding this image of the devout peasant, E. H. Carr asks:

> I wonder how we know this, and whether it is true. What we know as the facts of medieval history have almost all been selected for us by generations of chroniclers who were professionally occupied in the theory and practice of religion, and who therefore thought it supremely important, and recorded everything relating to it, and not much else. The picture of the Russian peasant as devoutly religious was destroyed by the revolution of 1917. The picture of medieval man as devoutly religious, whether true or not, is indestructible, because nearly all the known facts about him were preselected for us by people who believed it, and wanted others to believe it, and a mass of other facts, in which we might possibly have found evidence to the contrary, has been lost beyond recall.[2]

During medieval times, the keepers of the faith were also the keepers of the records, a historic fact still embodied in the French word "*clerc*," which can mean clergyman, scholar, or clerk; and in the English "clerical," an adjective pertaining both to clerks and clergy. Henry Charles Lea reports that ecclesiastics "monopolized . . . the educated intelligence of the age."[3] Similarly Frederick Engels mentions how the clergy's monopoly over the written word gave education "a predominantly theological nature."[4]

With the recording of history so thoroughly controlled by one favored estate, the peasants had virtually no opportunity to speak for themselves. While there do exist numerous studies of feudal communities, they rarely offer any direct testimony from the common folk. But, in 1965, not long after Carr voiced his regret that all contrary evidence "has been lost beyond recall," the three surviving volumes of the Inquisition Register of

Jacques Fournier, Bishop of Pamiers, transcribed in 1318–1325, were retrieved from the Vatican Library and published. These tomes contain exhaustive depositions elicited by the Inquisitional courts from the peasantry of Montaillou, a village in southern France suspected of being a hotbed of Albigensian heresy. They offer a richly detailed description of village life taken directly from the mouths of the peasants themselves.

Drawing from this Inquisitional record, Emmanuel Le Roy Ladurie wrote a detailed study of peasant life in Montaillou. The picture that emerges is of a people whose interests ranged far beyond religion to include such things as property, farming, cooperative communal services, crafts, festivals, family relations, and love affairs.[5] The peasants of 1318 were inclined to be loving toward their children, and wept more easily than we, both in happiness and sorrow. Nor were they particularly enthusiastic churchgoers, according to one of the religious dissidents. In his words: "Not half of [the priests'] parishioners go to hear them preach or understand anything of what they say."[6]

One villager remarked to a group of men in the community, "Instead of burning heretics they ought to burn Bishop Fournier himself, because he demands that we pay carnelages, or tithes in lambs."[7] While this statement would be treated by the inquisitors as a blasphemy against the church, in fact, it was a decidedly secular complaint about class exploitation. The peasant did not want his labor and property expropriated by a parasitic, high-living cleric. Bishop Fournier's efforts were not confined to theological policing. He imposed increasingly onerous tithes, extending them to previously exempt agricultural products. Two of the villagers contemplated paying someone to kill the bishop "So we won't have to pay tithes on the lambs."[8] Not without cause did some of the village heretics claim that "the priests do not do their duty, they do not instruct their flock as they should, and all they do is eat the grass that belongs to their sheep." And "The Pope devours the blood and sweat of the poor. And the bishops and priests, who are rich and honored and self-indulgent, behave in the same manner."[9]

Heresy in Montaillou seems to have stemmed less from theological disputes and more from a resistance to the economic thievery of the church hierarchy.[10] The impression one gets is that these peasants were not involved in church affairs so much as the church was involved in their affairs. They feared not God but the Inquisition. They were preoccupied not with eternal salvation but earthly survival.

Le Roy Ladurie's study of Montaillou confirms Carr's suspicions but it most likely will not overturn the conventional history that treats the feudal peasantry as devout rustics who accepted their station in life as vassals of paternalistic overlords. This was the picture created at the point of origin by the churchmen themselves in a feudal Europe that probably had as many ecclesiastical lords as secular ones. It remains to this day the picture of slaves, serfs, colonized indigenous peoples, and workers presented by those who see no reason to advertise the bleaker side of class history. Commoners are either depicted as more or less content with their lot, or they are "conveniently forgotten altogether by most of those who pass judgment on the past."[11]

What is underestimated in the conventional view of this "Age of Faith" are the material forces of class exploitation. Engels saw important material class interests at play in the peasant wars he studied. That they sometimes were cloaked in a religious idiom "may be explained by conditions of the time."[12] It would be a mistake to reduce all religious controversies to their economic corollaries. Disputes about Scripture, liturgy, and the nature of the godhead were often pursued as if one's salvation were at stake — as indeed was believed to be the case. At the same time, class interests frequently did come into play. In Europe, the imposition of tithes, the sale of indulgences, and various other church practices that were the burning issues of the Reformation were the means by which the ecclesiastic hierarchy expropriated the earnings of common people, a forced upward redistribution of income that could fuel mass unrest.

Not surprisingly, popular disaffection spilled over into theological issues such as the church's monopoly over Scripture and its unwillingness to publish a vulgate Bible or tolerate informal home-centered forms of worship. Religious oligarchy worked hand in hand with economic oligarchy, and popular struggle against one often entailed struggle against the other. Indeed, in many instances the two oligarchies were one and the same: often the feudal lord was a bishop and the manor a monastery. The church not only colluded with the landowners, it was itself the largest single landowner in most European countries, expropriating wealth from the labor of slaves and serfs as might any secular overlord.

Although conditions varied between regions, the overall plight of the medieval peasantry was far from enviable. Peasants faced a heartless burden of rents, tithes, taxes, bailiff charges, personal dues, and fees for the use of such monopolies as mills, communal ovens, and breweries. "Their yields and incomes were low, their feudal burdens were heavy, and the deductions for the various dues to the church, the manor and the state left them and their families with only very little for their own consumption." In addition, bad harvests, livestock disease, war, and armed raids easily turned their lot into "a living nightmare."[13]

Over the centuries, sporadic peasant uprisings against insufferable conditions assumed such scope and fury as to send tremors throughout aristocratic Europe. The year 579 saw a major peasant insurrection against the Merovingian king because of tax burdens. Serious revolts occurred in 841 and 843 against feudal rule in Saxony. Peasant rebellions in thirteenth-century northern and central Europe shook Drenter, West and East Frisia, Dithmarschen, and especially Stedingerland from 1207 to 1234. In Germany, there were four major upheavals in the 1300s and forty in the 1400s. Nor should we forget the

Jacquerie of 1358 in France, the massive peasant insurrections throughout England in 1381 and in Flanders between 1323 and 1328, the Hussite rebellion in Bohemia in the early fifteenth century, the peasant wars in Germany during the Reformation, and the revolts of the French townships in the early 1600s.[14] Even this incomplete list belies the image of a placid, rustic multitude living in mutually serviceable relations with their lords and bishops.

Conventional texts that deal with the medieval period sometimes give passing recognition to the poverty and wretchedness of the serfs' lives. What they seldom do is draw a causal link between that poverty and the lords' wealth. Contrary to conventional wisdom, class conflict in feudal times was not a rarity but a constant. Even in the early Middle Ages, various kinds of peasant resistance probably occurred more frequently than we realize: sabotage, fleeing the manor, violating prohibitions, and refusing to pay dues or perform certain services or abide by particular regulations.[15]

In her study of a community near St. Albans, England, during the thirteenth and fourteenth centuries, Rosamond Faith found a long struggle between peasants and landlords over rents, forced work service, communal rights, and access to game and fisheries.[16] For decades, the St. Albans townspeople made common cause with the peasants to resist the abbot's demand that villein tenants "owed suit," obliging them to have their cloth fulled and their grain ground at the abbey's mills, with a portion of each going to the abbot. This arrangement was both an expense and a nuisance for the peasants who preferred to perform such functions in their own homes.

The abbey's chronicler waxes indignant as he gives us his side of the story — which is the only side we have — an account that reverses the roles of victim and victimizer: "The men of this town rising up against us like wild people, began to propose a great outrage against us; to no little damage to our church they fulled their cloths and ground their own corn to please their own wishes and also—just as if they were allowed to do so—ventured to erect hand-mills in their own houses."[17] To settle the matter, the abbot sent armed bands of men to seize the tenants' hand mills, confiscate their cloth, and imprison the resisters.

The abbey's mills were large and expensive and represented a substantial capital investment and a source of considerable profit. The peasants' hand mills were small and cheap, consisting of two round millstones. It was, writes Faith, "a conflict over technology."[18] It was even more a conflict over class relations, an encapsulation of embryonic capitalism, involving:

§ the concentration of the means of production in the hands of the few who could afford a large capital investment (the abbey's mills cost £100);

§ the need to valorize that investment and realize an ongoing profit;

§ the de-skilling of ordinary people, divesting them of their tools and domestic crafts, transforming them into dependent consumers of a monopoly service;

§ the use of armed force to impose an exploitative social relationship upon a resistant population.

Rebellions against these conditions, and the brutal ways they were suppressed, seldom make it into our schoolbooks. Not surprisingly, writers who are in denial regarding the class oppression of their own day remain sedulously oblivious to class oppression long past.

The Curse of Eve

The gender of a society's deity is likely to be determined by the gender of those in power. In ancient Egypt, Ethiopia, Libya, Mesopotamia, and other early civilizations, women exercised public authority and played a preeminent role in society—and female deities were the main object of reverence.[19] These pre-Indo-European cultures are described by archaeologist Marija Gimbutas as matrifocal, agricultural, sedentary, egalitarian, and peaceful. They "contrasted sharply with the ensuing proto-Indo-European culture which was patriarchal, stratified, pastoral, mobile, and war-oriented, superimposed on all Europe, except the southern and western fringes . . . between 4500 and 2500 B.C."[20] In that patriarchal world from which Christianity emerged, the deities were fittingly male: Yahweh, the Lord Jehovah, God the Father, and the *Christos* god-king, Jesus the Son.

Some of the faithful claim, however, that the Christian veneration of the Virgin Mother helped to elevate women from the lowly status accorded them in Greco-Roman society. In fact, for all their Ave Marias, male church leaders repeatedly proclaimed the inferior nature of women. This accords with Max Weber's observation that nominal equality of women and men before God is no sure indication that women enjoy equality of opportunity anywhere in the religious community. Nor does the presence of female figures of veneration or female cult leaders denote or promote gender equality within the cult if that cult or religion has a male godhead and a male-dominated mythology.[21] Referring to rustic Christian communities, Jules Michelet summed it up: While the Virgin as ideal woman was more highly esteemed with each century, the woman of real life remained in low regard.[22] Nor should this surprise us, for Mary's idealized image was that of the male-dominated woman: the suffering, nurturing mother; gentle, passive, loyal, and pure.

The Christian view of woman draws less from Mary than from the Old Testament image of Eve, the corrupter of Eden, who partook of Satan's offerings, casting an affliction upon humanity, for which all women thereafter were to live in submissive atonement. In Genesis 3.16, Yahweh places a curse upon Eve for her disobedience: "I will greatly multiply thy sorrow and thy conception; in sorrow thou shalt bring forth children; and thy desire shall be to thy husband, and he shall rule over thee." The image of Eve as the corrupter of humankind obtains to this day in the Christian mythology. A hymn I recently heard at a High Episcopalian church contains the line, *mundi primam materiam, quam Eva turbavit* ("the primal matter of the world, which Eve threw into chaos"); another hymn tells of *plangentia vulnera mortis, que Eva edificavit in tormenta animarum* ("the sobbing wounds of death that Eve built into torments for souls").[23]

Some feminist scholars of theology tend to downplay the misogyny that inheres in early Christian theology. They emphasize how male supremacy was a product of the secular society in which the church happened to find itself; as Christianity developed from a sect into a church and moved into the mainstream of the Greco-Roman world, so did that world's gender ideology insinuate itself into the church community. Hence, these scholars say, we can conclude that misogyny is historically incidental rather than theologically central to Christianity. And one need not — and should not — abide by sexist prejudices to be a good Christian.[24]

Those of us who might welcome the notion of a nonsexist Christianity still should not downplay the misogynist strictures that clutter Scripture and other early church writings. The Old Testament, incorporated as part of the Christian Bible, reeks with fulminations against the idolatries and licentiousness that the Levite priests ascribed to the worshippers of the ancient female deity. In Jeremiah, Ezekial, Hosea, and elsewhere, devotion to the female godhead is equated with harlotry, infidelity, dissipation, and witchcraft.[25] Jezebel, wife of a Hebrew king of Israel, comes down to us as the prototypic vixen, the treacherously evil female, although her real sin was to follow the ancient religion of Asherah, a female godhead. For this, she was gruesomely murdered by one of Yahweh's approved agents.[26]

According to the Old Testament, a young woman should be

stoned to death if found not to be a virgin. If a man lies with a woman who is betrothed to another, they are both to be stoned to death, "the damsel, because she cried [out] not." But a man who rapes a virgin who is not betrothed simply must pay her father fifty shekels of silver "and she shall be his wife; because he has humbled her."[27] Note that the payment for injury is not to the victim but to the paterfamilias who owns her. The victim is now nothing more than unmarriageable damaged goods. She has no choice but to enter a forced marriage with her rapist in order to mitigate the shame that has been brought upon her by the rape. Meanwhile, the rapist suffers no shame for his crime and no serious sanction as long as he makes proper amends for the damage done to the patriarch's virginal property. Such attitudes still prevail in much of the world. Even in North America, there continue to exist communities where the rape stigma is greater for the victim than the victimizer.

Some Hebrew men had several wives, and some Old Testament kings collected as many concubines as they could sustain. But for women it was a different story. A woman who dared to be intimate with someone other than her husband was guilty of a shameful abomination often treated as a capital crime. Under the Levite law only the husband could obtain a divorce, and this by simply writing a note, a bill of divorcement. A married woman, even a faithful one who had borne children, had no legal standing whatsoever and in most cases could be "put away" at will.[28]

The New Testament offers little that is actually new in the way of gender relations. I Timothy 2.13–14, probably written decades after Paul's death but borrowing on his name and authority, tells us: "For Adam was first formed, then Eve. And Adam was not deceived, but the woman being deceived was in the transgression." That same epistle (2.11–12) instructs: "Let the woman learn in silence with all subjection. But I suffer not a woman to teach, nor to usurp authority over the man, but to be in silence." There are Paul's instructions in Ephesian 5.22–24: "Wives, submit yourselves to your husbands, as unto the Lord. . . . [A]s the church is subject unto Christ, so let the wives be to their own husbands in every thing"; and in I Corinthians 11.3,7: "[T]he head of every man is Christ; and the head of the woman is the man." The man "is the image and glory of God: but the woman is the glory of the man." Again in I Corinthians 14.34–35: "Let your women keep silence in the churches: for it is not permitted unto them to speak; but they are commanded to be under obedience. . . . And if they will learn any thing let them ask their husbands at home."[29] The apostle Peter (I Peter 3.1–2,6) instructs wives to "be in subjection to your own husbands," voicing only "chaste conversation coupled with fear."

Over a century later, Origen echoes Paul's admonition: "For it is improper for a woman to speak in an assembly, no matter what she says, even if she says admirable things or even saintly things; that is of little consequence since they come from the mouth of a woman."[30] Origen's older contemporary, Tertullian, writing probably in 202, advises women to walk about "as Eve mourning and repentent" the better to expiate the ignominy which all females collectively inherit from the first woman, the odium of "the first sin" that delivered ruination upon the human race. Warming to his subject, Tertullian goes on: "*You* are the devil's gateway. *You* are the first deserter of the divine law: *you* are she who persuaded him [Adam] whom the devil was not valiant enough to attack. *You* destroyed so easily God's image [which is] man," It is woman's fault that "even the Son of God had to die."[31]

Two centuries later, St. Ambrose, archbishop of Milan, declared, "It is just and right that woman accept as lord and master him whom she led to sin." And St. John Chrysostom, bishop of Constantinople, warned, "Among all savage beasts none is found so harmful as woman." St. Augustine, bishop of

Hippo, wrote that "woman is incomplete without man," but man is complete unto himself for only he is made in God's image. The progenitor of the Protestant Reformation in the sixteenth century, Martin Luther, believed that "the regiment and dominion belong to the man as the head and master of the house." And Luther's younger contemporary, John Calvin, maintained that political equality for women would be a "deviation from the original and proper order of nature."[32]

Women were not only inferior, they were carnally transgressive. Christian churchmen were long preoccupied with female concupiscence. They considered the female body to be perilously seductive, the source of lustful offenses for which the woman herself was at fault. The German inquisitors, Kraemer and Sprenger, described women as intellectually deficient, unable to grasp philosophy, burdened with weak memories, not inclined to self-discipline but ready to follow their impulses. A woman was an imperfect creature made from a bent rib, therefore always ready to deceive, more likely than a man to abjure her faith, more susceptible to inordinate affections and malicious passions, a shameless Jezebel given to lustful abominations, and more inclined to seek revenge through witchcraft or other means. All of which explains why so many more females than males were judged to be witches: they "cast wicked spells on countless men and animals" and they "consort with devils."[33]

Images of female lasciviousness enfevered the minds of abstemious Christian males, to be expunged only with uncompromising denunciations. In Revelation 2.20–23, St. John the Divine denounces a female leader of the church in Thyatira: "[T]hou sufferest that woman Jezebel, which calleth herself a prophetess, to teach and to seduce my servants to commit fornication. . . . Behold, I will cast her into a bed, and them that commit adultery with her into great tribulation, except they repent of their deeds. And I will kill her children with death. . . ."

88

Epiphanius reconstructs his theological contest with Gnostic female Christians as a self-flattering seduction scene: "Not only did women under this [heretical] delusion offer me this line of talk . . . with impudent boldness, moreover, they tried to seduce me themselves . . . because they wanted me in my youth."[34] Jerome relates an oddly kinky story about a young man who was chained naked on a bed of flowers, only to be sexually assaulted by a beautiful and wanton courtesan. To preserve his virtue and quell his swelling temptation, the youth bit off his tongue.[35]

Never to be outdone in rooting out concupiscence is Augustine, who wrote, "There is nothing which degrades the manly spirit more than the attractiveness of females and contact with their bodies." If a man were aroused by "the scent of a woman, or her long hair," or other "feminine attributes" but could not find "release of his passions" in a woman, he would turn "to sow his seed in a boy or man."[36] So the great church father blames female allure for causing male homosexuality and even pederasty!

On the subject of women, secular Christian rulers proved no less deranged than their ecclesiastical counterparts. The first Christian emperor, Constantine, ruled that females who were "willing accomplices" in a rape—whatever that might mean—were to be burned to death, while unwilling ones should still be punished for failing to scream and bring assistance from neighbors.[37] By putting the burden of proof on the victim, such a ruling must have discouraged women from seeking retribution, and served as a standing invitation to rapists.

There were women who spoke out against this dreary misogynistic litany. Christine de Pizan (c.1363–1431) argued that with Holy Mother Mary as queen of heaven and "head of the feminine sex," it was incumbent upon men to treat women with respect and reverence rather than reproach and abuse. Women were to be applauded for their many contributions to human society and civilization.[38] Such sentiments, when not suppressed altogether, were destined to leave the churchmen unmoved.

Christianity did not just happen to find itself in a sexist Greco-Roman society—not to mention a sexist Judaic society—it was an integral part of those worlds. Absent any conscious theological challenge to the contrary, Christianity became strongly supportive of patriarchal despotism. Just as it embraced ruling-class values relating to slavery and other politico-economic relations, so did it incorporate the dominant view on gender: the female's traditional virtues were chastity, modesty, submissiveness, silence, and familial dedication. Her realm was limited to hearth and home, and even there she had to defer to male judgment.[39]

It was not always so. A number of early semi-secret, household congregations were led by women priests, bishops, and prophesiers.[40] Women appear in early documents identified as *diakonos* (minister), *apostolos* (missionary), *presbyteros* (priest), and even *episcopos* (bishop). Paul's repeated counsel that women refrain from speaking in church and from exercising authority within congregations would have been oddly superfluous had women not been doing such things. St. Epiphanius (c. 315–402) complained that "women among them are bishops, presbyters, and the rest, as if there were no difference of nature."[41]

By Tertullian's day and in the two centuries to follow (A.D. 200–400) female church leaders came under heavy fire and were eventually pushed out of their positions. Male clergy were accorded the title "father," a term not found in early Christian texts and specifically rejected in Scripture.[42] (So we read in Matthew 23.9: "And call no man your father upon the earth: for one is your Father which is in heaven.")

In the polemics of that period, we first encounter the niggling arguments against female clergy that to this day are promoted by the Vatican hierarchy: women could not be ordained because Jesus had only male disciples; and women could not sermonize because Paul thought they should hold their tongues in church

I remember reading that

gatherings.[43] Male opposition to female clergy rested on the presumption that publicly active women were unnaturally masculine, shirking their obligations to home and family, and prone to be shameless and unchaste.[44]

We have no idea how women clergy defended their right to address the religious community since their writings were not deemed worthy of preservation by generations of male scribes. Some glimpses of their arguments survive in the works of male polemicists who repeat them only in order to rebut them. Thus, we hear that some Montanist women clergy attributed a special grace to Eve because she was the first to eat of the tree of knowledge. They also note that the sister of Moses was a prophetess, and that Philip the apostle had four daughters who prophesied. Such contentions are known to us only because they are alluded to by Epiphanius, a fourth-century defender of church orthodoxy, who dismisses them as "useless testimonies."[45]

Through much of Christian Europe over the centuries, women were forbidden to make depositions in court or give testimony. They were forced into marriages not of their choosing, and could be put away at their husband's caprice. During the Middle Ages "peasant women often suffered more under the burden of daily labor than men, especially among the lower peasant classes."[46] For hundreds of years throughout Christendom, lasting well into the eighteenth century, tens of thousands of women were burned as witches. Women were sometimes burned at the stake for other transgressions: talking back to a priest, stealing, prostitution, masturbation, adultery, and bearing a child out of wedlock.[47]

Michelet offers some suggestive statistics on witch burning: five hundred in three months in Geneva in 1513; eight hundred at Wurzburg—almost in one batch—and fifteen hundred at Bamburg, both of these exceptionally tiny bishoprics. In Toulouse, four hundred souls were treated to the horrors of the auto-da-fé on a single occasion. The numbers were even larger

is there such thing today of a priestess?

in Spain where Jews and Moors were thrown in with witches. One judge in Lorraine, who burned eight hundred women, boasted that sixteen of the accused had committed suicide — most likely to escape the impending torture and flames — which he took as certain evidence of their guilt.[48] Nor was there much concern if the blameless were snared. As one medieval theologian explained, "Why does God permit the death of the innocent? He does so justly. For if they do not die by reason of the sins they have committed, yet they are guilty of death by reason of [the Christian doctrine of] original sin."[49]

I have no words

Well into the nineteenth and twentieth centuries, in most Christian nations women were denied advanced education and could not vote. Catholic and Protestant clergymen were in the forefront of the fight against women's suffrage, arguing that female submission was ordained by God. Women could not serve on juries, obtain divorces, make wills, sign contracts, open bank accounts, or claim property rights against their husbands, including the right to control the money they earned or inherited. Women who struggled for legalized abortion and contraception encountered vehement resistance, most persistently from Protestant fundamentalists and the Roman Catholic Church, as remains the case today.[50]

As late as 1931, a papal encyclical by Pius XI proclaimed that married life presupposed subjection and obedience of the wife to the husband. The encyclical reaffirmed one by Leo XIII, from several decades earlier, which charged that female involvement in public affairs and other activities outside the home were likely to cause a woman to neglect her duties to husband and children and debase her womanly character.[51]

In 1977, the Vatican reaffirmed the traditional view that women could not be ordained into the priesthood for it would violate "the type of ministry willed by the Lord Jesus Christ and carefully maintained by the Apostles."[52] And in the 1990s, Pope John Paul II held fast to the policy of excluding women from the clergy and denying them the right to artificial birth control and safe legal abortion.

By the mid-twentieth century, after protracted debate, some mainstream Protestant denominations in the United States ordained female ministers and included women in their policy-making bodies.[53] Whatever the long overdue gains made by women, the Christian ministries remain overwhelmingly male-dominated to this day. At the same time, women continue to do most of the unpaid work in the churches. Ages ago there were the church dames or *bénédictes,* as they were called in sixteenth-century France, who kept the chapel in good order. Today we have the church ladies who teach Sunday school, organize the bazaars, cook the potluck dinners, do the mailings, raise funds, and volunteer for charity work.

Modern-day male theologians and historians continue to downplay the history of female clergy in early Christianity. "When a woman's name [in the early church] is associated with a title, both Catholic and Protestant translators tend to minimize the office," notes Karen Jo Torjesen. "Instead of translating *diakonos* as 'minister' as they do for male office holders, they arbitrarily translate it as 'deaconess,'" a lesser rank.[54] Luise Schottroff cites male theologians who decide on their own that *diakonia,* when applied to females, is an office of charitable service, but when applied to males it becomes the work done by missionaries like Paul. Schottroff finds numerous examples of such exegetical surgery performed by male theologians on early texts that contain no such differentiation.[55]

Today's German theologians seem even more unflinchingly retrograde than their American cohorts. Schottroff records how she was anathematized by her male colleagues in Germany when she put forth her anti-patriarchal, class-egalitarian thesis on Christianity.[56] When Torjesen, herself a professor of Women's Studies in Religion at Claremont Graduate University, sent her German mentor, Ekkehard Muhlenberg, a copy of her book *When Women Were Priests,* he wrote back saying "I'm afraid I cannot bring myself to read it." Likewise, when Karen King edited a book on feminine images in Gnosticism, which she gratefully sent her German mentor, Hans-Martin Schenke, she discovered that the subject held no interest for him; he gave the book to his wife, thinking she might have some use for it.[57]

In ancient times, Levite patriarchs and then Christian clergy sought to stamp out the deeply rooted worship of female deities. Many of Paul's attacks on idolatry were directed against the goddesses Artemis and Isis. The first Christian emperor, Constantine, suppressed the worship of Ashtoreth as "immoral." In 380, Emperor Theodosius closed the temples of Eleusis and Artemis. "It was said he despised the religion of women."[58] The campaign to obliterate the female deity continues to this day in the realm of scholarship. The overwhelming prevalence of male archeologists, historians, and theologians, who are imbued with a patriarchal Judeo-Christian perspective, heavily influences what is emphasized and what is considered hardly worth mentioning. Although female godhead temples were unearthed in nearly every Neolithic and historic excavation, one male scholar simply echoes the Old Testament by writing that the female deity was worshipped primarily on "hills and knolls." A leading archaeological authority describes the female religion as "orgiastic nature worship, sensuous nudity and gross mythology," replaced by Israel's "purity of life" and "lofty monotheism."[59]

Without benefit of evidence, various male scholars reduced the prehistoric female religion with its all-powerful female deity to nothing more than a fertility cult. "But archeological and mythological evidence of the veneration of the female deity as creator and lawmaker of the universe, prophetess, provider of human destinies, inventor, healer, hunter and valiant leader in battle suggests that the title 'fertility cult' may be a gross oversimplification of a complex theological structure," Merlin Stone argues.[60]

While the pre-Judaic female religion is labeled a "cult," a term that connotes something less fine than "religion," the primitive rituals and mythologies associated with the Judeo-Christian Yahweh (or Jehovah) and later the *Christos* godhead are always respectfully described by these same scholars as "religion," just as the words "God," "Lord," and even "He" are carefully endowed with capital letters, while "queen of heaven," "goddess" and "she" remain lower case. The female deity who was worshipped as creator of the universe is frequently accorded but a line or two, if mentioned at all, and although she is referred to in most historical documents of the Near East as the "Queen of Heaven," some writers are willing to know her only as the "Earth Mother."[61] Once again, the available evidence is no match for the established ideology.

The Burning of Books

An image likely to come to mind when thinking of the medieval church is of cloistered monks, the keepers of learning and literacy, toiling with quill pens to produce beautifully lettered manuscripts. Torjesen tells us that "these monasteries were the bearers of the literary culture of Roman imperial Christianity, preserving the literary wealth of the Roman period. . . ."[62] Harold Mattingly sees the church as "a bulwark against insurgent barbarism" during "the dark centuries."[63] Henry Lucas describes the medieval church as "the repository of ancient culture . . . transmitting the literature and learning of antiquity. . . . [P]hilosophy, theology, art, literature, and learning flourished under its protective wing."[64]

The reality is something else. Once the church gained official status under Constantine, there followed what Luciano Canfora describes as "the melancholy experiences of the war waged by Christianity against the old culture and its sanctuaries: which meant, against the libraries. . . . The burning of books was part of the advent and imposition of Christianity."[65] Book burning began rather early as a Christian practice. As recorded in the New Testament, Christian converts in Ephesus responded to Paul's preaching "and the name of the Lord Jesus" by destroying a large store of books valued at fifty thousand pieces of silver.[66] After bestowing legitimate status upon Christianity, Constantine demanded the surrender of heretical works under penalty of death. In 435, Theodosius II and Valentian III consigned all heretical Nestorian books to the bonfire. And punishment was threatened for those who failed to deliver up Manichean writings for burning.[67]

One chronicler described a scene in the capital during Justinian's reign that had numerous parallels throughout the empire: several pagan Greeks "were arrested and taken forcibly from place to place, and their books were burned in the *Kynegion* and so were the images and statues of their miserable gods."[68] The *Kynegion* was the site where the corpses of those condemned to death were flung.

In 391, in Alexandria, a Christian throng, led by the bishop Theophilus, destroyed a major portion of antiquity's greatest bibliotheca, the Serapeum, the annex or "daughter library" to the main edifice (the latter was known as the "Museum"). The Serapeum, wherein was housed the pagan temple of Serapis, contained an irreplaceable trove of scrolls and codices dealing with history, natural science, and literature.[69] Gibbon bemoans this destruction of the library of Alexandria: "and near twenty years afterwards, the appearance of the empty shelves excited the regret and indignation of every spectator whose mind was not totally darkened by religious prejudice."[70]

Canfora debunks the widely held misapprehension that Julius Caesar—himself a great supporter of libraries and learning—burned the library of Alexandria, a myth given renewed currency by George Bernard Shaw's play, *Caesar and Cleopatra*.

The fire that occurred during Caesar's expedition in Alexandria was on the waterfront and nowhere near the library. Documentary evidence shows the library was still flourishing decades after Caesar's expedition to Egypt. In the years after the Serapeum was gutted, the Christians also purged the Museum, the main library, so that by the time it was destroyed by Islamic invaders in 641, it housed mostly patristic writings.[71]

In pagan times, the Romans had libraries of up to 500,000 volumes. But with Christianity in command, the ancient academies were closed and in many dioceses laymen were forbidden to read even the Bible.[72] By the end of the fifth century, the profession of copyist had disappeared, as had the reproduction of most secular writings. The six largest monastic libraries in the sixth century contained collections numbering a paltry two hundred to six hundred volumes, mostly religious in content.[73] The Greeks and Romans had produced a rich literature, but in Christendom, from A.D. 500 to A.D. 1100, hardly a book was written that currently wins our attention. Michelet describes the medieval church's scholastic "schools" as "lighted by the merest glimmer of day through a tiny slit." For hundreds of years "between Abelard and Occam the progress made is—nil!"[74]

The great Greco-Roman tradition of secular learning and education was undone not only by the general decline of Roman civilization but also by the ideological force of Christianity triumphant. While depicted as an oasis of learning amidst the brutish ignorance of the Dark Ages, the church actually was a major purveyor of that ignorance, a regressive influence in such fields as literature, philosophy, art, theater, science, medicine, anatomy, astronomy, mathematics, and commerce, suppressing these subjects entirely or confining them to theological servitude.

During the Dark Ages there were few instances of book burning because there were few books left to burn. The revival of learning and inquiry that came with the growing prosperity of the eleventh and twelfth centuries (labeled the "High Middle Ages" by some historians) also brought a revival of the church's bonfires. In 1210, the writings of suspected heretics at the University of Paris along with works by Aristotle were torched. In 1229, the Council of Narbonne condemned the possession of any portion of Holy Writ by laypersons. Works by Jayme I of Aragon and William of St. Amour were burned. The forbidden writings of Albigensians and Waldensians were flung into the flames. In 1239, Pope Gregory IX attempted to cleanse western Europe of Jewish books, especially the Talmud, which he and his associates incorrectly believed contained blasphemous allusions to the Savior and the Virgin. From the thirteenth to the early fifteenth centuries, in Paris, Aragon, Castile, Toulouse, and other such places, wagonloads of the Talmud and other purportedly blasphemous Hebrew books were publicly burned.[75]

Up until the late sixteenth century or so, the church hierarchy viewed unbridled literacy among the masses as a threat to religious and social order. Secular learning was perceived as a gateway to heresy. But from the seventeenth century onward, with the growing dissemination of the printed word, the guiding policy of both Catholic and Protestant churches was not to attempt the impossible task of completely denying access to reading materials, but to control what texts were read and how they were interpreted.[76]

The Christian church of late antiquity and the Middle Ages also waged war against nature and the flesh, including concerted campaigns against bodily hygiene. The Roman Empire's great public baths were closed. Saints were saluted for having never washed. A naked display of one's body risked mortal sin. Personal ablutions were deemed a kind of defilement, not only in the cloister but also among laypersons. "Never a bath known for a thousand years!" hoots the irrepressible Michelet.[77] No wonder so many of the faithful were afflicted with boils, skin ulcers, and other dermatological torments.

Upon becoming the official religion of the empire, the church waged war on the thousands of beautiful edifices that served as pagan sites of worship. "Many of these temples were the most splendid and beautiful monuments of Grecian architecture," laments Gibbon. The emperor had an interest to maintain the splendor of his own cities and the value of his possessions. But as long as they stood, and regardless of what neutralized use they might be put to, such buildings remained lures for a possible pagan restoration. So, during the 380s, throughout the Roman world, "an army of [Christian] fanatics, without authority and without discipline," invaded peaceful pagan precincts and perpetrated "the ruin of the fairest structures of antiquity. . . ."[78]

The goal of the triumphant Jesus worshippers was to convert "the whole world to Christianity. The thrust was forward, outward, and global."[79] This expansionist missionary zeal continues into modern times, contributing to the obliteration of the historical memories and cultural heritages of indigenous peoples around the world. As Christianity expanded into distant lands so did its suppressive mechanisms—including its time-honored practice of book burning. For example, in Mexico in the early sixteenth century, church authorities, assisted by the swords of conquistadores, denounced all Aztec and Mayan hieroglyphic books as the works of the devil, and systematically torched them, so depriving us of invaluable sources of historical data on Mexico's early civilizations.[80]

In 1995, a best-seller by Thomas Cahill breathed new life into the myth of the church as a citadel of light and learning. Cahill portrays the monastic clergy as having "saved" classical civilization from those whom he calls "unwashed barbarians," who "descended on the Roman cities, looting artifacts and burning books."[81] While the barbarians certainly looted, Cahill offers not a scrap of evidence to support his repeated assertions that they burned books or waged—as the Christians long had been doing—a Kulturkamp against lay literacy and learning. The barbarians seemed little interested one way or the other in written texts.

The one actual incident Cahill offers of books being damaged by invaders occurred centuries after the fall of Rome, in Ireland, when "Viking terrorists," as he called them, looted some monasteries and "destroyed books by ripping off bejeweled covers for booty."[82] Note, even in this instance their interest was in the valuable gems, not in the destruction of books as such.

Cahill offers the interesting theory that, from the last days of the empire until what he calls "the rise of medieval Europe," the less rigid and more literate Irish clergy rescued from extinction the classical and ancient folk literature (including Ireland's own rich contributions), and reintroduced such works to Scotland, England, and the Continent in the seventh and eighth centuries. Cahill's thesis is not of his own invention. Other historians have noted that Irish monastics produced an impressive flowering of classical learning. They not only preserved Greek and Latin literature but relished them with true literary enthusiasm.[83] If the Irish thereby "saved civilization," it was not from the barbarians but from their fellow ecclesiatics on the Continent.

Actually there were places in addition to the Irish monasteries in which literature and learning were preserved and even advanced: in the private manors of some few learned aristocrats, in the cities of the Byzantine Empire of southeastern Europe, among the Moors of northern Africa and Spain, and in other locales peripheral to Christendom. But Cahill's book, *How the Irish Saved Civilization,* would have had far less sales appeal had he more accurately entitled it, *How the Irish Played a Limited but Valuable Role Along with Others in Preserving a Portion of What Might be Called "Civilization."*

Cahill offers not a word about the closing of academies, the destruction of libraries, the banning of books, and the overall intellectual repression waged by the Christian church well before the fall of Rome and continuing long afterward. From about 320 to 395, the twenty-eight public libraries in Rome "like tombs, were closed forever," as he quotes the lamenting Ammianus Marcellinus—whom he fails to identify as a pagan and a noted fourth-century historian.[84] Again, the impression left is that the barbarians were to blame, but the closings occurred during the time of Christian domination, years before the barbarians sacked Rome in 410.[85]

Cahill does drop a few hints regarding Christianity's war against learning, mentioning Pope Gregory's hostility toward pagan classics, and St. Jerome's fear of damnation for having read Cicero. Ironically, the one actual case Cahill gives of book burning is by a pope: Honorius III's order in 1225 to torch all copies of a metaphysical work of some originality by Irish philosopher John Scotus Eriugena.[86]

Along with the closing of academies came the closing of minds. There was no limit to the enmity that leading churchmen felt toward secular arts and learning. The church fathers "despised all knowledge that was not useful to salvation," along with every earthly and corporeal delight including the enjoyment of music, art, and literature.[87] Early in the third century Tertullian related how in the next life he would laugh and exult when he beheld the proud monarchs, sage philosophers, deluded scholars, celebrated poets, tragedians, dancers, and others all groaning in the abyss and burning in the eternal flames.[88] With equal vehemence, Augustine disdains the "so-called liberal arts" that occupied his earlier years when he was "the vile slave of vile affections." Secular learning was worse than superfluous, it was pernicious. His studies in rhetoric, logic, music, geometry, and arithmetic had led him not to God but to his own "perdition." But now, as a Christian, he felt he could spend a lifetime studying only the Scriptures yet not fully plumb their rich mysteries.[89]

Before we blame the barbarians for destroying classical civilization, we might question whether the terms "civilization" and "barbarian" convey an accurate impression of the respective cultural levels of contending forces in the fifth century. In the mind of the modern reader, "civilization" probably suggests a higher degree of social development and literacy than was actually enjoyed in fifth-century Christendom, and "barbarian" conjures up images of hairy brutes in animal skins. In fact, the northern peoples had a level of civil organization, folk culture, agriculture, and military technology that in many respects was the same or not much less advanced than what existed to the south. In the first century B.C., long before the sacking of Rome, Gaul was "more extensive in area, more populous, richer in resources and only slightly less advanced technologically than Italy."[90] Something of the same might be said of Germany. On various occasions during the early centuries of the Christian era, contingents of Germans and other northerners were allowed to settle within the empire and even join the Roman army. "Many of these German officers were men of brilliant talents, fascinating address and noble bearing."[91]

Another familiar but misleading image is of Rome being sacked and the empire being overturned by a horde of marauding barbarians. In 410, the Visigoths, led by King Alaric, entered the city in an attempt to force the emperor to accept their demands for a homeland. Many Roman commoners — demoralized by the heavy taxes, corruption, and despotism of the late empire — were either indifferent to the invaders or actually welcomed them.[92] Roman servants and slaves joined in the looting of wealthy residences and the killings that ensued. On orders from Alaric, the invaders did little damage to churches, public buildings, and the city in general.[93] After six days, the Visigoths departed. They may have sacked Rome but they hardly brought down Roman civilization.

Even with the subsequent takeover of Roman territory and

the appearance of Germanic tribes along much of the Mediterranean shore, as Henri Pirenne notes, the northern tribes thought to settle themselves "in those happy regions where the mildness of the climate and the fertility of the soil were matched by the charms and the wealth of civilization." Their aim was not to disassemble the Roman Empire "but to occupy and enjoy it." What they preserved far exceeded what they destroyed or introduced anew.[94]

To be sure, from the sixth to the tenth centuries, successive invasions by Slavs, Bulgars, and Magyars from the east, piratical Scandinavians from the north, and Saracens from the south had a seriously disruptive effect on Greco-Roman society and commerce. The point to remember, however, is that much of the civic impoverishment was effected *before* these invasions, and must be credited to the narrowly spirited Christian orthodoxy that strove without stint for monopoly control over all cultural and intellectual output. While a Christianized western and central Europe slumped into the Dark Ages, there was no comparable devolution in the Byzantine Empire of southeast Europe, and there was an extraordinary intellectual burgeoning throughout much of the Arabic world.[95]

In sum, contrary to the conventional wisdom, we should spend less time blaming the barbarians and more time scrutinizing the role played by Christianity in ushering in a stagnation that lasted for the better part of a millennium.

Preparing the Holocaust

Upon emerging as the established religion early in the fourth century, the Christian church launched a reinvigorated war against other beliefs. Responding to the exhortations of their bishops and priests, Christian mobs destroyed pagan temples and sanctuaries, along with places of worship used by Jews, Donatists, Manichaeans, and other infidels and heretics, many of whom paid with their lives, most of whom had fared better under the pagan emperors than under their Christian successors.[96]

The treatment measured out to Jews composes an especially horrid record. Up until the early fifth century A.D., official Roman policy recognized the right of Jews to practice their strange religion (strange to the Romans because it was monotheistic) as long as they lived peaceably with their Gentile neighbors and with each other.[97] In A.D. 41, Emperor Claudius cautioned the Alexandrians "to behave gently and kindly toward the Jews . . . and not to dishonor any of their customs in their worship of their god."[98] Christian bishops were generally unsuccessful in inducing the emperors to stop treating Judaism as a protected religion. Even decades after Constantine's edict that led to Christianity's emergence as the official state-supported religion, Emperor Theodosius (379–395) issued decrees pointing out that the Jewish sect was prohibited by no law and that Jewish assemblies were not to be suppressed nor synagogues destroyed or despoiled.[99]

In time, the civic immunities that had been granted to the Jews were gradually rescinded by Christian rulers.[100] For the better part of two thousand years, papal proclamations, church sermons, pastoral letters, hymns, council edicts, and the pronouncements of bishops and leading theologians heaped contumely upon the Jews for their refusal to embrace Christianity and for the crucifixion of Jesus. If we rely on Scripture, which is all we have on this question, there seems to be no evidentiary grounds for blaming the Jews for the murder of Christ. The gospels of Matthew, Mark, and Luke clearly indicate that the Jewish multitude had nothing to do with the plot against Jesus. If anything, the populace enthusiastically endorsed the sermons he directed against a corrupt and privileged priestly class. Jesus's potentially seditious remarks caused the pharisees and elders to conspire against him, but because of his popularity among Jewish commoners, they moved cautiously. "And the

104

scribes and chief priests . . . sought how they might destroy him: for they feared him, because all the people were in admiration of his doctrine. . . . And they sought to lay hold on him, but feared the people."[101]

The crowd that eventually called for Jesus' crucifixion composed but a minute and unrepresentative segment of the two million or so Jews in Palestine, most of whom probably never had any direct contact with the preacher from Galilee. The other three or four million Jews living in Antioch, Alexander, Rome, and elsewhere throughout the empire had little sense of what was happening in Jerusalem and most likely had never heard of Jesus.

Scripture aside, only a grotesquely racist blood theory of inheritable and collective guilt can blame Jesus' death on millions of Jews who had no part in the incident—and millions more born in the centuries that followed. Historically speaking, the crucifixion was the work of the Roman secular authorities who carried out the deed, egged on by a handful of upper-class pharisees.

The image of the Jews as Christ-killers took shape in the fourth Gospel (ascribed to St. John), the author of which, writing from a hostile perspective outside the Jewish world, tirelessly uses the phrase "the Jews" where the earlier gospels talked of pharisees, scribes, elders, and priests as plotting against Jesus.[102] The slander was repeated down through the ages, hardening into an informal dogma. In 200, Origen charged that Jews had committed the most heinous crime of all: the murder of Christ, for which they suffered the destruction of their nation.[103] At about that time, St. Clement, serving as pope, ruled that the Jews were to blame for Nero's persecution of Christians.[104] A half-century later, St. Cyprian demanded the expulsion of all Jews from his diocese at the point of the sword, if need be.[105] More than a century later, St. John Chrysostom, bishop of Constantinople and a leading church father, sermonized, "The Jews sacrifice their children to Satan. . . . They are worse than wild beasts . . . lower than the vilest animals. . . . Their religion is a sickness. . . . God always hated the Jews. It is incumbent upon all Christians to hate the Jews."[106] The synagogue, he told his congregations, was "worse than a brothel"; it was "a criminal assembly of Jews . . . a den of thieves, a house of ill fame, a dwelling of iniquity, the refuge of devils." The Jews "know only one thing, to satisfy their stomachs, to get drunk, to kill and beat each other up like stage villains and coachmen," and Christians were strongly admonished never to associate with these "lustful, rapacious, greedy, perfidious robbers . . . this nation of assassins and hangmen!"[107]

This same Chrysostom is described by one Protestant divine as "the most eloquent of preachers" who brought "tidings of truth and love." And Cardinal Newman described Chrysostom as "a bright cheerful gentle soul" with an emotional temperament "elevated, refined, transformed by the touch of heaven."[108] In our own day, sociologist Rodney Stark strives in that academic fashion to present himself as a neutral commentator by neutralizing his subject matter. Stark argues that we should not dismiss Chrysostom as a "raving bigot," but see him as one among a number of ecclesiatical leaders who labored hard to separate the church from the synagogue in an age when the two were still closely intertwined. Chrysostom's attacks on Judaism "reflect efforts to consolidate a diverse and splintered [Christian] faith into a clearly defined catholic structure."[109] In fact, there is no reason to assume that these two views of Chrysostom are mutually exclusive: the bishop did indeed labor manfully to consolidate the faith, and he also was a raving bigot.

Consider the other saintly bishops. St. Ambrose, archbishop of Milan, defended the burning of a synagogue by a Christian mob, telling Emperor Theodosius with deliberate defiance, "I hereby declare that it was I who set fire to the synagogue: indeed, I gave the orders for it to be done so that there should no longer be any place where Christ is denied."[110] In A.D. 415 St. Cyril, bishop of Alexandria, incited a Christian mob to expel the Jews from the city and seize their property.[111] At about that time, St. Augustine, bishop of Hippo, declared that the fate of the Jews is to be downtrodden and dispersed, and that "the true image of the Hebrew is Judas Iscariot, who sells the Lord for silver. The Jew can never understand the Scriptures and forever will bear the guilt for the death of Jesus."[112] St. Jerome warned, "Jews are congenital liars who lure Christians to heresy. They should therefore be punished until they confess."[113]

Jerome, Ambrose, Augustine, and others were not obscure friars. They were leading doctors of theology and influential churchmen, whose writings had a widespread and lasting impact. They bestowed a respectablity on anti-Semitic preachments that continued through the Middle Ages and into modern times.[114] In the thirteenth century St. Thomas Aquinas considered it lawful and desirable "according to custom, to hold Jews, because of their crime, in perpetual servitude. . . ."[115] Several centuries later, Martin Luther, convinced that his modified version of Christianity would be readily accepted by the Jews, was furious to discover otherwise. It was their malevolent obstinacy that made them reluctant to convert, he concluded, and not any deficiencies in his doctrine or practice. So he attacked the Jews with the full measure of his hatred, urging that their synagogues and homes be destroyed and they be driven out of the country: "Verily a hopeless, wicked, venomous and devilish thing is the existence of these Jews . . . our pest, torment, and misfortune."[116]

Eric Meyers reports a wealth of archaeological findings in Italy and near Galilee of closely related communities of Jews and Christians living harmoniously together, a condition that did not survive Christianity's emergence as the triumphant religion in the fourth century.[117] In Spain and other parts of western Europe, during the Dark Ages (A.D. 500–1000), there was a stream of decrees from church and state officials ordering the populace and lower clergy to refrain from friendly relations with Jews. This suggests that the people paid little heed to such directives, preferring to continue their everyday social intercourse with Jews, failing to perceive them as demonic or dangerous.[118] As Joshua Trachtenberg comments:

> The constantly reiterated fulminations of Church authorities against close social and religious intercourse between the two groups ("It comes to such a pass that uneducated Christians say that Jews preach better to them than our priests," complained Agobard), against eating and drinking and living with Jews, testify to their unimpaired and cordial intimacy. Even the clergy had to be forbidden from time to time to be friendly with Jews. . . . Christians took service in Jewish homes as nurses and domestics, and Jewish traders dealt in ecclesiastical articles. Business relations were markedly free and close, and there are many instances of commercial partnerships between adherents of the two faiths.[119]

The Jew of Christian legend, the Christ-killer who rejected and was rejected by God, the devil incarnate who allegedly indulged in secret poisonings, blood rites, anti-Christian sorcery, ritual murder of Christian children, desecration of the sacred host, and other abominations—such a creature bore little relationship to the real Jew whom the common people knew. The demonized Jew "was entirely the creation of theological thinking; an exotic plant that did not speedily take root in the newly converted lands. The European peasant had to learn— and he learned slowly—that he was expected to equate the theological Jew with the neighbor whose friendship he enjoyed and with whom he worked and dealt."[120]

Anti-Semitism is usually ascribed to popular prejudice and a more or less spontaneous mass hysteria. In fact, anti-Semitic campaigns—like other such political, racial, and religious witchhunts—are frequently initiated and engineered from on high. Much of political life involves the rational manipulation of irrational sentiments by ruling elites. During the early centuries of Christianity, anti-Semitism was primarily the hyped product of ecclesiastic and secular leaders whose interest was to secure their hold over the populace. The problem was that the mass of people did not share their preoccupation with heretics and infidels. Nor did the peasantry have any great interest in Christianity itself, retaining for centuries a sub rosa attachment to magic, sorcery, and ancient pre-Christian practices.[121] If they needed centuries of prodding to become fullblown anti-Semites, perhaps it was partly because they were such lukewarm Christians from the start.

The officially proscribed Jew served as a convenient scapegoat, blamed for famines, plagues, pestilence, pillage, material want, and other supposed manifestations of divine displeasure. Anti-Semitism helped distract the populace from their real grievances about land, taxes, and tithes. Better the people storm the synagogue than wreak their fury upon the manor, the monastery, and the cathedral, inhabited as these latter were by their fellow Christians—who also happened to be their real oppressors.

Throughout the Middle Ages and into later times, Jews were afflicted with a gamut of legal and social disabilities that diminished their social status and stigmatized them in the eyes of Christians. They were subjected to forced conversion, periodic confinement, expulsion, special taxes, extortion, ghettoization, confiscation of property, bans on their religious observances, and the burning of their synagogues. Jews were banned from public office and most professions. They were forbidden to own farmlands or engage in export and import business. In various locales, authorities prohibited marriage and all other social contact between Christians and Jews. And there were occasions when Jewish children were forcibly removed from their families and handed over to Christian households or monasteries.[122]

What business monasteries had with children is not explained.

In 1215, at the initiative of Pope Innocent III, the Fourth Lateran Council (an ecumenical council) adopted a series of measures to degrade and impoverish the Jewish population of Europe: trade boycotts, social ostracism, expulsion from all positions of authority and trust, and the wearing of a distinctive badge that visibly branded Jews as a race of outcasts.[123]

Not all classes were eager to inflict such injuries upon the Jews, notes Malcolm Hay. "Hatred was the product of a clerical propaganda." During the Middle Ages, in countries like Spain, "no social class except the clergy showed any inclination to attack the Jews, who, owing to their intelligence and their industry, were contributing to the prosperity of the country. . . . But Jewish prosperity anywhere was regarded by the papacy as contrary to Holy Writ and a menace to Christendom."[124] As church leaders made clear in repeated pronouncements, the infidel Jews should be allowed to live, but only in a state of misery under the Christian yoke so that they might bear witness to the true faith which they stubbornly abjured. "Their own sin consigned them to eternal slavery," wrote Pope Gregory to his bishops in 1233.[125]

By the early medieval period, church efforts at setting Christians against Jews was having the desired effect. Even then, the anti-Semitism of the common folk was "supported by the official policy of the Church, actively propagated by all its organs of popular instruction, given added weight by the legislative enactments of secular and ecclesiastical authorities."[126] The mobs that attacked and despoiled Jews, reducing them to desperate levels of impoverishment, were often led by nobles and higher clergy who saw opportunities for stealing property or evading repayment of debts to Jewish creditors.[127]

One notable exception to a millennium of Jew-hating popes and bishops was Innocent IV, who in the mid–thirteenth century vigorously and repeatedly called for humane treatment of

Jews and who urged secular authorities to defend Jewish communities from Christian avarice. His proclamations "will surprise readers who have been brought up on history books [in which] Jews never appear except as greedy usurers. . . ."[128] Speaking of which, Christian usurers were far worse than their Jewish counterparts, who tended to lend at lower rates. Numerous observers from Geoffry of Paris, a medieval chronicler, to Thomas Witherby, an early-nineteenth-century Englishman, offer similar testimony regarding the willingness of Jewish lenders to incur greater risk at more reasonable rates. Even Bishop Grosseteste, no friend of the Jews, advised the faithful to patronize the more reasonable Jewish moneylenders and shun the Christian usurers because they were "all without mercy." Some of the unscrupulously rapacious Christian moneylenders were financed by bishops and princes, who shared in the profits.[129]

If anyone was obsessively engaged in the pursuit of money, it was the wealthy ecclesiastic and secular leaders of Christendom, who in this regard differed little from most other ruling classes in history. The authorities who engaged in mass expulsions of Jews from England, France, Germany, and Spain from the late thirteenth to late fifteenth centuries may have been propelled by a desire to preserve the "Christian purity" of their lands, but another more substantial motive was cupidity. Jewish property, homes, gold, silver, and precious stones were confiscated. As Malcolm Hay notes, the bishops and princes who attacked Jewish communities "were all animated by the same profit-making motive." Whatever the defammatory charges leveled against the Jews, "the result was always the same: Jewish money went into the pockets of the hunters." Jews who had any money or property were hunted to death.[130]

Entire Jewish communities were massacred, often at the urging of popes, bishops, priests, and nobility. Major massacres occurred in Germany, one of the worst in 1196. There were massacres in England in 1290, and in various European cities during the Black Death epidemic of 1347–1350. The next two centuries saw massacres in Hungary, Spain, and the Ukraine.[131] In 1451, John of Capistrano led the Inquisition against Jews in northern Europe in an orgy of criminal blood-letting that did not prevent his being canonized a holy saint and defender of the faith. During the crusades, at the urging of church leaders, Christian troops deemed it their duty to massacre Jewish populations as a prelude to their campaigns against infidels in the Holy Land.[132]

There were instances during the Middle Ages when church and state authorities issued condemnations of anti-Semitic outrages and mob passions. But never was there a denunciation of the theological ill will that incubated such violence. And the mildness of papal letters deploring the brutal mistreatment of Jews stands in striking contrast to the vehemence and venom expressed by the church hierarchy when denouncing Jewish misdemeanors (such as employing Christian domestics or failing to show a proper humility).[133] Thus, St. Bernard, though credited with criticizing the massacre of Jews by crusaders, himself delivered hate-ridden homilies against the Jews who were lower than "brute beasts," "a race who had not God for their father, but were of the devil, and were murderers."[134]

By the fourteenth and fifteenth centuries conversion to Christianity was no longer a way to escape persecution. A prime target of the Spanish Inquisition were Jews who had converted but were suspected of secretly practicing Judaism. Thousands of *conversos* were burned at the stake. Thus "Jewish blood taint" continued to be treated by church inquisitors as a contaminant irrespective of religious subscription, laying the grounds for the racialist anti-Semitism of Nazism.[135] In Russia and eastern Europe in the mid–seventeenth century, killings of Jews were accompanied by dreadful tortures; victims had their hands and feet amputated, were split asunder, flayed alive, roasted on coals, burned at the stake, or boiled alive in scalding hot water.[136]

From the nineteenth century onward, Jews gained emancipation in Christian countries throughout Europe, yet continued to confront serious discrimination. In 1800, in the United States, Jews were barred from holding state and local public office by provisions in most state constitutions that required officials to believe in the divinity of Jesus.[137] In Germany, Russia, Rumania, and elsewhere, Jews continued to suffer limitations on where they could live, and were barred from certain trades, professions, and government posts. Whole communities of Jews were subjected to forced conversion or deracination.[138] In Russia, the Czarist government fingered the Jews as exploiters of the peasants. Through the nineteenth century and at least until the Bolshevik Revolution of 1917, peasants launched pogroms against hundreds of Jewish settlements while police looked the other way.[139]

Toward the end of the nineteenth century, Pope Pius IX unsuccessfully opposed an Italian law that granted Jews equal rights in Italy. And to divert the public's attention from the anticlerical attacks of the day, Pius issued a series of anti-Jewish pronunciamentos. Meanwhile, Catholic publications throughout Europe launched Jew-baiting attacks.[140] Political conservatives founded anti-Semitic political organizations and publications in Germany, France, Austria, Hungary, and elsewhere.[141]

Former Jesuit theologian Peter de Rosa noted that, while the Roman church published over one hundred official anti-Semitic documents through the centuries, "not one conciliar decree, not one papal encyclical, bull, or pastoral directive suggests that Jesus' command, 'love your neighbor as yourself,' applied to Jews."[142] Not until 1959, on orders from Pope John XXIII—described by *Encyclopedia Judaica* as "the first pope to show a high personal regard for Jews and Judaism"—were anti-Semitic passages expunged from the Good Friday prayer, including a reference to the "perfidious Jews."[143] And it was not until the Second Vatican Council in 1965 that church leaders formally condemned anti-Semitism and repudiated the notion of Jewish guilt for the crucifixion of Jesus.

Seen in this historical context, the Holocaust is not the mysterious enormity it is sometimes made out to be. To ask incredulously, "How could such a thing have happened?" is to overlook the fact that Jewish people had been maligned, persecuted, and massacred for almost two millennia. When the Nazis came along, their venomous message fell on ground long fertilized by Christianity's age-old war against the Jews. Pierre van Paassen concludes "that Hitler neither could nor would have done to the Jewish people what he has done . . . if we had not actively prepared the way for him by our own unfriendly attitude to the Jews, by our selfishness and by the anti-Semitic teaching in our churches and schools."[144] Others such as Trachtenberg, Cohn, Schottroff, Grosser, and Halperin agree that "the underlying spirit of the Holocaust is almost 2,000 years old."[145]

Hannah Arendt sharply disputes that view, claiming that modern anti-Semitism is a uniquely contemporary phenomenon; a chasm separates the modern world from both antiquity and the Middle Ages with respect to Jewish affairs. Furthermore, she argues, modern anti-Semitism is racial in form, with no roots in Christianity, and is itself anti-Christian.[146] (Here Arendt must be thinking of the anti-Christian strain in Nazism and in some of the atavistic German *volk* cults.)

Arendt's view is open to serious challenge. To posit a sharp discontinuity between the modern world and earlier ages, as she does, "runs against common sense and sound historiography," argues John Gager.[147] There are no fixed and distinct periods in history other than those percolated in the minds of historians, who out of necessity must impose some organization upon time and social experience. Certainly the New Testament has made the transition from antiquity to the modern age, and in regard to Christian anti-Semitism, portions of the New Testament provided the first seeds. There are passages in the fourth Gospel and elsewhere that fuel the myth of the Jews as Christ killers.

Arendt notwithstanding, the images of the Jew as the cause of economic disasters; the Jew as carrier of a blood taint, as beastial, diabolic, avaricious, treacherous, murderously preying upon the Gentile community, and deserving of perpetual suffering and even extermination—such cruel caricatures propagated by popes, bishops, and saints over the centuries can also be found *mutatis mutandis* in Nazi propaganda. Nazi minister of propaganda Joseph Goebbels made clear his debt to Christian demonology when he exclaimed: "Such is their wickedness that no one should be surprised to see a Jew as the personification of the Devil among our people, representing everything that is evil."[148]

To be sure, not all Nazi anti-Semitic caricatures were appropriated directly from Christian sources; some came via nineteenth-century rightist political organizations and other secular propagandists. But these latter images, in turn, had a theological source. A study by Uriel Tal shows the impact in Germany during the Second Reich (1870–1914) of two anti-Semitisms, one Christian, propagated widely by pastors and theologians, and the other explicitly anti-Christian. The latter variety had borrowed heavily from Christian sources.[149] For instance, the expression, "the Jews are our misfortune," adopted as a slogan by the leader of the Christian-Socialist Party in Germany in the late nineteenth century, later became a popular Nazi motto. While erroneously ascribed to the nationalist ideologue Treitschke, it actually comes from Luther.[150]

More significant than words were Christianity's terrible *practices:* ghettoization, forced deracination, denying legal and eco-

nomic rights, expropriating property, defiling synagogues, looting and destroying Jewish homes and businesses, burning sacred
and secular Jewish literature, forcing the wearing of badges of
dishonor, humiliating assaults, unspeakable torture, and
repeated massacres — all were part of Christianity's war against
the Jews centuries before the Nazis put these same practices into
more systematic operation from 1933 to 1945, exterminating six
million Jews in what became known as the Holocaust.

Nazi anti-Semitism served a scapegoating function similar to
the older Christian Jew-baiting. Hitler's propagandists blamed
the Jews for just about all existing social ills in an effort to direct
popular grievances away from the giant cartels that were the
major authors of economic injustice and hard times.[151]

The Vatican itself belatedly seems to have recognized a link
between traditional Christian anti-Semitism and the Nazi variety. In 1998, it issued a formal statement denouncing crimes
against the Jews perpetrated over the centuries, and deploring
the generally dismal record of Christian nations in assisting the
Jewish people during the Nazi oppression:

> Erroneous and unjust interpretations of the New Testament
> regarding the Jewish people and their alleged culpability have
> circulated for too long, engendering feelings of hostility toward
> this people. The fact that the Shoah took place in Europe, that
> is, in countries of long-standing Christian civilization, raises the
> question of the relation between the Nazi persecution and the
> attitudes down the centuries of Christians toward the Jews. . . .
> The history of relations between Jews and Christians is a tor-
> mented one. . . . [T]he balance of these relations over 2,000
> years has been quite negative. . . . The spoiled seeds of anti-
> Judaism and anti-Semitism must never again be allowed to take
> root in any human heart.[152]

While praiseworthy for the sentiments expressed, the Vatican
statement also can be criticized for what is left unsaid. Anti-
Semitism is seen solely as an "attitude" entertained by an undif-

ferentiated population of Christians, a product of something vaguely described as "Christian civilization." Relations between Jews and Christians are equivocally described as "tormented" and "negative" in what amounts to a false balancing act. What is missing is any reference to the crucial role played by the church itself, the centuries of calumny and atrocity against a law-abiding minority by popes, bishops, saints, monks, church-inspired mobs, and inquisitors. Also omitted from the Vatican statement is any mention of the collaboration between prominent members of the church hierarchy and the Nazis before, during, and after World War II.[153]

Although the persecution of Jews throughout Christendom continued for the better part of two millennia, it often goes unmentioned in textbooks on European history, except for references to the Nazi Holocaust. The great contributions of the Jewish people to science, medicine, art, literature, commerce, and politics are seldom mentioned, though there sometimes is a reference to how the Jews were forced to become usurers (with nothing said of Christian usury).

In sum, contrary to popular notions, from early in its history Christianity supported secular and ecclesiastical autocracy, class oppression, slavery, sexism, and anti-Semitism. For centuries it had a severely regressive effect upon just about every area of learning. In addition, church officials tortured and executed tens of thousands of "witches," and exterminated whole populations of heretics, infidels, and Jews.

Far from being a purveyor of human rights, Christianity has more often been an antagonist. Most of the struggles for class justice, emancipation, gender equality, religious tolerance, and other rights have been waged by secular, not religious, groups, a fact seldom acknowledged in our classrooms.

In recent decades, those within the Roman Catholic Church who have struggled for human rights and social justice have been repeatedly suppressed by the Vatican under the aegis of

Pope John Paul II. In the late 1970s, the Vatican threw its weight against the liberation theology movement. John Paul II packed the College of Cardinals with conservatives. In Latin America he appointed a large number of conservative bishops to impoverished urban dioceses, transferring liberal ones to remote rural areas. He suppressed liberation theology curricula in seminaries and imposed Vatican manuals, silenced liberation theology theorists, and forbade liberal and radical clergy from holding public office.[154] The prelates were to administer to souls and avoid engaging in political struggles. Meanwhile, John Paul II, that most political of all popes, actively supported the political involvements of his more conservative clergy and laity who operated in a quasi-fascist organization, Opus Dei.[155] The pope himself continually intervened in world affairs, remaining up to his ears in counterrevolutionary politics, even entering into a clandestine alliance with President Reagan in an attempt to hasten the dissolution of Communism in eastern Europe.[156]

In the average school, instructors who raise serious questions about the theory and practice of Christianity run the risk of encountering uncomfortable pressures from parents, clergy, or superiors.[157] Those who engage in a critical research of Christianity's history face certain hurdles. As Gager puts it:

> For the most part the task of dismantling the orthodox version of the past consists of laborious deconstruction and intelligent guesswork. Frustration is a constant companion. The problem is not merely that sources for the "other voices" are missing. Such sources, after all, belong to the spoils of victory and frequently have been consumed in the celebratory bonfires. An even more persistent frustration lies in the difficulty of altering our habitual ways of thinking. Without knowing it, we perceive the past according to paradigms first created many centuries ago.[158]

Today, one would have to search long and hard to find a critical discussion of the darker side of Christian history in the major media, history schoolbooks, or in mainstream publications and other avenues of public discourse. History has been kind to the Christians, even the worst among them, because the Christians have written so much of it and because the varieties of organized Christianity persist as highly coercive forces in Western society.

NOTES:

1. Carlton J. H. Hayes, Marshall Whithed Baldwin, and Charles Woolsey Cole, *History of Europe,* rev. ed. (New York: Macmillan, 1956), 308.
2. Edward Hallett Carr, *What is History?* (New York: Random House, 1961), 12–13.
3. Henry Charles Lea, *The Inquisition of the Middle Ages: Its Organization and Operation* (New York: Citadel Press, 1961), 5.
4. Frederick Engels, *The Peasant War in Germany* (New York: International Publishers, 1966), 52.
5. Emmanuel Le Roy Ladurie, *Montaillou, The Promised Land of Error* (New York: Vintage, 1979). The original Inquisition record from the Vatican Library is cited by Le Roy Ladurie as: Jean Duvernoy (ed.), *Le Registre d'Inquisition de Jacques Fournier, evêque de Pamiers (1318–1325),* 3 vols. (Toulouse, 1965).
6. Le Roy Ladurie, *Montaillou,* 246. Devotion to orthodoxy might be measured by the testimony of one peasant woman who admitted having an affair with a clergyman. She considered it not displeasing to God because "I liked it." Cynics among us might suspect it was the priest who self-servingly fed her this unusual theology. In fact, she herself was careful to add: "But now, with him, it does not please me any more. And so now, if he knew me carnally, I should think it a sin!": ibid., 151 and 159.
7. Le Roy Ladurie, *Montaillou,* 69.
8. Le Roy Ladurie, *Montaillou,* 321. In 1334 Bishop Fournier was elected pope of Avignon under the name of Benedict XII.
9. Le Roy Ladurie, *Montaillou,* xi, 317, and 333.
10. Le Roy Ladurie, *Montaillou,* 231 and 243.
11. G. E. M. de Ste. Croix, *The Class Struggle in the Ancient Greek World* (Ithaca, N.Y.: Cornell University Press, 1981), 351.
12. Engels, *The Peasant War in Germany,* 50–51. In similar fashion, Finley describes the turbulence in Judaea during the first century A.D., "The people were divided, bitterly, and it is characteristic of Jewish history in this period that class divisions and political conflicts were indistinguishable from sectarian religious disputes": M. I.

Finley, *Aspects of Antiquity* (New York: Viking Penguin, 1968), 181. See my discussion of Josephus in chapter 3.

13. Werner Rösener, *Peasants in the Middle Ages* (Urbana and Chicago: University of Illinois Press, 1992), 140 and 272.

14. Rösener, *Peasants in the Middle Ages,* 237–251, also the various German, French, and English sources Rösener cites: ibid., 310, n6; and B. H. Slicher van Bath, *The Agrarian History of Western Europe, 500–1850* (New York: St. Martin's Press, 1964), 189ff; Roland Mousnier, *Peasant Uprisings* (New York: Harper & Row, 1970); A. L. Morton, *A People's History of England* (New York: International Publishers, 1968 [1938]), 120–127; Ye. Agibalova and G. Donskoy, *History of the Middle Ages* (Moscow: Progress Publishers, 1982), 112–113, 133–144; Engels, *The Peasant War in Germany*; Marc Bloch, *French Rural History* (Berkeley: University of California Press, 1966); Yves-Marie Berce, *History of Peasant Revolts: The Social Origins of Rebellion in Early Modern France* (Ithaca, N.Y.: Cornell University Press, 1990).

15. All this leads Rösener to observe, "It is not necessarily a reversion to rigid class-war truisms to acknowledge that peasant revolts and peasant resistance occurred throughout the Middle Ages, although they were more frequent in some centuries than in others." Rösener does not explain why it is necessary to allude dismissively to "rigid class-war truisms" when studying class-war realities, nor what he means by such a term in this context: *Peasants in the Middle Ages,* 237.

16. Rosamond Faith, "The Class Struggle in Fourteenth-Century England," in Raphael Samuel (ed.), *People's History and Socialist Theory* (London: Routledge & Kegan Paul, 1981), 50–60.

17. Faith, "The Class Struggle in Fourteenth-Century England," 52.

18. Faith, "The Class Struggle in Fourteenth-Century England," 54.

19. For a discussion of some of the pertinent literature, see Merlin Stone, *When God Was a Woman* (New York: Harcourt Brace, 1976), 30–61.

20. Marija Gimbutas, *The Goddesses and Gods of Old Europe,* new edition (Berkeley, Calif.: University of California Press, 1982), 9 and passim.

21. Max Weber, *Economy and Society,* vol. 2, edited by Guenther Roth and Claus Wittich (New York: Bedminster Press, 1968) 488ff. Ironically, as the devotion to Mary grew, so did the power of the male clergy, and so were the clerical roles of women diminished or eliminated altogether: Caroline Walker Bynum, *Fragmentation and Redemption: Essays on Gender and the Human Body in Medieval Religion* (New York: Zone Books, 1991), 58–59.

22. Jules Michelet, *Satanism and Witchcraft: A Study in Medieval Superstition* (New York: Citadel Press, 1939), 22.

23. The hymns were respectively "O Splendidissima Gemma" and "O

Clarissima Mater," offerings in a benefit concert, Grace Cathedral Church, San Francisco, March 14, 1999.

24. Karen Jo Torjesen, *When Women Were Priests* (San Francisco: Harper-SanFranciso, 1995), 155–172 and passim; and the overview in Cullen Murphy, *The Word According to Eve: Women and the Bible in Ancient Times and Our Own* (Boston: Houghton Mifflin, 1998), 140ff; also Leonard Swidler, "Jesus Was a Feminist," *Catholic World*, January 1971: 177–183.

25. Jeremiah 3.6–13, 20–1; Ezekiel 23.7–8, 36–39; Hosea 2.10–11, 17, 3.1–3, 4.17–19.

26. II Kings 9.5–6, 22, 30–37; and Stone, *When God Was a Woman*, 188–189.

27. All these strictures are in Deuteronomy 22.20–24, 28–29.

28. Stone, *When God Was a Woman*, 191–192.

29. In that very same epistle, somewhat contradictorily, Paul recognizes that women "prophesieth" in the church, which he seems to accept as long as they keep their heads covered as a gesture of modesty: I Corinthians 11.5–6.

30. Origen quoted in Torjesen, *When Women Were Priests*, 114.

31. Tertullian, "On the Apparel of Women," reprinted in Barbara J. MacHaffie (ed.), *Readings in Her Story: Women in Christian Tradition* (Minneapolis: Fortress Press, 1992), 27.

32. Augustine, Luther, and Calvin are quoted in Stone, *When God Was a Woman*, 226–227; and Madalyn Murray O'Hair, *Women and Atheism* (Austin, Texas: American Atheist Press, 1979), 11–12.

33. Heinrich Kraemer and Jacob Sprenger, *Malleus Maleficarum*, published in 1486, excerpted in MacHaffie (ed.), *Readings in Her Story*, 53–56. Michelet describes Sprenger as "dull witted," an "imbecile monk" and "intrepid fool," perfectly suited to fashion dogmatic justifications for the Inquisition's slaughter of witches and wizards: Michelet, *Satanism and Witchcraft*, xii, 129–130, 145. On the way women were especially targeted, Michelet quotes King Louis XIII: "For one Sorcerer, ten thousand Sorceresses": ibid., viii.

34. Epiphanius *Panarion* 37.2, cited in Torjesen, *When Women Were Priests*, 112.

35. Jerome's "strange story," as Gibbon calls it, is from his "Legend of Paul the Hermit": Gibbon, *The Decline and Fall of the Roman Empire*, chapter 16, 209n.

36. Augustine, *Soliloquia* I.40.

37. Sarah B. Pomeroy, *Goddesses, Whores, Wives and Slaves: Women in Classical Antiquity* (New York: Schocken Books, 1975), 160. Even Augustine was more enlightened on this point than the emperor, arguing that since it was not of their volition, rape victims "have no guilt to be ashamed of" and remain pure of soul, with only their bodies defiled: *The City of God*, I.16–18 and II.2.

38. Christine de Pizan, *The Book of the City of Ladies* (New York: Persea Books, 1982).
39. Torjesen, *When Women Were Priests,* 118–121.
40. On the gender mutuality of the early household church, see Luise Schottroff, *Lydia's Impatient Sisters: A Feminist Social History of Early Christianity* (Louisville, Kentucky: Westminister John Knox Press, 1995), 214–218.
41. Torjesen, *When Women Were Priests,* 5 and 44. On the positions of authority held by women in the early church, see also W. H. C. Frend, *The Rise of Christianity* (Philadelphia: Fortress Press, 1984), passim.
42. Schottroff, *Lydia's Impatient Sisters,* 31, 230n.
43. Torjesen, *When Women Were Priests,* 6.
44. Torjesen, *When Women Were Priests,* 7, 37–39, 114–121.
45. Torjesen, *When Women Were Priests,* 43–44.
46. Rösener, *Peasants in the Middle Ages,* 184.
47. O'Hair, *Women and Atheism,* 14.
48. Michelet, *Satanism and Witchcraft,* xi–xii, 144–147.
49. Michelet quoting Spina: *Satanism and Witchcraft,* xii–xiii.
50. For a general summary of patriarchal oppression and some of the relevant literature, see my *Land of Idols: Political Mythology in America* (New York: St. Martin's Press, 1994), 142–156.
51. "On Christian Marriage: Encyclical Letter of His Holiness Pope Pius XI," *The Catholic Mind,* January 22, 1931, excerpted in MacHaffie (ed.), *Readings in Her Story,* 163–166.
52. "Declaration on the Question of the Admission of Women to the Ministerial Priesthood," in Leonard and Arlene Swidler (eds.), *Women Priests: A Catholic Commentary on the Vatican Declaration* (New York: Paulist Press, 1977), 38–40.
53. See MacHaffie (ed.), *Readings in Her Story,* 191–207. For a critique of the persistence of mysogynist notions embedded in the Christian theology and practice, see Mary Daly, *The Church and the Second Sex* (Boston: Beacon Press, 1985).
54. Torjesen, *When Women Were Priests,* 5.
55. Schottroff, *Lydia's Impatient Sisters,* 219–220.
56. Schottroff, *Lydia's Impatient Sisters,* 17–19.
57. Both Torjesen's experience and King's are reported in Murphy, *The Word According to Eve,* 207.
58. Stone, *When God Was a Woman,* 193–194.
59. Stone, *When God Was a Woman,* xviii–xix.
60. Stone, *When God Was a Woman,* xix–xx.
61. Stone, *When God Was a Woman,* xx–xxi.
62. Torjesen, *When Women Were Priests,* 224.
63. Harold Mattingly, *Christianity in the Roman Empire* (New York: W. W. Norton, 1967), 76.

64. Henry S. Lucas, *A Short History of Civilization* (New York & London: McGraw-Hill, 1943).

65. Luciano Canfora, *The Vanished Library* (Berkeley: University of California Press, 1987), 192.

66. Acts 19.17–19.

67. Lea, *The Inquisition of the Middle Ages,* 250.

68. An Antioch chronicler, quoted in Canfora, *The Vanished Library,* 193.

69. Canfora, *The Vanishing Library,* 91, 192.

70. Gibbon, *The Decline and Fall of the Roman Empire,* edited by D. M. Low (New York: Harcourt, Brace, 1960), chapter 28, 417.

71. Canfora, *The Vanishing Library,* 82–99 and passim. Canfora notes that the last famous figure associated with the great library of Alexandria had been Theon, whose daughter, the celebrated Hypatia, a student of geometry and musicology, was barbarously murdered in 415 by Jesus believers who suspected her of being a heretic.

72. Helen Ellerbe, *The Dark Side of Christian History* (San Rafael, Calif.: Morningstar Books, 1995), chapter 4.

73. J. W. Thompson, *The Medieval Library* (New York: Hafner Publishing Co., 1939).

74. Michelet, *Satanism and Witchcraft,* xviii. In their 1,089-page *History of Europe,* Hayes, Baldwin, and Cole devote a very brief section to the "Development of Christian Literature and Art" in the fourth and fifth centuries, that deals entirely with the religious writings of church fathers, with brief references to the religious frescoes and sculpture found in the catacombs. No mention is made of the Christian campaign to suppress secular art, literature, philosophy, and science.

75. Lea, *The Inquisition of the Middle Ages,* 249–252.

76. Francois Furet and Jacques Ozouf, *Reading and Writing: Literacy in France from Calvin to Jules Ferry* (Cambridge: Cambridge University Press, 1982); and Harvey Graff, *The Literacy Myth* (New York: Academic Press, 1979).

77. Michelet, *Satanism and Witchcraft,* 79.

78. Gibbon, *The Decline and Fall of the Roman Empire,* chapter 28, 414–415.

79. Burton L. Mack, *Who Wrote the New Testament: The Making of the Christian Myth* (New York: HarperCollins, 1995), 291, 294–295.

80. Fogel, *Junipero Serra, the Vatican, and Enslavement Theology,* 25.

81. Thomas Cahill, *How the Irish Saved Civilization* (New York: Doubleday, 1995), 3.

82. Cahill, *How the Irish Saved Civilization,* 210.

83. Hayes, Baldwin, and Cole, *History of Europe,* 124–125.

84. Cahill, *How the Irish Saved Civilization,* 181–182. Vogt considers Ammianus "Rome's last great historian" who "often surpasses his

master Tacitus in factual accuracy and unprejudiced observation":
The Decline of Rome, 148.

85. Cahill does point out that the barbarian raids were used as an
excuse for the big landowners to extend their "protection" over a
free but besieged peasantry, expropriating their lands and indentur-
ing them and their families into a lifetime of serfdom: *How the Irish
Saved Civilization,* 36–37.

86. Cahill, *How the Irish Saved Civilization,* 158–159, 182, 210.

87. Gibbon, *The Decline and Fall of the Roman Empire,* chapter 15, 166.

88. Gibbon, *The Decline and Fall of the Roman Empire,* chapter 15, 160.

89. Saint Augustine, *The Confessions of Saint Augustine* (New York:
Modern Library, 1949), IV. 71, 72, and XII passim. Augustine even
struggled over church music, fearing it led to the "peril of pleasure,"
a consideration that caused him — in a rare recognition of his own
puritanical excesses — to admit, "I err in too great strictness": ibid.,
X.228–229.

90. Arthur D. Kahn, *The Education of Julius Caesar* (New York: Schocken
Books, 1986), 235.

91. Samuel Dill, *Roman Society in the Last Century of the Western Empire*
(New York: Meridian Books, 1958), quoted in Edward Goldsmith,
The Great U-Turn, De-industrializing Society (Hartland Bideford,
Devon, 1988), 6; see also Finley, *Aspects of Antiquity,* 150.

92. Carcopino, *Daily Life in Ancient Rome,* x; Cantor, *The Civilization of
the Middle Ages,* 103.

93. Augustine cites Alaric's failure to sack the Christian churches as
proof of Christ's influence: Augustine, *The City of God,* I.1–7.

94. Henri Pirenne, *Medieval Cities* (Garden City, N.Y.: Doubleday,
1956, originally 1925), 3, 5; Cantor likewise notes that the Visigoths
"sought to get into the empire not to destroy it, but to participate in
its higher standard of living":
The Civilization of the Middle Ages, 90 and 101–102.

95. Hayes, Baldwin, and Cole, *History of Europe,* 141–142.

96. Michael Grant, *History of Rome* (New York: Charles Scribner, 1978),
458.

97. John G. Gager, *The Origins of Anti-Semitism: Attitudes Toward Judaism
in Pagan and Christian Antiquity* (New York and Oxford: Oxford
University Press: 1983), 41–53.

98. Gager, *The Origins of Anti-Semitism,* 48.

99. Gager, *The Origins of Anti-Semitism,* 97–98; see also 16–17 and
134–159 for related points. At the same time, Roman leaders themselves did not hesitate to repress politically rebellious populations in
Judea in a thoroughly brutal fashion. Josephus refers to "the
unprecedented character of the Romans' cruelty" in quelling a
Jewish uprising by massacring 3,600 people in one day; and in
Alexandria he reports that 50,000 Jews were slaughtered in one day

in A.D. 66: Josephus, *The Jewish War* II.306–308, 326–328, 496–498.

100. Gibbon, *The Decline and Fall of the Roman Empire*, chapter 22, 361.

101. Mark 11.18, 12.12; see also Matthew 21.46, 27.20; and Luke 19.47–48.

102. See John 5.10, 5.16–18, 7.1, 7.11–13, 10.31–33, 18.29–40, 19.1–6; see also Acts 10.39, 13.45–50; Titus 1.10–14; I Thessalonians 2.14–16; Charlotte Klein, *Anti-Judaism in Christian Theology* (Philadelphia: Fortress Press, 1978); John Dominic Crossan, *Who Killed Jesus: Exposing the Roots of Anti-Semitism in the Gospel Story of the Death of Jesus* (San Francisco: HarperSanFrancisco, 1996); and Hay, *Europe and the Jews*, 12–16.

103. Origen, *Against Celsus,* quoted in Paul E. Grosser and Edwin G. Halperin, *Anti-Semitism: The Causes and Effects of a Prejudice* (Secaucus, N.J.: Citadel Press, 1976), 57.

104. Edward H. Flannery, *The Anguish of the Jews: Twenty-Three Centuries of Anti-Semitism* (New York: MacMillan, 1965), 27.

105. Dagobert Runes, *The Jew and the Cross* (New York: Philosophical Library, 1966), 41.

106. Quoted in Fred Gladstone Bratton, *The Crime of Christendom* (Boston: Beacon Press, 1969), 84–85; see also Runes, *The Jew and the Cross*, 61–62.

107. Quoted in Hay, *Europe and the Jews*, 27–30

108. Both quoted in Hay, *Europe and the Jews*, 27.

109. Rodney Stark, *The Rise of Christianity: A Sociologist Reconsiders History* (Princeton, N.J.: Princeton University Press, 1996), 66–67.

110. Dagobert Runes, *The War Against the Jews* (New York: Philosophical Library, 1968), 113.

111. Heinrich Graetz, *History of the Jews,* cited in Grosser and Halperin, *Anti-Semitism*, 79.

112. Augustine, *The City of God* 18.46; and Runes, *The War Against the Jews*, 58.

113. Runes, *The War Against the Jews*, 96.

114. Grosser and Halperin, *Anti-Semitism*, 80–81.

115. Flannery, *The Anguish of the Jews*, 95.

116. Hay, *Europe and the Jews*, 166–167; and Bauer, *A History of the Holocaust*, 22.

117. Meyers's studies are summarized and cited in Stark, *The Rise of Christianity*, 68.

118. Grosser and Halperin, *Anti-Semitism*, 86.

119. Joshua Trachtenberg, *The Devil and the Jews* (New Haven: Yale University Press, 1943), 159–160.

120. Trachtenberg, *The Devil and the Jews*, 162.

121. On this see Michelet, *Satanism and Witchcraft*, passim.

122. Grosser and Halperin, *Anti-Semitism*, 58–103.

123. Hay, *Europe and the Jews,* 86–87.
124. Hay, *Europe and the Jews,* 35.
125. Hay, *Europe and the Jews,* 104–105.
126. Trachtenberg, *The Devil and the Jews,* 7, 14 and passim.
127. Hay, *Europe and the Jews,* 98, 117–118 and passim.
128. Hay, *Europe and the Jews,* 112–119.
129. Hay, *Europe and the Jews,* 95–102. The bishop's comment is in ibid., 96.
130. Hay, *Europe and the Jews,* 152.
131. Yehuda Bauer, *A History of the Holocaust* (New York: Franklin Watts, 1982), 10.
132. Grosser and Halperin, *Anti-Semitism,* 58–103, 146, and passim; Flannery, *The Anguish of the Jews,* 52; Hay, *Europe and the Jews,* 41–42.
133. Hay, *Europe and the Jews,* 68–69, 103–104.
134. Hay, *Europe and the Jews,* 54–56.
135. Grosser and Halperin, *Anti-Semitism,* 154; see also Yitzhak Baer, *History of the Jews in Christian Spain,* vol. 2 (Philadelphia: Jewish Publication Society of America, 1961), passim; Bauer, *A History of the Holocaust,* 21.
136. S. M. Dubnov, *History of the Jews in Russia and Poland* (Philadelphia: Jewish Publication Society of America, 1920), 146–148, 164–165.
137. Flannery, *The Anguish of the Jews,* 248–251.
138. Dubnov, *History of the Jews in Russia and Poland,* 346–358, 404–406, and passim.
139. Flannery, *The Anguish of the Jews,* 189–190; Dubnov, *History of the Jews in Russia and Poland,* 114–120.
140. Runes, *The War Against the Jews,* 144; Norman Cohn, *Warrant for Genocide* (New York: Harper & Row, 1966), 39; and Hay, *Europe and the Jews,* 107–108 and passim.
141. Grosser and Halperin, *Anti-Semitism,* 206–254.
142. De Rosa quoted in James Haught, *Holy Horrors* (Buffalo, N.Y.: Prometheus Books, 1990), 157–165.
143. *Encyclopedia Judaica* (Jerusalem: Keter Publishing House, n.d.), vol. 10, 159.
144. Pierre van Paassen, *The Forgotten Ally* (1943), quoted in Hay, *Europe and the Jews,* 12.
145. The quotation is from Grosser and Halperin, *Anti-Semitism,* 3; see also Trachtenberg, *The Devil and the Jews,* 5–6; Cohn, *Warrant for Genocide,* passim; and Schottroff, *Lydia's Impatient Sisters,* 16.
146. Hannah Arendt, *The Origins of Totalitarianism* (New York: Harcourt, Brace, 1966), xi.
147. Gager, *The Origins of Anti-Semitism,* 267.
148. Goebbels quoted in Jean Bacon, *The Greater Glory* (Bridport,

Dorset/San Leandro, California: Prism Press, 1986), 34.

149. Uriel Tal, *Christians and Jews,* 304, cited in Gager, *The Origins of Anti-Semitism,* 267.

150. Hay, *Europe and the Jews,* 337n and see 18–19 and 310ff.

151. See my *Blackshirts and Reds: Rational Fascism and the Overthrow of Communism* (San Francisco: City Lights Books, 1997), 16.

152. Commission for Religious Relations with the Jews, *We Remember: A Reflection on the Shoah* reprinted in *New York Times,* March 17, 1998.

153. On the church's accommodations with Nazism before and during the war, see Guenter Lewy, *The Catholic Church and Nazi Germany* (New York: McGraw-Hill, 1964).

154. *Los Angeles Times,* September 4, 1984; *Washington Post,* September 4, 1984; *Attenzione,* May 1981: 16–20; *Guardian,* April 19, 1989; Daniel Fogel, *Junipero Serra, the Vatican, and Enslavement Theology* (San Francisco: Ism Press, 1988), 165–173. John Paul II will always be the CIA pope to me.

155. Penny Lernoux, "Opus Dei and the 'Perfect Society,'" *Nation,* April 10, 1989: 482–487; Curtis Bill Pepper, "Opus Dei, Advocatus Papae," *Nation,* August 3/10, 1992: 139–140.

156. Carl Bernstein, "The Holy Alliance," *Time,* February 4, 1992: 28–32; David Willey, *God's Politician, John Paul at the Vatican* (New York: St. Martin's Press, 1993).

157. See Edward Jenkinson, *Censors in the Classroom* (Carbondale and Edwardsville, Ill.: Southern Illinois University Press, 1979); Joan DelFattore, *What Johnny Shouldn't Read: Textbook Censorship in America* (New Haven and London: Yale University Press, 1992).

158. Gager, *The Origins of Anti-Semitism,* 266.

4

HISTORY IN THE FAKING

Those engaged in the manufacturing of history often introduce distortions at the point of origin well before the history is written or even played out. This initial process of control is not usually left to chance but is regularly pursued by interested parties who are situated to manipulate the record. Here are some examples of the phenomenon.

Suppression at the Point of Origin

Consider how the Inquisition kept its records. Although it committed horrible crimes against hundreds of thousands of innocent people without ever questioning its own rectitude and overweening power, inquisitors did take pains to leave certain things out of the record. Torture was the centerpiece of their modus operandi, yet in the official records of tribunal proceedings, references to torture are curiously few. Confessions were extracted but there is seldom anything to indicate by what means. In over six hundred cases entered into the register of Toulouse from 1309 to 1323, only one mentioned that the accused had retracted a confession made under torture. But in the original confession itself there was no reference to torture.[1]

The testimony of surviving victims and other observers tells us that, despite its absence from the official record, torture was a standard way of wringing confessions from hapless innocents. Charles Henry Lea observes that the chief inquisitor of Toulouse, "too emphatically expressed his sense of the utility of torture on both principals and witnesses for us to doubt his readiness in its employment."[2] Still, it is interesting that Inquisitional authorities avoided mentioning the practice in the official records, perhaps sensing that references to torture would detract from the validity of an investigatory system that was, to put it mildly, self-confirming in its methods.

Probably the most famous victim of the auto-da-fé is Jeanne d'Arc (known in the English-speaking world by the curious misnomer "Joan of Arc"[3]). Her trial, execution, and subsequent rehabilitation demonstrate not only how history is distorted at the point of origin by the victors, but in this uncommon case, accorded an honest reconstruction when the victors are eventually vanquished. Born in 1412, Jeanne d'Arc was an illiterate peasant who began having mystical visions during adolescence. At age seventeen, she led a French force to lift the English siege of Orléans. After a number of other remarkable feats of arms, the Maid of Orléans, as she became known, was captured, put on trial in Rouen, and charged with heresy. The political character of the trial was not doubted even at the time. The Inquisition presided, but it was the English who paid the court expenses and controlled the proceedings. And whatever the outcome of the trial, they intended to retain custody of the prisoner, whom they saw as a serious threat to their rule.[4]

Having not the slightest evidence of Jeanne's "heresy," the prosecution fixed on her male attire as visible proof of her unwomanly, unnatural spirit and her refusal to submit to church authority and therefore confirmation of "heresy." Jeanne herself proffered a more mundane explanation: "It is more licit and fitting to have man's clothes since I am with men than to have woman's clothes."[5] Toward the end of her trial, when she finally realized that neither God nor the French were likely to rescue her, she abjured, agreeing to sign a document of penitence and to wear women's clothing, remarking that she preferred signing to burning. *("Eh bien, je préfère signer plutôt qu'être brûlée.")* Still, she was found unrepentent and guilty of heresy and burned at the stake in 1431.[6]

Twenty-five years later, French forces under Charles VII liberated Rouen and all of Normandy, making it possible to ascertain how the Maid's trial had been conducted. The documents were preserved at the archbishopric; and a number of the witnesses were still alive, including the court notaries who had faithfully transcribed Jeanne's testimony. In a Trial of Rehabilitation ordered by Charles, it was discovered that the twelve articles of accusation against the Maid, including the charge that she would not submit herself to the determination of the church, had never even been read to her, yet they contained testimony that was the very opposite of what she had given.[7]

The official document of abjuration *(cédule)* found in the court record was a lengthy statement in which Jeanne repeatedly accused herself of having feigned revelations, blasphemed God and his saints, incited schism, desired "cruel effusion of human blood," and worn clothes that were "dissolute" and "against natural decency." Would Jeanne d'Arc really have confessed to such self-damning abominations? The answer came during the Trial of Rehabilitation, when the notaries and other eyewitnesses revealed the existence of another *cédule,* differing from the implausible one inserted into the official record, one that the illiterate Jeanne had actually signed with an X, after it had been read to her. As various witnesses recalled, it was a brief statement of not more than seven or eight lines in which she agreed to forsake male attire and submit to the authority of the church, the agreement she had been led to believe would save her from the stake. That document had disappeared from the trial record.[8]

A pretrial report investigating Jeanne's early life—which had evoked the bishop's wrath because it showed her in a most favorable light as a decent and well-regarded person—was also not to be found. In addition, Jeanne agreed to submit to a physical examination (if properly conducted by a reputable matron) to prove she was still a virgin. This report too does not appear in the record, doubtless because it failed to support the image of "excommunicated whore," concocted by some of her antagonists.[9]

Regarding the Maid's "relapse," which became the excuse for burning her, the official record leaves the impression that she defiantly returned to wearing male clothing at the first opportunity and by this wicked practice demonstrated her heretical insubordination. But the rehabilitation uncovered something else about her sartorial recidivism. One account noted that her jailers had hid her female garments and given her only male clothes which she was forced to wear when taken from her cell. Other witnesses recalled that the English had done "much wrong and violence" to her in prison when she was dressed as a woman, leaving "her face covered with tears, disfigured and outraged." There is testimony that an English lord raped or attempted to rape her when she was dressed as a woman, causing her again to don male attire even though it would seal her doom.[10]

Some of the participants in the original trial who had served the prosecution were not too happy about the new inquiry. When brought before the rehabilitation court, they insisted that it was all so long ago; and, of course, they could not remember much of anything; and in any case they had played a minor part in the proceedings.[11]

The heresy charges brought against Jeanne d'Arc twenty-five years earlier were refuted from the evidence obtained during the new trial.[12] In sum, our understanding of the history of her trial, both its content and process, would have been decidedly different had not French forces driven the English out of Normandy and taken the opportunity to set the record straight.

When it comes to suppressing historical materials, no ruling coterie can match the Roman Catholic hierarchy. While governments withhold documents for decades, the Vatican withholds them for centuries. Consider the plight of Filippo Tamburini, a priest who in 1995 wrote a scholarly book on crimes committed centuries ago by monks, nuns, priests, and some nobles and merchants. Murder, sodomy, fornication, adultery, castration, bestiality, theft, forgery, and piracy were among the transgressions. Tamburini used documents dated from 1451 to 1586, drawn from the secret Vatican archive *(l'archivo segreto vaticano)* where he had worked for twelve years. They consisted of public statements of penitence from sinners who sought a return to their ecclesiastic or secular stations in life. In every case, the church granted a pardon to the well-appointed murderers, rapists, thieves, and other felons.[13]

But there was no pardon for Father Tamburini, who was destined to suffer the fate of whistleblowers everywhere. Like most organizations, the Vatican is inclined to deal more harshly with those who publicize institutional crimes than with those who commit them. Summoned before an archbishop, Tamburini was barred from the archives and issued a severe condemnation for having published Vatican documents without permission. His only solace might be the knowledge that in an earlier era he would have suffered more severe sanctions.

When interviewed, Tamburini remarked, perhaps too naively: "Maybe they thought it was material from sacramental confessions and I had published something I shouldn't have. But they are public cases."[14] Obviously, what aggrieved the Vatican was the release of "public cases" that had been kept snugly under lock and key for five hundred years, cases that revealed the hierarchy's tolerance for the worst sort of crimes when committed by the best sort of people.

Governments are among the prime suppressors and fabricators of historical information. And war records are among the most readily concealed and thoroughly doctored. There is the famous and utterly disastrous battle of Passchendaele in World War I, also known as the Third Battle of Ypres, in which British commander in chief Sir Douglas Haig sent an entire army to its destruction in order to advance nine thousand yards deeper into an indefensible bog. The costs at Passchendaele were so devastating that British army records were virtually combed clean to conceal the truth from the public. Official histories put British casualties at a fictional 238,000. Haig's own horrified private admission: "Have we really lost half a million men?" was closer to the truth.[15] Even a standard reference book like Langer's encyclopedia puts Passchendaele casualties at 400,000, a figure much higher than the official toll.[16] Though the battle was fought in 1917, most of the extant documentation in the United Kingdom continues to be withheld from the Public Record Office.

In his revealing reassessment of Haig, Dennis Winter discovered that the official record of World War I was "systematically distorted" both during the conflict and in the subsequent official history.[17] Winter ascertained that Commander Haig had rewritten his diary after the events, inserting his seemingly uncanny anticipations of those same events, calculated to make him seem brilliantly prescient and to disguise his unerring ability to choose the most catastrophic time and place for military engagements.[18]

Haig's woeful lack of tactical skill was evident as early as 1915 at the "battle" of the Marne, a series of bungled maneuvers and lost opportunities. On one occasion he opined that "artillery only seems likely to be really effective against raw troops"; the machine gun is "a much over-rated weapon"; and "cavalry will have a larger sphere of action in future wars."[19] To demonstrate the latter two hypotheses, Haig actually sent massed cavalry against machine guns at Monchy les Proeux, with predictably horrifying results.

Haig was not the only one tampering with history at the point of origin. The most detailed transcripts of British Cabinet records of 1914–1918 still remain inaccessible to the public. War Office records, the prime minister's minutes and diary, and the personal papers of various officers and officials have either been locked away, severely weeded, or have disappeared altogether. So many orders, intelligence reports, unit command diaries (which commanders were required to keep), and conference minutes have been destroyed as to make impossible any real check of the official history.[20]

The historian originally assigned to write an official popular narrative of the Great War (as World War I was called) was Sir John Fortescue, former royal librarian and author of a highly respected study of the British Army. Considered "an ideal choice, sound to the point of tedium," as Winter describes him, Fortescue produced a volume in 1918 that violated all official expectations. It stated that the government had failed to prevent the war when it had the power to do so, that Haig had panicked during the retreat from Mons and deserted a fellow commander at the battle of Le Cateau, and that Sir John French (Haig's predecessor as commander in chief) had been overwhelmed by events and reduced to a bewildered spectator. For committing such truths, Fortescue was sacked and his manuscript suppressed.[21]

Behind all this cover-up was something more than a desire to protect personal egos and public reputations. British leaders had witnessed four monarchial dynasties—Romanov, Hapsburg, Hohenzollern, and Ottoman—swept away in popular uprisings. In Britain itself, as Winter reminds us, the rulers faced trade-union militancy, Irish rebellion, and an embittered people who suspected they had not been told the whole story about a bungled war that had lasted four terrible years, killed 1 million Britons, wounded another 2.5 million, and left the German Army unbroken. It was feared that a candid revelation of all the losses and deceptions might only incite public outrage and threaten the whole structure of upper-class rule. As one cabinet secretary put it: "Is it really to the public advantage that our national heroes should be hauled off their pedestals? It has somewhat the same effect as would be produced if some distinguished churchman were to marshal the historical evidence against the Saints."[22]

Even more remarkable, the cover-up remained operative over seventy years later. In the 1980s, when Winter embarked on his study of Haig, he discovered that Staff College conference minutes "would abruptly disappear when I requested access. The Earl of Derby's diary appeared and disappeared within a few weeks." Lord Rawlinson's diary, which Winter and several other historians had previously consulted, suddenly "dematerialized" from the Army Museum with an assurance that it had never been there. And so it went throughout his ten years of research, moving Winter to comment wryly, "Few historians have the good fortune to receive such clear indication that their research is proceeding on the right lines."[23]

An example of how a dominant class can control what is said about its own history is offered by historian Carroll Quigley, who for twenty years studied the Cecil Rhodes–Alfred Milner Round Table group that had such a decisive influence on British policy from 1891 through World War II. Quigley himself was close to establishment elites in this country and Great Britain. After teaching at Princeton and Harvard he spent the rest of his career at Georgetown's School of Foreign Service, was a consultant for the Brookings Institution, the Pentagon, and the State Department, and taught Western Civilization and history. Not surprisingly, Quigley was in agreement with most of the

Round Table elites, but he was bothered by some of their methods and thought their inherited wealth and power held serious implications for democratic governance. He was disturbed both by their influence over events and their control over the recording of those events:

> No country that values its safety should allow what the Milner Group accomplished in Britain — that is, that a small number of men should be able to wield such power in administration and politics, should be given almost complete control over the publication of the documents relating to their actions, should be able to exercise such influence over the avenues of information that create public opinion, and should be able to monopolize so completely the writing and teaching of the history of their own period.[24]

This comment is from Quigley's first book, *The Anglo–American Establishment,* which was rejected by fifteen publishers, and finally appeared posthumously more than thirty-two years after its completion. His major work, *Tragedy and Hope,* supposedly went out of print immediately after publication in 1966. Quigley was entitled to recover the plates from Macmillan, but after much stalling, the publisher claimed that the plates had been "inadvertently" destroyed.[25]

Cold War in the Archives

With political victory comes the opportunity to monopolize the historical record. After the German Federal Republic (West Germany) annexed the German Democratic Republic (East Germany) in 1990 (misleadingly described as a "reunification"), GDR official records, libraries, and school texts were systematically purged of materials and ideas that conflicted with the orthodox procapitalist, anti-Communist, West German perspective. The prestigious Otto-Suhr Institute in Berlin was closed and its 230,000-volume library disbanded, including collections that had replaced the ones destroyed by Nazi book burnings of the 1930s. The institute's materials on anti-Semitism were dispersed through auctions, along with its 78,000-volume collection of leftist history and politics, and the 31,000 volumes pertaining to the conservative connivance that preceded the Nazi takeover in Germany.[26]

The willful destruction of any library is egregious. In the case of the Otto-Suhr Institute, progressive scholars around the world who are studying the history of the Third Reich, Nazism, and anti-Semitism have been deliberately deprived of a rich informational resource. The dissolution of the institute and its library "is part of a larger pattern, both in Germany and world-wide," observes Patricia Brodsky. Public and factory libraries in the former German Democratic Republic "have been burned or emptied of books pertaining to GDR history, Marxism-Leninism, and the like." Police raided and temporarily closed down the Central Party Archive at the Institute for the History of the Workers Movement in Berlin, another internationally significant research facility. Alternative bookstores in several German cities were raided, copies of a leftist newspaper seized, and bookstore personnel threatened with prosecution for distributing the "subversive" publication.[27]

Federal Republic officials also launched a concerted campaign to distort or erase the historical record preserved in antifascist memorials and concentration camp museums. One whole wing of the museum at Buchenwald, dedicated to such topics as international solidarity in the camp, the war crimes tribunal, and "the well-documented continuity between the Third Reich and the political and industrial leadership of the Federal Republic has been dismantled," reports Brodsky. In its place there is now a special memorial to postwar internees—who were for the most part Nazi collaborators implicated in Holocaust crimes. Such assaults on historic materials that shed a critical light on fascism and reactionism are not random.

"They illustrate the revival of the Cold War campaign to downplay, obscure, and, where possible, destroy all traces of antifascist culture."[28]

As might be expected, the struggle to define Germany's history has extended into education and scholarship. For more than two decades after World War II, critical inquiry into the Third Reich was not encouraged in the Federal Republic. West German schools taught almost nothing about Nazism (while East German schools took a vigorously damning approach to the subject). The erstwhile Nazi affiliations of leading figures in the Federal Republic's economy went unmentioned. Nazism was regarded as a passing aberration. Its horrific crimes were acknowledged but attributed mainly to the personal demonic genius of Adolf Hitler, as was the entire Nazi movement.[29]

By the 1970s, scholarly studies began to take a more critical tack, leaving no doubt about the enormities of Nazism. Yet the process was limited, and many Nazi sympathizers remained in positions of authority.[30] Some leading West German historians still did not think too harshly of the Hitlerian past. Biographies were written of Hitler that emphasized his skills and performance, while saying little about the massive crimes he perpetrated against humanity.[31] Historians like Ernst Nolte seemed to blame Nazism on Communism, arguing that the threat of Bolshevism caused the German bourgeoisie to rally around a militant reactionism. Hitler and his followers feared that the Soviet Communists would target Germany with their fell designs, so the Nazis launched a campaign to save their nation. The war itself was an attempt by Hitler to build a unified West as a bulwark against the Red tide, argues Nolte. In response, Richard Evans points out that through 1940 and well into 1941, Hitler committed nearly his entire force to subjugating Western Europe, offering not the slightest suggestion in his military conferences and discussions that he feared a Russian attack. According to Hitler's propaganda minister, Joseph Goebbels, the Nazi leadership believed (correctly) that the USSR would stay out of the conflict for as long as it could, preferring to let the warring capitalist powers exhaust each other.[32]

There are those of us who have argued that the Nazis saw the Soviet Union as the ultimate target of their aggression.[33] This differs from saying, as does Nolte, that Hitler was acting to defend the West from a Soviet Union readying for a war of conquest, or that Moscow so menaced the supposedly freedom-loving politico-economic elites in Germany as to justify their accepting and, in many cases, actively supporting a monstrous movement like Nazism.

Nolte and others also downplay the scope and ferocity of German military brutality during the war, including the Holocaust. Facing the Red Menace, Germany supposedly had no choice but to act decisively and harshly in the East. Andreas Hillgruber, Joachim Fest, and other well-known, neoconservative West German historians share Nolte's position in part or whole, having made little effort to explore the German Military Archives at Freiburg or captured Nazi documents and other materials that offer a fuller picture of mass atrocities in the Nazi-occupied portions of Eastern Europe and the Soviet Union.[34] Their work, while not identical to outright Holocaust deniers, does have the same effect of blurring the line between fact and fiction, persecuted and persecutor.[35]

The attack against East German socialist history launched by capitalist West Germany should remind us that the cold war is not over. It continues full force in the realm of ideology and historiography. A decade after the overthrow of the Soviet Union, a stream of television documentaries, books, and articles continue to propagate the old claim that the USSR was implacably bent on world conquest. The specter of Communism still haunts the bourgeois world. The goal of anti-Communist ideologues is to make certain that no alternative system ever again challenges the hegemony of global capitalism.

Until the early 1990s, historians of the cold war relied almost exclusively on Western records to draw inferences about Soviet intentions. But in recent years, the Russians and their former Warsaw Pact allies have begun opening their archives for research. This has allowed some mainstream historians and other cold warriors to exercise a tailor-made selectivity of documents in order to buttress their view of a besieged "Free World" acting defensively against a relentlessly menacing Soviet Juggernaut.[36]

A more careful reading of the newly attained Soviet archival materials and of the books and articles based on them suggests a markedly different view. Surveying the literature, Melvyn Leffler concludes that "the cold war was not a simple case of Soviet expansionism and American reaction. . . . Soviet leaders were not focused on promoting worldwide revolution." Rather they were primarily concerned with rebuilding their country, maintaining its security, and protecting its immediate borders. "Governing a land devastated by two world wars, they feared a resurgence of German and Japanese strength. They felt threatened by a United States that alone among the combatants emerged from the war wealthier and armed with the atomic bomb." Soviet officials had no premeditated plans "to make Eastern Europe Communist, to support the Chinese Communists, or to wage war in Korea."[37]

Standard histories of the cold war assume that the Soviet Union exercised a lockstep control over docile "satellite nations," the latter being little more than puppets within a monolithic "Soviet bloc." The new documents throw a different light on the relationship between Moscow and its allies. Communist leaders in Poland, Hungary, East Germany, Cuba, Afghanistan, and elsewhere "could and did act in pursuit of their own interests, sometimes goading the Kremlin into involvements it did not want."[38]

The newly excavated archival materials also reveal that Stalin was not determined to impose a fixed design upon the economies and societies of Eastern Europe. Even as late as 1947, he seemed chary of acting too precipitously, especially when relations with the Western powers remained uncertain.[39] The documents show, as a number of scholars have pointed out, that Stalin nursed no desire for an overarching confrontation with the West. Above all, Soviet policy was based on realpolitik and security considerations.[40] Such a view of history has yet to win much attention in U.S. corporate-owned media or corporate-produced textbooks that see the cold war as the product of Soviet aggrandizement against the "Free World."

Classified History, USA

U.S. leaders point with pride to the free flow of information in our supposedly open society. Yet these same leaders regularly withhold or destroy official materials, thereby seriously distorting the historical record at the point of origin. Millions of U.S. government documents have remained classified for fifty years or more. The War Department records on the Abraham Lincoln assassination were kept secret for sixty years, finally placed in the public domain in the mid-1930s. When researching the conspiracy behind Lincoln's murder, Theodore Roscoe discovered that some records of the "U.S. Army secret intelligence" were still classified almost one hundred years after the assassination.[41] What question of national security could be involved here? How many Confederate spies were prowling behind Union lines in 1960, the year Roscoe's book was published?

Perhaps the most famous disclosure controversy in recent U.S. history concerns the study that became known as the Pentagon Papers, an extensive top-secret history of U.S. involvement in Indochina from World War II to May 1968. The report was commissioned by Secretary of Defense Robert McNamara, and compiled by thirty-six anonymous historians, mostly academicians who worked for the State Department and

Defense Department. It revealed how for two decades officials deceived the Congress and the U.S. public while pursuing a war of aggression and attrition in Indochina. A Department of Defense consultant, Daniel Ellsberg, risking prison and sacrificing his government career, managed to copy the papers and get them into the hands of the *New York Times* and the *Washington Post* with a commitment to publish. In the interests of "national security," President Nixon's Justice Department went to court to get prior judicial restraints placed upon publication of the documents. In its final decision, the Supreme Court decided that the newspapers could continue publishing the documents — an unusual instance in which judicial action rescued a fragment of history from official suppression.[42] By exposing the deceptive and criminal methods of the war waged in Indochina, the Pentagon Papers did not harm national security, as some officials claimed, but it did raise troublesome questions about the legitimacy of U.S. policy in Indochina, and *that* was the real cause for concern.

Suppressing documents is a major industry of the national security state. In 1995, the Department of Defense, the Central Intelligence Agency (CIA), and the Justice and State Departments performed some 3.6 million classification acts. In 1996, the number climbed to more than 5.8 million, or about 21,500 classifications every workday of the year.[43] As much as $16 billion is consumed annually on classifying a growing stockpile of secret documents, involving the efforts of 32,397 full-time federal employees. All this despite President Clinton's much publicized executive order to promote declassification.[44] Issued in 1995, presidential executive order 12958 mandates automatic release of documents that have been kept secret for twenty-five years or longer, and sets a ten-year limit on current secrets. However, in what amounts to a giant loophole, the order does allow exceptions for "very sensitive" materials. At the same time, the Clinton administration extended to the

National Security Council the same broad protection from public scrutiny that is reserved for White House papers.[45]

From 1993 to 1996, as part of the declassification effort, the National Security Agency (NSA), the Pentagon's spy service, released more than 1.3 million pages of documents, all of which were more than fifty years old, some dating from before World War I. NSA officials were at a loss to explain why these materials had remained secret for so long. The released records represented but a small fragment of the billions of pages still classified within that agency's archives.[46]

It becomes extremely difficult if not impossible to set the historical record straight when vital information is classified, then circulated among small interconnecting circles within the national security state, and then grudgingly released piecemeal over a period of decades or centuries.[47] It recalls Carroll Quigley's warning about the Milner group: how a secret unaccountable coterie of policymakers wields such power over events while monopolizing the information about those same events, thereby thwarting democratic accountability.

Researchers are further frustrated when materials are so heavily redacted as to be of no real value even when declassified. FBI documents in my possession, dating from 1956 and finally declassified forty years later in 1996, relating to the activities and suspicious death of noted labor union leader Walter Reuther, had their entire texts inked out.[48] The same with completely inked out FBI documents relating to Lee Harvey Oswald and the assassination of President John Kennedy, stamped "Top Secret," dating from 1963, and declassified thirty-one years later in September 1994 only after much pressure from dedicated researchers.[49] Such unreadable specimens put a curious twist on the concept of "freedom of information," leaving one to wonder, what is there to hide?

The late FBI director J. Edgar Hoover and his counterparts in the CIA and the military intelligence agencies amassed files on scores of famous writers, poets, and artists, including such notables as William Faulkner, Ernest Hemingway, Archibald MacLeish, Robert Frost, and Georgia O'Keeffe. Government agents not only monitored their writings and speeches but wiretapped and bugged them, opened their luggage, intercepted their mail, and intimidated their associates. FBI agents even bullied librarians to report what books the surveilled individuals were reading. Hoover parceled out the damaging personal or political information to cooperative politicians and journalists in order to deny the targeted persons jobs, promotions, passports, and awards. When Herbert Mitgang used the Freedom of Information Act to demand the files these agencies kept on famous authors and artists, much of what he requested was refused and much of what he got was heavily redacted, even in regard to writers who had been dead for forty years.[50] Again this raises the question, what is there to hide? And how can we keep police state agencies from fabricating a self-serving version of history, including the history of how they themselves violate our democratic rights?

The CIA and other U.S. intelligence agencies have had a close collaboration with Guatemalan military and paramilitary forces, dating back to the U.S.-sponsored overthrow of the democratically elected reformist government in Guatemala in 1954. These U.S. agencies have extensive files on the more than 200,000 murders and disappearances in Guatemala. Under pressure from the CIA, President Clinton retreated from earlier commitments to release the files. In 1996, after much protest by critics of U.S. policy, the Clinton administration declassified thousands of documents concerning human rights abuses, mostly relating to cases in which U.S. citizens in Guatemala had been raped, tortured, and killed. Guatemalan officials hoped that the papers might reveal useful information about the longstanding links between the CIA and the Guatemalan military, which was accused of committing most of the crimes. But the documents that arrived were so thoroughly excised as to contain little that was not already known. "[N]ot one of these documents has any value at all in a judicial proceeding. . . . These are not declassified documents; they are censored documents," announced Julio Arango Escobar, head of the special prosecution team appointed by the Guatemalan government. Guatemala's leading newspaper, *Prensa Libra,* complained that, as in the past, "all that became known was what the CIA wanted." And Helen Mack, a human rights campaigner whose sister was killed by the Guatemalan military, pointed out that Washington continued to cover up its knowledge of abuses by exempting the CIA and the Defense Department from public disclosure.[51] In sum, much of the terrible history of U.S.-sponsored political murder in Guatemala was suppressed by the very agencies that participated in the deeds.

After several more years of pressure, enough pertinent information was finally released for the Guatemalan Historical Clarification Commission to report that the Guatamalan military had committed "acts of genocide" against the Mayans during the thirty-six-year war against the poor. The declassified documents revealed how the United States government gave money and training to the Guatamalan military, and along with U.S. private companies "exercised pressure to maintain the country's archaic and unjust socio-economic structure." In addition, the U.S. government and its various agencies, including the CIA, lent direct and indirect support to illicit state operations, many of which were carried out "without respect for any legal principles or the most elemental ethical and religious values, and in this way completely lost any semblance of human morals. . . ."[52]

The Freedom of Information Act [FOIA] "allows the [CIA] to be exceedingly stingy in responding to requests from historians, journalists and citizens for documents."[53] Confronted with an FOIA lawsuit regarding its role in the 1954 coup in

Guatemala, the CIA released barely 1,400 of 180,000 relevant pages, nearly half a century after the events. The agency reportedly destroyed most of its files on other covert actions in the 1950s and 1960s, including all records relating to its role in the overthrow of reformist prime minister Mohammed Mossadegh of Iran in 1953.[54] A volume of State Department papers on Iran, published in 1990, omitted any mention of the CIA's part in that coup. In protest, Warren I. Cohen, a historian at Michigan State, resigned his post as chair of the State Department's advisory committee on historical diplomatic documentation, complaining that "the State Department is playing games with history." This expurgated *Foreign Relations of the United States* volume now sits authoritatively on thousands of library shelves.[55]

The CIA promised that it would release documents on the 1953 coup in Iran, the 1961 Bay of Pigs invasion of Cuba, its covert operations supporting political interests in France and Italy in the 1940s and 1950s, insurgencies in Indonesia and Tibet in the 1950s and 1960s, insurrections in the Belgian Congo and the Dominican Republic in the 1960s, and secret actions in North Korea and Laos. But little has been forthcoming.[56] The agency did not mention releasing materials about CIA involvement in the brutal wars of attrition it waged against revolutionary governments in Nicaragua, Mozambique, Angola, and Afghanistan during the 1980s, which resulted in millions of deaths and laid waste to all four countries. Nor was there any mention of its support for the death squads that have killed hundreds of thousands of peasants, trade unionists, students, clergy, and others throughout Latin America and parts of Asia and Africa.[57]

In 1996, fed up with unfulfilled promises to release records, George C. Herring of the University of Kentucky resigned from the CIA's Historical Review Panel, a group that was supposed to assist in declassifying data. Herring called the CIA's promises merely "a carefully nurtured myth."[58] Another panel member, historian John Lewis Gaddis, remarked, "It can only be to the advantage of the agency to come clean and release the stuff. Not releasing it conveys the impression of there being something to hide."[59] Is there something to hide?

Numerous reasons are given to explain the CIA's resistance to declassification:

§ The agency is said to be steeped in "a culture of secrecy" and cannot quite grasp the idea of open information.[60] In fact, the agency has no problem swiftly declassifying information that might benefit it or one of its operations.

§ The CIA's declassification efforts supposedly are bogged down in bureaucratic inertia. Actually, the CIA suffers little bureaucratic inertia when mobilizing vast resources for terroristic intervention abroad. With a budget of about $3 billion a year, the agency has allocated less than $1 million to declassification.[61] Not bureaucratic inertia but deliberate political intent is behind the logjam.

§ It has been suggested that the CIA does not want to be embarrassed by having to expose failures such as the Bay of Pigs.[62] In fact, the Bay of Pigs is already well known as a CIA fiasco. More likely the agency does not want to disclose too much about its more successful machinations.

§ Agency officials say they must be careful about declassification so as not to compromise their "sources and methods." Here they are inching closer to the truth.[63] Sources from a half-century ago are not likely to be still operative, but the CIA certainly does not want its *methods* advertised. Throughout its history, the agency has resorted to every conceivable crime and machination to make the world safe for the *Fortune* 500, using false propaganda, economic warfare, bribery, rigged elections, sabotage, demolition, theft, collusion with organized crime, narcotics trafficking, death squads, terror bombings, torture, massacres, and wars of attrition.

In short, there *is* something to hide even with cases that are fifty or sixty years old. It is a mistake to think that the CIA or any other national security agency is unnecessarily uptight for refusing to declassify materials that passed long ago into history. The agency understands that to publicize the violent and criminal methods of its covert operations from decades past would (a) reflect poorly upon its present image and current undertakings, causing an outcry that might threaten its funding and functioning; (b) call into question the entire legitimacy of U.S. global interventionism, its goals and purpose; and (c) invite inquiries as to whether the CIA is still committing those same crimes today—and there is no reason to believe it is not.

Besides being classified or excised, U.S. government documents are often destroyed or "lost." Sometimes the loss is not only to suppress history but to thwart justice. Thus, for over a century Native American Indians have been deprived of a simple accounting of money and land held in trust for them by the federal government. The lands were managed by the government and usually leased out to gas, oil, and timber corporations. As many as a half-million Native American beneficiaries may have lost up to $10 billion over the last century in extracted revenues. Pursuing the matter in the federal courts, plaintiffs were informed by government officials that "records of nearly century-old oil, gas, or timber leases have disappeared in many cases."[64] In fact, official government records never just "disappear," and they are seldom just "lost." More often, someone removes and destroys them for reasons best known to that someone.

Consider the Iran-contra conspiracy. Before two congressional investigative committees, Colonel Oliver North calmly described how he shredded hundreds of pages of pertinent materials, in effect changing the history of that covert operation before it could ever be written. In 1986, it was discovered that the Reagan administration had been sending millions of dollars' worth of secret arms shipments to Iran, a country the White House had publicly accused of supporting terrorism. Then, North's secret team circumvented the Congress, the law, and the Constitution, by funneling the funds from the Iranian arms sale to Nicaraguan mercenaries known as the "contras," who were waging a CIA-sponsored war of terror and attrition against the Nicaraguan population and its reformist Sandinista government. Evidence indicated that the contra war was supported also with money from drug trafficking, involving many of the CIA's closest allies and operatives. Some of the same secret routes used to bring arms to the contras brought cocaine back to the United States.[65] The congressional report that emerged from the Iran-contra hearings did more to cover up than uncover the operation, avoiding any probe of the CIA's role in drug trafficking.[66] Much of this Iran-contra story remains untold and is probably lost to history.

For every Pentagon Papers controversy or Iran-contra scandal that bursts into national headlines there are scores of other cases that get only passing attention, if that. In 1992, in the wake of the Gulf War, when Representative Henry Gonzalez, chair of the House Banking Committee, attempted to investigate U.S. loan policy toward Iraq, the National Security Council convened a top-level interagency meeting to suppress the release of all germane materials. Gonzalez accused the Department of Agriculture of spending an entire weekend shredding documents pertaining to the investigation. A senior administration official confirmed that there had been a "wholescale destruction" of documents in the Justice Department, "more extensive than anything in anyone's memory." In numerous other instances, the administration simply refused to produce the records that Gonzalez had subpoenaed, or claimed that they had been "lost."[67]

After landing in Haiti in 1994, ostensibly to restore stability and democracy to that battered country, U.S. troops seized more than 150,000 pages of documents and photographs from the headquarters of the Haitian military and from FRAPH, the previous regime's most feared paramilitary group. Officials of the democratically elected government of President Jean-Bertrand Aristide said that the return of the documents was indispensable to their efforts to disarm and prosecute human rights violators connected with the previous military regime. Human rights groups in Haiti blamed FRAPH for most of the three thousand people killed in the 1991–1994 period, along with thousands of other incidents of rape, torture, beatings, and arson. But Washington continued to stall because, in the view of one Aristide adviser, the purloined records were likely to contain data about the finances and activities of U.S.-supported Haitian death squads, as well as information about the location of arms caches hidden around the country by rightist groups. Washington, the adviser noted, did not want to see the assassins and torturers go on trial in Haiti and "have it emerge that they were paid and supported by American intelligence."[68]

In 1975 Congress ordered the release of the Nixon White House tapes, thirty-seven hundred hours of private conversations between President Nixon and his aides. Twenty-one years later only sixty-three hours had been released.[69] Ex-president Nixon litigated furiously to keep the tapes secret. Nixon exercised what amounted to a posthumous grip on the recordings, seeing to it that after he died the executors of his estate would continue the fight to delay release. Under court order they won the right to excise and destroy "private" portions of the tapes, a process that was to take three to six years and cost the taxpayers more than $600,000. Most of the "private" portions, critics maintained, were actually political discussions by Nixon and others, which National Archive officials deemed "private" because the president was acting not as president but as head of the Republican Party or in some other such capacity.[70] This decision assumed that Nixon could don or discard his historically significant presidential status like a cloak.

Along with government secrecy, there are many centers across the country that retain a tight grip on the private papers of people who once served in positions of public trust. Families of notable personages also are often slow in opening their archives. Public and private corporations release only a thin stream of papers. In all, "the amount of actual truth that makes it through the classification process to the general population each year is scant indeed."[71]

Additional problems are presented by presidential libraries, which often seem less intent upon serving history than preserving the image of a particular president. Various researchers have complained about materials made available at the Kennedy library that were so severely excised as to distort our understanding of John F. Kennedy's presidency.[72] The Kennedy library is administered by the National Archives and Records Administration, which is supposedly obliged under the law to run it impartially. Likewise, the Ronald Reagan Presidential Library and Center for Public Affairs in Simi Valley, California, seems to be more a mausoleum than a research center. Even its director, Richard Norton Smith, allowed that many of its displays were too hagiographic. Although Reagan left office in January 1989, most of the library's documents remain inaccessible for "security" reasons or because they still have not been processed.[73]

As with textbooks, schools, and presidential libraries, so too history museums have become "one way the dominant classes in the United States—wittingly or unwittingly—appropriated the past," writes historian Mike Wallace. He argues that the museums tended to "falsify reality and become instruments of class dominance. They generated conventional ways of viewing history" that justified the capitalist mission as something natural and inevitable.

> And perhaps more importantly, they generated ways of not seeing. By obscuring the origins and development of capitalist society, by eradicating exploitation, racism, sexism, and class

struggle from the historical record, by covering up the existence of broad-based oppositional traditions and popular cultures, and by rendering the majority of the population invisible as shapers of history, the museums inhibited the capacity of visitors to imagine alternative social orders—past and future.[74]

The same sanitized, mythologized McHistory is presented by numerous corporate-sponsored historic theme parks, from Williamsburg to Disneyland.[75] The memorials and equestrian statues found in public parks, government centers, and town halls offer a similarly skewed historical record. Mount Rushmore features colossal heads of Washington, Jefferson, Theodore Roosevelt, and Lincoln: two slaveholders, an imperialist, and a reluctant emancipator. In 1999, there was serious discussion about giving Ronald Reagan a place on Rushmore, the president who did so much for the rich while leaving the world a dirtier, poorer place.

All over the United States monuments pay homage to military figures who participated in unjust wars, including the defense of the southern slavocracy and the slaughter of Native Americans, Mexicans, Spaniards, Filipinos, and others. Far fewer are the monuments to abolitionists, pacifists, anarchists, socialists, labor radicals, civil libertarians, and other champions of egalitarianism whose efforts have afforded us the modicum of democracy and social justice we possess today. In the entire United States there exists not a single monument to the heroic volunteer veterans of the Abraham Lincoln Brigade who fought fascism in Spain during the Spanish civil war (1936–1939), save one obscure memorial plaque at the City College of New York to the fallen students who served in the brigade.[76]

The idea that official documents contain the real history of what transpires within the circles of power is a questionable assumption made by too many historians, Daniel Ellsberg maintains. So much of the official public record is deceptive, written as a cover or justification for existing policy. "It's almost never the case that a government official feels that his boss and his policy is best served by the whole truth and nothing but the truth." The public record—consisting of official statements, interviews, even background interviews, and released documents "is always distorted and a great deal of it is lies," concludes Ellsberg from his own insider experience. Top-secret classified material is more reliable but still inadequate; much is left unwritten for fear of leaks. The dedicated investigator must rely on a combination of official documents, unofficial materials, private letters, diaries, confidential or overheard conversations (when they come to light), anonymous interviews, and other testimonies. Even then there is no guarantee that the truth will out.[77]

Among the things rarely recorded in official communiques, Ellsberg notes, is the top policymakers' overriding preoccupation with domestic political costs. Though constantly kept in mind, such a concern is seldom admitted in the foreign policy area, where the reigning myth is that tawdry partisan calculations play no part in statecraft. Other deliberations and decisions never committed to writing include the use of nuclear threats and the risks arising from them; bribing officials of foreign governments; conspiracies to commit political assassination; political coups against other governments; financing death squads, torturers, and terrorists; involvement in massacres; and connections with organized crime and drug trafficking. According to Ellsberg, most such concealment is not intended to protect operations from foreign enemies but to avoid public accountability, limit the political costs, or avoid criminal prosecution.[78]

Listening to the Muted Masses

If much of history is written by the victors, who then speaks for the muted masses? Through the centuries there has been scarcely anyone to record their glory and misery; few to take note of those obscure souls who wept for loved ones lost in famous wars, the peaceful villages obliterated by the conquerer's holocaust, the women torn from their hearths by the military plunderers and rapists.

It was Caesar, not those he vanquished, who chronicled the conquest of Gaul.[79] We can read much about the greatness of Charlemagne but who records the miseries of the people enslaved in Charlemagne's mines? Volumes aplenty have appeared chronicling the exploits of Darius the Great, Alexander the Great, Catherine the Great, Peter the Great, Frederick the Great, and other self-styled "greats" whose major accomplishments were the forceful exploitation and suppression of toiling populations. Fewer have been the chroniclers who recorded how the course of history was changed by the women and men who created the crafts and generated the skills of civilization; those who developed horticulture and designed the first wagons, seafaring vessels, and fishing nets, the first looms, lathes, and kilns; who cultivated the first orchards, vineyards, and terraces; discovered the use of medicinal herbs, and invented the written word, arithmetic calculations, and musical instruments; those who did what Thorsten Veblen called "the work of civilization."[80] One is reminded of Bertolt Brecht's poem, "Questions from a Worker Who Reads":

Who built the seven gates of Thebes?
The books are filled with names of kings.
Was it kings who hauled the craggy loads of stone?
And Babylon, so many times destroyed,
Who raised that city up each time?
In which of Lima's houses, glittering with gold, lived those who built it?
On the evening that the Wall of China was finished
Where did the masons go? . . .
Philip of Spain wept when his fleet went down.
Was there no one else who wept?
Frederick the Great won the Seven Years War.
Who won it with him? . . .

A victory on every page
Who cooked the victory feast?
A great man every ten years.
Who paid the costs? . . .

Giving the people their due involves more than just giving them credit for performing the drudgery of society. A people's history recognizes ordinary people as the source of most of the positive contributions that have made life tolerable and even possible. To the princes and presidents, plutocrats and prime ministers, we owe the horrors of war and conquest, the technologies of destruction and control, and the rapacious expropriation that has enriched the few and impoverished the many. It is from the struggles of ordinary populations that gains have been made on behalf of whatever social betterment and democracy we have.

A people's history should give us (a) an uncompromising account of the crimes of ruling interests, so many of which have been ignored or glossed over by mainstream historians, and (b) a full account of how the common people of history struggled against the oppressions of each age, a subject that mainstream history seldom mentions, except in passing and often disapprovingly.[81]

The gentrification of history takes place even before it is written, at the point of origin. Public and personal papers and news reports are heavily skewed in an upper-class direction, having been written and preserved by those with the education, authority, or leisure to do so. In her study of the struggles of southern womanhood, Anne Firor Scott notes: "This book deals largely with women who left a mark on the historical record, which means for the most part women of educated or wealthy families. In antebellum times the wives of small farmers and the slave women lived, bore children, worked hard, and died, leaving little trace for the historian coming after."[82]

While too often the case, this is not entirely true. There does exist a historical record consisting of more than the thoughts and deeds of the prosperous. Doubtless, it is easier to locate the papers left by them. Certainly the newspapers—owned by members of their class—bestowed well-established individuals a degree of attention seldom accorded those of lesser station (as remains the case today). But information about the muted masses can be found even among the papers of the oppressors themselves. As Herbert Aptheker reminds us, by reading against the grain, one can glean revealing data from plantation accounts, court records, prison documents, police reports, newspapers, letters, and diaries. Furthermore, ordinary working people, including African American women, arguably the most oppressed of all, had dozens of organizations and left a record of impressive struggle.[83]

Looking at the struggles in England during the Tudor-Stuart centuries, 1485–1688, Christopher Hill finds that the poor and illiterate did not leave much written evidence—so he searches for their voices and ideas in popular plays, in such literature as *Pilgrim's Progress,* in oral folklore about Robin Hood, and tracts written by Levelers and Diggers. Some of what the common people did can be detected in the distressed and apprehensive letters, speeches, and official statements of the gentry, nobility, and upper clergy.[84]

An example of how mass political consciousness might be reflected in the records of the oppressor are the miles of files accumulated by the secret police in Mussolini's Italy, revealing an extensive opposition to fascism. Police reports about suspicious doings in factories and neighborhoods, oppositional flyers secretly circulated, isolated acts of sabotage, and revolutionary graffiti on public buildings and even toilet walls, hailing Lenin and Stalin and displaying the hammer and sickle, all duly recorded by the police, provide an entirely different image of Italy under fascism, and help explain the resilient and major role played by the Italian Communist Party during the partisan war and after World War II.[85]

While it is frequently assumed that working people were too illiterate to leave written records, in fact, by the early nineteenth century, through the work of self-help agencies, there was in England a growing literacy among large sections of the working class. It is also assumed that the lives of ordinary people were too dull and obscure to merit recording, or that they lacked sufficient time for literary exertions. Nevertheless, "intermittent journals, and autobiographies written over a period of years and, often, toward the end of life, are common enough," reports John Burnett. "In the main, working people who wished to write found time and energy to do so—late at night, on their Sundays and rare holidays, in periods of unemployment and in old age." "But it remains true," Burnett adds, "that the direct, personal records of working people have not so far been regarded as a major historical source, and that the whole area of such materials remains largely unexplored territory."[86]

All this speaks to the question of how the historical record is shaped by forces that are often beyond the historian's reach. These larger forces also impact directly upon historians themselves, as we shall see in the next chapter.

NOTES:

1. Henry Charles Lea, *The Inquisition of the Middle Ages: Its Organization and Operation* (New York: Citadel Press, 1961), 119–120.
2. Lea, *The Inquisition of the Middle Ages,* 120.
3. Jeanne's family name was d'Arc. Her father was Jacques d'Arc, her mother Isabelle d'Arc. Changing Jeanne d'Arc to "Joan of Arc" would be like changing Alexis de Tocqueville to "Alex of Tocqueville."
4. Régine Pernoud, *Joan of Arc: By Herself and Her Witnesses* (New York: Stern and Day, 1982), 160–162.
5. Pernoud, *Joan of Arc,* 221.
6. Pernoud, *Joan of Arc,* 179, 196, 212–214, and André-Marie Gerard, *Jeanne, la mal jugée* (Paris: Bloud et Gay, 1964), 324.
7. Gerard, *Jeanne, la mal jugée,* 320–331; Pernoud, *Joan of Arc,* 261–268. The Trial of Rehabilitation is also pointedly referred to by some as the Trial of Vindication: see Daniel Rankin and Claire

Quintal in their notation to *The First Biography of Joan of Arc, With the Chronicle Record of a Contemporary Account* (Pittsburgh: University of Pittsburgh Press, 1964), 4.

8. Pernoud, *Joan of Arc*, 214–215; Gerard, *Jeanne, la mal jugée*, 329–330.
9. Pernoud, *Joan of Arc*, 167–169.
10. "*[U]n grand seigneur anglais qui tenta de la prendre par force*": Gerard, *Jeanne, la mal jugée*, 332; also Pernoud, *Joan of Arc*, 218–220.
11. Pernoud, *Joan of Arc*, 263.
12. "The work was very thoroughly done and thereafter nothing was left of the heresy charge": Pernoud, *Joan of Arc*, 268.
13. Filippo Tamburini, *Santi e Peccatori: Confessioni e Suppliche dai Registri della Penitenzieria dell'Archivo Segreto Vaticano, 1451–1586* (Milano: Instituto di Propaganda Libraria, 1995).
14. Daniel Wakin, "Vatican Stirred Up Over Book on Clerical Sins," *San Francisco Chronicle*, March 25, 1995.
15. Denis Winter, *Haig's Command: A Reassessment* (New York: Viking, 1991), 95, 110–113. Winter found much documentation in Australia and Canada supporting the higher casualty figures and demonstrating that British war records had been drastically purged, which is not to say that Australian and Canadian records were pure and untouched. For a recent attempt at giving a full account, see Robin Prior and Trevor Wilson, *Passchendaele: The Untold Story* (New Haven: Yale University Press, 1996).
16. William Langer, *An Encyclopedia of World History*, 5th ed. (Boston: Houghton Mifflin, 1980), 960. Relying on British sources, one otherwise informative work estimates only 244,897 killed and wounded at Passchendaele: John Ellis, *Eye-Deep in Hell: Trench Warfare in World War I* (New York: Pantheon Books, 1976), 95.
17. Winter, *Haig's Command*, 3–4; for specifics, see 225–257 and 303–315.
18. Winter, *Haig's Command*, 225–257 and passim.
19. Alan Clark, *The Donkeys* (London: Pimlico, 1991, originally 1961), 17–18, 22. The peculiar title of Clark's book is taken from an exchange between Field Marshal Ludendorff, who said "The English soldiers fight like lions," and General Hoffman, who replied "True. But don't we know that they are lions led by donkeys." Also John Laffin, *British Butchers and Bunglers of World War One* (Herndon: International Publishers Marketing, 1996), documents how inept British generals repeatedly sent troops to slaughter in World War I.
20. Winter, *Haig's Command*, 247, 307–308, and passim.
21. Winter, *Haig's Command*, 241–243.
22. Winter, *Haig's Command*, 239, quoting Maurice Hankey.
23. Winter, *Haig's Command*, 5.
24. Carroll Quigley, *The Anglo-American Establishment* (New York: Books in Focus, 1981), 197 and xi.

25. Carroll Quigley, *Tragedy and Hope: A History of the World in Our Time* (New York: MacMillan, 1966); also the discussion in Daniel Brandt, "Philanthropists at War," *NameBase NewsLine,* no. 15 (October–December 1996): 1–2.
26. Patricia Brodsky, "Germany Report: The Selective War on History," *Progressive Clearinghouse Bulletin* 5 (1998): 13, drawing upon an article by Klaus Hartung in *Die Zeit* (Hamburg), November 7, 1997.
27. Brodsky, "Germany Report: The Selective War on History," 13–14.
28. Brodsky, "Germany Report: The Selective War on History," 14. These events have been documented in great detail in Monika Zorn (ed.), *Hitlers zweimal getötete Opfer: Westdeutsche Endlösung des Antifaschismus auf dem Gebiet der DDR* [Hitler's Twice-Killed Victims: The West German Final Solution of Antifascism in the Territory of the German Democratic Republic] (Freiburg: Ahriman Verlag, 1994).
29. Richard J. Evans, *In Hitler's Shadow: West German Historians and the Attempt to Escape from the Nazi Past* (New York: Pantheon Books, 1989), 11–14.
30. Consider the pro-Nazi sympathies of the Federal Republic's courts: Ingo Müller, *Hitler's Justice: The Courts of the Third Reich* (Cambridge, Mass.: Harvard University Press, 1991), 201–298.
31. For instance, Werner Maser, *Hitler: Legend, Myth & Reality* (New York: Harper & Row, 1973).
32. *The Goebbels Diaries 1939–1941,* cited in Evans, *In Hitler's Shadow,* 46. Ernst Nolte produced a central text: *Der europäische Bürgerkrieg 1917–1945: Nationalsozialismus und Bolshewismus* (Frankfurt, 1987), summarized and critiqued by Evans, 27ff.
33. See my *The Sword and the Dollar: Imperialism, Revolution, and the Arms Race* (New York: St. Martin's Press, 1989), 141ff; for additonal comments on Nazism, see my *Blackshirts and Reds: Rational Fascism and the Overthrow of Communism* (San Francisco: City Lights Books, 1997), 1–22.
34. Evans, *In Hitler's Shadow,* 57–91.
35. See also the critical discussion of Nolte and Fest in Deborah Lipstadt, *Denying the Holocaust: The Growing Assault on Truth and Memory* (New York: Plume/Penguin, 1994), 211–215.
36. For instance, John Lewis Gaddis, "The Tragedy of Cold War History," *Foreign Affairs* (January/February 1994): 142–154; and Douglas J. MacDonald, "Communist Bloc Expansion in the Early Cold War: Challenging Realism, Refuting Revisionism," *International Security* (Winter 1995–96): 152–188.
37. Melvyn P. Leffler, "Inside Enemy Archives: The Cold War Reopened," *Foreign Affairs* (July/August 1996): 120–135.
38. Leffler, "Inside Enemy Archives: The Cold War Reopened," 122, 129–131; also William A. DePalo Jr., "Cuban Internationalism: The

Angola Experience, 1975–1988," *Parameters* 23 (autumn 1993): 61–74; and Hope M. Harrison, "Ulbricht and the Concrete 'Rose': New Archival Evidence on the Dynamics of Soviet-East German Relations and the Berlin Crisis, 1958–1961," Cold War International History Project Working Paper No. 5, Woodrow Wilson International Center, 1993, cited in Leffler, 130.

39. Leffler, "Inside Enemy Archives: The Cold War Reopened," 122–123.

40. Vladislav Zubok and Constantine Pleshakov, *Inside the Kremlin's Cold War: From Stalin to Khrushchev* (Cambridge, Mass.: Harvard University Press, 1996), 74, 125, and 276–277; Sergei Goncharov, John Lewis, and Xue Litai, *Uncertain Partners: Stalin, Mao and the Korean War* (Stanford: Stanford University Press, 1993), passim.

41. Theodore Roscoe, *The Web of Conspiracy: The Complete Story of the Men Who Murdered Abraham Lincoln* (Englewood Cliffs, N.J.: Prentice-Hall, 1959, 1960), ix.

42. David Rudenstine, *The Day the Presses Stopped: A History of the Pentagon Papers Case* (Berkeley: University of California Press, 1996); also R. W. Apple Jr., "25 Years Later, Lessons From the Pentagon Papers," *New York Times*, June 23, 1996.

43. Information Security Oversight Office, *Report to the President* (Washington, D.C.: National Archives and Records Administration, 1995 and 1996); Executive Order 12829, "National Industrial Security Program," *Federal Register*, vol. 58, no. 5, January 8, 1993; Office of Management and Budget, "Information Security Oversight Office; Classified National Security Information" 32 CFR Paret 2001, *Federal Register*, vol.60, no. 198, October 13, 1995.

44. Information Security Oversight Office, *Report to the President*, 1995, 1; and *Washington Post*, May 15, 1994. Over 80 percent of classification costs consists of billings from defense industry contractors.

45. Executive Order 12958, "Classified National Security Information" *Federal Register*, vol. 60, no. 76, April 20, 1995; and *New York Times*, March 26, 1994.

46. *New York Times*, April 5, 1996.

47. Dennis Effle, "The Second Crucifixion of Oliver Stone," *Probe*, May 22, 1995: 13–14.

48. On Reuther, see the investigative piece I wrote with Peggy Karp: "The Wonderful Life and Strange Death of Walter Reuther," in my *Dirty Truths* (San Francisco: City Lights Books, 1996), 192–207.

49. The documents on Reuther were supplied to me by William Gallagher, investigative reporter at WJBK TV, Detroit, who obtained them under the Freedom of Information Act. The ones on Oswald, procured by investigator Peter Dale Scott, were reproduced in *Open Secrets* (newsletter of the Coalition on Political Assassinations, Washington, D.C.), January 1995, 7.

50. Herbert Mitgang, *Dangerous Dossiers: Exposing the Secret War Against America's Greatest Authors* (New York: Donald I. Fine, 1988).

51. The comments by Arango Escobar, *Prensa Libra,* and Mack are from *New York Times,* August 9, 1996; see also Guatemala News and Information Bureau newsletter, July 1998.

52. "Guatemala, Memory of Silence," report of the Historical Clarification Commission, Guatemala City, February 25, 1999 and *New York Times,* February 26, 1999.

53. David Corn, "Secrets From the CIA Archives," *Nation,* November 29, 1993, 660. Corn summarizes a number of CIA atrocities revealed in the newly released 500,000 pages related to the John F. Kennedy assassination.

54. *New York Times,* May 29, 1997; Stephen Schlesinger, "The CIA Censors History," *Nation,* July 14, 1997, 20–21; and Eric Alterman, "The CIA's Fifty Candles," *Nation,* October 6, 1997, 5–7.

55. R. J. Lambrose, "The Abusable Past," *Radical History Review,* spring 1992, 152.

56. *New York Times,* April 8, 1996.

57. See the discussion on "The Mean Methods of Imperialism" in my *The Sword and the Dollar* (New York: St. Martin's Press, 1989), 37–62; and my *Against Empire* (San Francisco: City Lights Books, 1995) 23–30 and passim.

58. *New York Times,* May 20, 1997.

59. *New York Times,* April 8, 1996.

60. Writing in the *New York Times,* April 8, 1996, Tim Weiner sees a clash of cultures pitting CIA cold warriors against open-minded historians.

61. *New York Times,* April 8, 1996.

62. Peter Kornbluh thinks further disclosures of the Bay of Pigs operation would "embarrass the CIA's covert operations directorate"; see his op-ed: "The CIA's Cuban Cover-Up," *New York Times,* April 16, 1996.

63. As one agency official argued in the *New York Times,* May 20, 1997.

64. *New York Times,* February 23, 1999.

65. On the contra-CIA-drug connection, see Peter Dale Scott and Jonathan Marshall, *Cocaine Politics: Drugs, Armies, and the CIA in Central America* (Berkeley: University of California Press, 1991); also Jonathan Marshall, Peter Dale Scott, and Jane Hunter, *The Iran-Contra Connection* (Boston: South End Press, 1988), 34–47, 64–68, 134–139; Christic Institute Special Report, *The Contra-Drug Connection* (Washington, D.C.), November 1987; "Is There a Contra Drug Connection?" *Newsweek,* January 26, 1987; and *New York Times,* January 20, 1987. President Reagan admitted full knowledge of the arms sales to Iran, but claimed he had no idea what happened to the money earned from the sales. He asked the public to believe

that unlawful policies of such magnitude were conducted by subordinates, including his own National Security Advisor, without being
cleared with him. In subsequent statements, his subordinates said
that Reagan had played an active role in the entire affair.

66. *Report of the Congressional Committees Investigating the Iran-Contra
    Affair* H.-Rep. 100–433, S-Rep. 100–216, 100th Congress, 1st
    Session (Washington, D.C.: Government Printing Office, 1987).
67. Jack Colhoun, "White House 'loses' evidence," *Guardian,* March 23,
    1992; and Stephen Pizzo with Mary Fricker and Kevin Hogan,
    "Shredded Justice," *Mother Jones,* January/February 1993, 17.
68. *New York Times,* November 28, 1995. At least one highly placed
    FRAPH operative boasted of his links with U.S. intelligence agencies.
69. In 1996, historian Stanley Kutler finally won a legal battle that
    promised to lead to the eventual release of the remaining hours,
    though no firm schedule was set. Kutler maintained that the tapes
    would reveal a history far different from the "self-serving memoirs" of
    President Nixon and his former aides: *New York Times,* April 13, 1996.
70. *Washington Post,* August 11, 1998.
71. Dennis Effle, "The Second Crucifixion of Oliver Stone," *Probe,* May
    22, 1995: 13.
72. Ronald Kessler, "History Deleted," *New York Times,* April 30, 1996.
73. Edmund Morris, "A Celebration of Reagan, What the Presidential
    Library Reveals About the Man," *New Yorker,* February 16, 1998, 48
    and 54.
74. Mike Wallace, *Mickey Mouse History and Other Essays on American
    Memory* (Philadelphia: Temple University Press, 1996), 24–25.
    Thanks to the efforts of public historians, industrial museums of late
    have shifted the focus from industrial objects and entrepreneurs to
    the struggles and contributions of the working class: ibid., 88ff.
75. Wallace, *Mickey Mouse History and Other Essays on American
    Memory,* 134–174.
76. Letter to me from Edward L. Remais, Committee for the Founding
    of an Association for the Study of the Spanish Republic and the
    Spanish Civil War, May 1997. The same bias is found in other bour-
    geois political cultures. Thus in Italy one can find many statues
    of the emperors but few devoted to the Gracchi or other popular
    leaders of antiquity.
77. Daniel Ellsberg, interviewed by Christian Parenti and me,
    Kensington, California, February 8, 1999.
78. Ellsberg interview, February 8, 1999.
79. According to Pliny the elder, Caesar's wars cost 1,192,000 lives,
    which may explain why Caesar mentions no casualty figures in his
    writings. The number Pliny gives is precise enough to lead one to
    question its reliability. Still, the casualties must have been high
    enough: Pliny, *Natural History* VII. 91–92.

80. This is not to deny that mainstream history has provided us with worthwhile accounts of social life through the ages; for instance, Henri Pirenne, *Economic and Social History of Medieval Europe* (New York: Harcourt, Brace & World, 1937); Edmund Morgan, *The Puritan Family: Religion and Domestic Relations in 17th Century New England* (New York: Harper & Row, 1966); and Peter Laslett, *The World We Have Lost: England Before the Industrial Age,* 2nd ed. (New York: Charles Scribner's Sons, 1971).

81. The public's interest in people's history and alternative views in general can be measured by the popularity of such worthwhile works as Howard Zinn, *A People's History of the United States* (New York: Harper & Row, 1980); and James W. Loewen, *Lies My Teacher Told Me* (New York: New Press, 1995).

82. Anne Firor Scott, *The Southern Lady: From Pedestal to Politics, 1830–1930* (Chicago: University of Chicago Press, 1970), xi.

83. Herbert Aptheker, *Racism, Imperialism, & Peace: Selected Essays by Herbert Aptheker,* edited by Marvin Berlowitz and Carol Morgan (Minneapolis: MEP Publications, 1987), 130–131. Tera W. Hunter restores some of the voices of the African American masses by combing through unsympathetic sources: see her *To 'Joy My Freedom: Southern Black Women's Lives and Labors After the Civil War* (Cambridge, Mass.: Harvard University Press, 1997). See also Jesse Lemisch, "Listening to the 'Inarticulate': William Widger's Dream and the Loyalties of American Revolutionary Seamen in British Prisons," *Journal of Social History* 3 (fall 1969): 1–29. Lemisch has made other important contributions to "history from the bottom up"; see Jesse Lemisch, "The Radicalism of the Inarticulate: Merchant Seamen in the Politics of Revolutionary America," in Alfred F. Young (ed.), *Dissent: Explorations in the History of American Radicalism* (De Kalb: Northern Illinois University Press, 1968), 37–82; and his "The American Revolution Seen From the Bottom Up," in Barton J. Bernstein (ed.), *Towards a New Past: Dissenting Essays in American History* (New York: Vintage 1969), 3–45.

84. Christopher Hill, *Liberty Against the Law: Some Seventeenth Century Controversies* (London and New York: Penguin/Allen Lane, 1996); and Christopher Hill, *The World Turned Upside Down: Radical Ideas During the English Revolution* (Harmondsworth, Middlesex, and New York: Penguin, 1972, 1975).

85. Franco Andreucci, "'Subversiveness' and anti-Fascism in Italy," in Raphael Samuels (ed.), *People's History and Socialist Theory* (London: Routledge & Kegan Paul, 1981), 199–204.

86. John Burnett (ed.), preface to *Annals of Labour: Autobiographies of British Working-Class People 1820–1920* (Bloomington & London: Indiana University Press, 1974), 9–10.

5

IN RANKE'S FOOTSTEPS

For centuries, the writing of history was largely the avocation of lawyers, clergy, businesspeople, and men of private fortune. There were court scribes who chronicled events in a manner pleasing to their monarchs. And there were gentlemen amateur historians who wrote for gentlemen readers. As late as the mid–nineteenth century there existed almost no professors of history in U.S. universities. In 1884, when the American Historical Association was organized, there were no more than fifteen professors and five assistant professors teaching history exclusively; others combined history with political science, philosophy, and other subjects. In time, the growth of industrial society saw an increase in the nation's college population and a commensurate professionalization of academic disciplines, including history.[1] By the time the *American Historical Review* was founded in 1895, there were about one hundred full-time college teachers of history, almost half of whom had studied at a German university. "Thus the professionalization of history meant a gradual transformation of the historian from a gentleman-scholar into a teacher-scholar, who earned the support he received by the instruction he provided."[2]

Today the monarch's scribes are gone but others continue to do service as court historians.

His Majesty's Servant

One of the most renowned nineteenth-century European historians was Leopold von Ranke, whose loathing of popular revolution and unflinching devotion to absolutism won him the favor of German monarchs. The Revolution of 1830 was seen by Ranke as the opening salvo in a series of popular rebellions that would threaten monarchist rule throughout Europe. He believed that Europe was the region that God had selected for the growth of the one true religion, Christianity, and that monarchy was Christianity's best protector. In 1831 he agreed to edit a political journal sponsored by the Prussian government. Two years later, elevated to a professorship at the University of Berlin, he launched a series of attacks in the journal against liberalism, including the "dangerous ideas" of the French Revolution. Ranke had nothing to say on behalf of individual rights. He opposed a constitution for Prussia and argued against the establishment of a Prussian parliament, no matter how circumscribed its powers.[3]

For Ranke, history was to be objectively grounded on facts, and facts were to be ascertained in documents. But since documents were produced mostly by the state, "objective factual history" tended to be history heavily refracted through official lenses, fitting nicely with Ranke's own conservative predilections. Lord Acton saw Ranke as a scholar of great stature, "almost the Columbus of modern history." Yet, even Acton noted that Ranke was better attuned to the shifting relations of cabinets and factions than to the broader forces that make history.[4]

In 1841, King Friedrich Wilhelm IV of Prussia appointed Ranke official historiographer of the Prussian state. Wilhelm subsequently called on him as an adviser and in 1854 appointed him to the Council of State. Ranke's other royal admirer,

Maximilian II of Bavaria, offered him a university position in Munich, which he refused, then appointed him chair of the newly formed Historical Commission of the Bavarian Academy of Sciences. With the financial support it received from the Bavarian government, the commission formed an institution for the scholarly study of German history that subsequently supported publication of *Historische Zeitschrift,* the premier journal of the German historical profession to this day.[5]

What is evident from all this is that the German monarchs of Ranke's day took history seriously. They financed chairs, commissions, journals, and professional societies, taking care that these be staffed by gentlemen who shared their own views about how past and present should be defined.

Further honors came to Ranke from the United States. In 1885, undeterred by his antidemocratic sentiments, the gentlemen historians of the newly formed American Historical Association elected Ranke as the AHA's first honorary member, on which occasion George Bancroft dubbed him "the father of historical science" and "Germany's greatest historian."[6]

Coexisting with conservatives like Ranke within Germany's history profession were dedicated democrats and liberals, but they were not likely to be granted awards, editorships, or special funding, nor be appointed to state commissions, honorary societies, and choice academic posts. Ranke's contemporary, Theodore Mommsen, is a case in point. Early in his career, on a recommendation from his teacher Otto Jahn to the Ministry of Culture in Saxony, Mommsen was appointed a professor of law at the University of Leipzig. After two years, he was dismissed for his democratic sympathies, along with his sponsor Jahn and another scholar Moritz Haupt. This was during the repressive aftermath of the 1848 revolution, and the government was purging the university of dissidents. Mommsen survived in his profession by moving to Switzerland, winning an invitation from the University of Zurich, a less beleaguered institution.[7] In 1881, he was elected to the Reichstag, and became increasingly liberal as he grew older. Much of his active political life came after he had made his reputation as a leading historian of antiquity, which may explain how he survived in his early and middle years in academia.[8]

Within the German history profession there were even some left Hegelians like the notable Wilhelm Zimmermann, whose work on the German peasant war stood as a classic in radical history for over a century, serving as the basis for Engels's book on the same subject. Scarcely off the press in 1841, his first volume was banned in Bavaria and Württemberg. Not long after his involvement in the struggle of 1848, Zimmermann was dismissed from his post as professor at the Karlsruhe Polytechnic and lived out the rest of his life as a parson of a poor parish near Stuttgart, in marked contrast to the well-paved road traveled by Ranke.[9]

In the 1830s and 1840s, with politics being too dangerous a topic for open debate, the Young Hegelians focused on theological and philosophical questions.[10] But given the close ties between state and church in Germany, it was foreordained that a movement of religious criticism would crystallize into one of political opposition. Not surprisingly, Friedrich Wilhelm IV, the same monarch who was heaping honors upon Ranke, sought to, in his own words, "root out the dragon-seed of Hegelianism."[11]

One casualty of Wilhelm's repression was Bruno Bauer, who was deprived of his teaching post because of his unorthodox philosophical views, including his renowned critique of the Gospels and his denial of the historicity of Christ. Another victim was Arnold Ruge, who was exiled from university teaching after being refused a chair. Then there was Karl Marx, a close companion of both Bauer and Ruge. Though endowed with a doctoral degree and exceptional capabilities, Marx never even got his foot in the university door.[12]

In England, too, "the university intelligentsia, from the beginning, were coopted by the ruling class," serving as trainers of the domestic and colonial administrative cadre.[13] Nevertheless, here and there could be found historians iconoclastic enough to have their careers brought to a sorry finish. There was the prominent case of Thorold Rogers, who labored from the 1860s to the 1880s to bring forth a monumental social and economic history, the abridged version of which served as a text for the socialist movement well into the twentieth century.[14] Though he frequently took pains to inject unfriendly comments about socialism into his writings, Rogers supported striking farm workers and voiced enough anti-Tory opinions to get himself run out of his professorship at Oxford.[15]

As in monarchist Germany and aristocratic Britain, so in republican America: outspoken radicals had a markedly low survival rate in academia. There was Daniel DeLeon, who received the prized lectureship at the newly formed School of Political Science at Columbia College in 1882. Elected president of the Academy of Political Science in 1884–85, DeLeon seemed securely launched upon a promising career. But one day, while he sat with some of his colleagues, a crowd of workers trundled by in the street below. They were celebrating their victory after a hard-fought strike in which they had been treated brutally by management and police. Hastening to the window to view the procession, DeLeon's colleagues expressed such utter contempt for the laborers as to infuriate him. In short time, DeLeon threw his support to Henry George, the radical single-tax advocate, whom the unions were backing for mayor of New York. He began speaking publicly for George, identified as "Professor DeLeon of Columbia College." President Barnard, supported by Columbia officials, acted swiftly to end the "outrage" of associating the name of their institution with a "monstrous agitation" that threatened to "overthrow the entire structure of civilized society."[16]

Columbia was a pillar of the established order, preparing young men for leadership roles in the financial and legal world and upper echelons of government service. DeLeon's political activities prevented him from ever becoming a regular member of the Columbia teaching staff.[17] Even though he had demonstrated considerable ability as a scholar and a teacher he was not, as would normally have been the case, offered a professorship. In 1889 he left the faculty in disgust.[18]

In twentieth-century United States, a dismaying number of radical academics came under fire. Among the better known victims were E. A. Rose, Scott Nearing, Edward Bemis, and Paul Baran. Of special note was Thorstein Veblen. Although his formal training was in economics, Veblen regularly challenged the received truths of bourgeois history and social science, which he saw as little more than an extended apologetic for the existing politico-economic system. Common lore has it that his personal lifestyle, including a stormy divorce and illicit liaisons with various women, was the cause of his checkered career in academia. One of his editors sets the record straight, noting that what really upset Veblen's academic employers and peers "was less his unstable *ménage* than his dangerous thoughts. They got back at him in many ways. He was 'not sound,' they said; 'not scholarly.'" They froze his meager salary and delayed his promotions. Despite his fame, his productivity, and the relatively wide readership he had gained, his choice of teaching posts shrank and never was he awarded a grant for any research project he submitted.[19]

In 1918 Veblen published *The Higher Learning in America,* a slashing critique of the mummery and cant that composes so much of the academic world. When asked what the subtitle would be, he answered only partly in jest: "A Study in Total Depravity." In 1925, unable to completely ignore his great scholarly contributions and his celebrity among a literate public, the American Economic Association tendered Veblen the nomination for its presidency, a shamefully long-overdue recognition. Even then the invitation came only after some heated clashes within the association's ranks. Veblen refused the offer, remarking with some bitterness that it came too late.[20]

An "Aristocratic Profession"

If it is true that people frequently perceive reality, past and present, in accordance with the position they occupy in the social order, then it is no mystery that so much of the history handed down to us has an affluent, Anglo-Protestant gentlemen's perspective. In both England and the United States until recent times, the history departments of leading universities were populated largely by relatively well-off Christian Caucasian males of politically conventional opinion, who viewed the struggles of the world *de haut en bas,* never knowing serious economic insecurity and having little understanding of the tribulations of working-class life.

As late as 1890, many gentlemen historians — in the words of one — had "no ambition to be known as a Professor of American History," and emphasized their European training and orientation so to avoid "being regarded as an American provincial."[21] Relatively few courses in American history were offered at Harvard and Yale, and none at all at Princeton. This snobbery began to recede after the Spanish-American War of 1898, when the United States was recognized as a world power by the European nations. During the next fifty years American history became the most assiduously cultivated field in both teaching and research.[22]

In the United States, through the first half of the twentieth century, a noticeable number of prominent historians were wealthy (George Beer in tobacco, Rhodes in iron, Beard in dairy farming), or editors of big business publications (Oberholtzer), or quasi-official scribes for Rockefeller and Ford (Nevins), or U.S. Navy admirals (Mahan and Morison).[23] One of them, Rhodes, remarked in no uncertain terms that they conceived of history as an "aristocratic profession" and "the rich man's pastime."[24] Herbert Aptheker describes the gentlemen historians of that time as ultra-nationalist, male chauvinist, white supremacist, and class elitist:

> [They] wrote and taught history in very much the same way as bourgeois judges have traditionally interpreted and administered the law, and for very much the same reasons. . . . Naturally such individuals had "a somewhat careful solicitude for the preservation of wealth," as a sympathetic commentator remarked of Schouler. Of course, in their books, the "wage earner and farmer rarely appears," as was said of McMaster. Certainly one like Fiske would detest the Populists, and Rhodes thought of workers as "always overbearing and lawless," while to Oberholtzer, labor organizers were veritable demons, guilty of "follies and excesses," who turned "foreign rabble" into "murderous mobs."[25]

The founders of the history profession in the United States, writes Mark Leff, "defined themselves and their immediate audiences as gentlemen, as a genteel intellectual and social elite," working in tandem with the patrician class "to rein in the democratic excesses that so repelled them."[26] No surprise that Henry Adams could not recollect ever having heard the names of Karl Marx or August Comte mentioned during his student days at Harvard College, the two radical writers whom he considered the most influential of his time.[27] As almost foreordained by his lineage, Adams himself developed into a full-blown historian of the gentleman amateur variety, who bemoaned the democratic intrusions of mass society and the passing of preindustrial gentility.[28]

Some gentlemen historians have been more conservative than others. Samuel Flagg Bemis, for instance, so zealously trumpeted the United States' role in world history that his students dubbed him "American Flagg Bemis." A few like David Saville Muzzey and Henry Steele Commager had liberal leanings on some issues, though gravely marred by the worst sort of ethnic prejudice. Thus, for Muzzey, Native American Indians manifested "a stolid stupidity that no white man could match." The Reconstruction era was a "travesty" for it placed "the ignorant, superstitious, gullible slave in power over his former master"; it handed over southern state governments to scalawags and inferior blacks who indulged in "an indescribable orgy of extravagance, fraud, and disgusting incompetence."[29]

Henry Steele Commager assisted Samuel Eliot Morison in writing a best-selling American history textbook that had only kind words for southern slavery and only one name for four million enslaved Africans: "Sambo, whose wrongs moved the abolitionists to wrath and tears . . . suffered less than any other class in the South from its 'peculiar institution.'" And "the majority of slaves were . . . apparently happy. . . . There was much to be said for slavery as a transitional status between barbarism and civilization. The negro learned his master's language, and accepted in some degree his moral and religious standards."[30] The Morison-Commager textbook continued in subsequent editions for more than twenty years.

The gentleman historian's ethno-class bias was evident from the start. The 1895 premier issue of the *American Historical Review* featured an opening statement by William M. Sloane, a future president of the American Historical Association: "We are Europeans of ancient stock" who "brought with us from England, Scotland, Ireland, Holland, Germany, and France" a "well-ordered, serious life" and created "a set of distinctively American institutions." The radicalism of European democracy—which Sloane compared unfavorably to the "orderly, modern democracy" of "English America"—if unchecked, would bring "anarchy and ruin" and "destroy all greatness both in the making and in the writing of history."[31] Like many of his associates, Sloane feared that the leveling tendencies of radical democracy could only threaten his professional and class privileges and detract from the quality of life as he and his kind knew it.

In the United States, before World War II, the accepted patrician norms of the university "often debarred from academic life people whose ethnic or racial background was different from that of the white, Anglo-Saxon, Protestant ascendancy"[32]: Jews, Catholics, African Americans, Latinos, and Asians. In the post–World War II era, the growth in enrollments and in federal and state funding for higher education brought a greater diversity in ethnicity, class background, and — to a lesser degree — political orientation among academic historians. The conservative Anglo-patrician grip on the profession was loosened though not broken. And with the loosening came an improvement in the quality of historiography, with at least some scholarship directed toward understanding the historical realities of class power and exploitation.[33]

Such transitions did not go unnoticed among the patricians. In 1957, at Yale, as class barriers and religious restrictions gave way to the post-war influx of bright young men with G.I. Bill benefits, the chairman of the history department confided his concerns to the university's president, noting that while the graduate program in the English department "still draws to a degree from the cultivated, professional, and well-to-do classes, by contrast, the subject of history seems to appeal on the whole to a lower social stratum." Referring to the doctoral applicants in his own department, he complained that "far too few of our history candidates are sons of professional men; far too many list their parents' occupation as janitor, watchman, salesman, grocer, pocketbook cutter, bookkeeper, railroad clerk, pharmacist, clothing cutter, cable tester, mechanic, general clerk, butter-and-egg jobber, and the like."[34]

What was wrong with having historians who were drawn from "a lower social stratum"? Addressing the annual meeting of the American Historical Association in 1962, President Carl Bridenbaugh, himself a product of Protestant Middle America, vented his ethno-class concerns in regard to this "great mutation" (his term). Aware that the postwar G.I. Bill ushered in all sorts of people who could not have gone to college in earlier times, Bridenbaugh lamented, "Many of the young practitioners of our craft, and those who are still apprentices, are products of lower middle-class or foreign origins, and their emotions not infrequently get in the way of historical reconstructions." Urban-bred and influenced by the Old World attitudes of their parents, they suffered from "environmental deficiency." Through no fault of their own, they lacked the understanding "vouchsafed to historians who were raised in the countryside or in the small town."[35]

Bridenbaugh's reference to urban, foreign-born, lower-class mutants (mostly Jews, it was understood) who were intruding upon his profession, made clear his bigoted conviction, shared by other members of his profession, that only middle- to upper-class white Protestant males from "solidly American" towns had the proper intellect and rooted experience to divine the complexities of America's history.[36]

Patrician conservatives were not the only ones to indulge in this sort of self-inflating pap. Even an independently-minded radical like William Appleman Williams often claimed that his small-town Midwest origins explained his insights into U.S. history.[37] One might just as easily argue that a limited small-town, Anglo-Protestant, ethno-class background was a handicap, rather than an advantage, when trying to fathom the multivariated, largely urban "American experience." A case in point is John Franklin Jameson, the first editor of the *American Historical Review*, who — according to his biographer — felt that his "ambition to write the social history of America was thwarted by his obvious distaste for people in the mass and for ethnic groups other than his own."[38]

The affirmative action programs beginning in the early 1970s brought still greater ethnic and gender diversity to academe. But the journey from undergraduate to graduate school and eventually to a tenured faculty slot at one of the better colleges or universities still remained essentially a conservative socialization process unconducive to iconoclastic critiques. Nor did the lifestyle change all that much. As historian Theodore Hamerow describes it:

> By now the descendants of the *Mayflower* or the Sons of the American Revolution are outnumbered on many campuses by members of the B'nai B'rith or the Knights of Columbus.
>
> Yet in a fossilized form, the old, genteel WASP tradition lives on. The ethos of academic life still reflects the manner of the New England Brahmin or the Southern gentlemen—sedate, dignified, poised, and slightly aloof. Today those who earn their livelihood in colleges and universities may come from a broader social and ethnic background, but they are still expected in many places to adapt in speech and appearance to the old patrician style. They gradually become absorbed and assimilated. . . . The donnish refinement cultivated in the better schools is reminiscent of academic life at the turn of the century, with its courtly manner and aristocratic studiousness. If the founders of the American Historical Association could visit a contemporary campus, they might be puzzled by the swarthy complexions among the professors, they might wonder at the strange-sounding Celtic, Latin, or Semitic names, But the flavor, the atmosphere of college life would not be unfamiliar to them.[39]

Purging the Reds

Of the new arrivals who made their way into academia by midcentury, those who encountered the most difficulty by far were the Communists and other radicals. Consider the career of Herbert Aptheker, a prolific historian and for most of his lifetime a prominent member of the Communist Party. Aptheker produced groundbreaking works on antebellum slave revolts; he edited a seven-volume documentary history of African Americans, and the papers of W. E. B. Du Bois. He describes the job discrimination he encountered early in his career:

My graduate degrees from Columbia included the Ph.D. granted in February 1943. Prior to that my efforts at job hunting had been quite unsuccessful in colleges within New York, and the reason clearly was political. When I returned from combat overseas and inquired of the late Prof. W. L. Westermann of the possibilities of appointment at Columbia, he gently remarked that while he thought I belonged there it was not possible for Columbia to hire one with my political beliefs. Thereafter letters to the employment office and to the history department at Columbia went unanswered. Efforts to obtain an appointment continued through the forties and fifties and sixties. I applied at Howard, University of Wisconsin, Reed and many more. Departments indicated interest in employing me at Reed, Northern Illinois, Buffalo and other places but these were always cut off at the administatrative level—usually without anything in writing—though from Buffalo there was first an enthusiastic offer from the chairman and then a curt note from the same person to the effect that the administration did not look with favor at the appointment.[40]

Aptheker goes on to relate how subsequently he was invited for an occasional lecture or course at various schools, sometimes only after protracted struggle, as at the University of North Carolina, Chapel Hill, where he brought suit against the university after being invited to speak and then denied access to the campus by the administration, and at Yale University where he was asked to teach one guest course which the administration initially refused to honor.[41]

Another prolific but underemployed historian was Philip Foner, who authored or edited scores of pioneering books on labor history, African American history, and related subjects. Foner and his three brothers were among more than forty faculty and staff fired from the City College of New York in 1941 during the anti-Communist witchhunt conducted by the notorious Rapp-Coudert Committee of the New York State Legislature. It was twenty-five years before Foner found another teaching post.[42]

177

During the 1940s and 1950s, hundreds of instructors were denied contracts or turned down for tenure on political grounds at universities around the nation. Opponents of such purges were intimidated into silence. Many had to sign humiliating "loyalty oaths" as a prerequisite to keeping their jobs. In some instances, the FBI actually set up office on campus, working closely with university administrators to comb student and faculty records and recruit students to spy upon their fellow students and professors. According to one study, undergraduate William F. Buckley was a regular campus informant, as was Henry Kissinger. A protégé of Arthur Schlesinger Jr., Kissinger opened the mail of fellow graduate students and sent the contents to federal authorities.[43]

Of the left academics who did manage to survive within the university system, many had a hard row to hoe, as William Appleman Williams discovered. In the early 1950s, Williams developed a critical view of the prevailing cold war orthodoxy, seeing U.S. containment policy as counterproductive, foolish, and shortsighted. He believed that normal and friendly relations between the United States and the Soviet Union were possible.[44]

Williams's critique of U.S. foreign policy was not Marxist as such. He seemed unaware that U.S. ruling circles had no interest in reaching an understanding with Moscow and were dedicated to undermining any country that departed from the global capitalist system.[45] Yet his work was critical enough for him to be targeted by academic and governmental cold warriors. He could not get his articles published in the two major journals of the history profession, the *American Historical Review* and the *Mississippi Valley Historical Review*. One essay of his that offered a critical overview of U.S. policy in Latin America from 1917 to 1933, with every single footnote from a primary source and almost all from archival materials, was returned by the editors as "insufficiently researched." Another of his submissions was rejected by a noted conservative figure in foreign relations because Williams had cited documents not ordinarily used, ones that went beyond officially sanctioned State Department records.[46]

Williams won a following among both students and the politically literate public. Still, he endured the cancellation of book contracts on political grounds, Red-baiting from colleagues, ferocious hectoring from cold war operatives like Theodore Draper, slaps from publications like *Time* magazine, and persistent badgering from the U.S. House Un-American Activities Committee and the Internal Revenue Service.[47] Williams's biographers conclude: "Offered very few grants, fewer jobs, and no particularly prestigious ones over the course of his career, and awarded only one honorary degree (by a Black community college) despite his later presidency of the Organization of American History, Williams evidently never entirely escaped an informal blacklist."[48]

In a most unscholarly fashion, Harvard historian Oscar Handlin attacked Williams's *The Contours of American History*, calling it "a scandalously intemperate polemic," "farcical," and "an elaborate hoax."[49] In 1971, Michael Harrington, a "democratic socialist" and dutiful anti-Communist, accused Williams of being a "Leninist" because of his critical views on U.S. imperialism.[50] One of Williams's most persistent detractors was noted historian Arthur Schlesinger Jr., who repeatedly attacked him for being the "pro-Communist scholar" who failed to see that Marxist ideology and Stalin's "paranoia" made the cold war inevitable. Schlesinger took to the *New York Times* and other mass circulation media (which readily accommodated him) to wage an ideological crusade against all "the sentimentalists," "the utopians, the wailers," and "fellow travelers" who were "softened up . . . for Communist permeation and conquest."[51] In contrast, Williams's articles and commentaries, including his responses to Schlesinger's attacks, found an outlet only in publications of much smaller circulation, such as the *Nation* and *Monthly Review*.

A staunch purveyor of the jingoist persuasion was Samuel Eliot Morison. In his 1950 presidential address to the American Historical Association, entitled "Faith of an Historian," Morison called for an end to the "imprecatory preaching" of antiwar critics that is "unbalanced and unhealthy." He wanted U.S. history to be written from "a sanely conservative point of view" which he seemed to equate with objectivity and reliability. Morison, a former admiral, then launched into his own imprecatory preaching, beating the drum of cold-war anti-Communist conformity, firing salvos at those in his profession who took a critical view of U.S. military involvements and war in general. The historian, he warned, "owes respect to tradition and to folk memory." Lacking sufficient patriotic enthusiasm, historians were largely responsible for youth's "spiritual unpreparedness" for World War II. In the two decades before that conflict, they robbed "the people of their heroes," and "repelled men of good will and turned other men, many not of good will, to Communism." Reviewing Morison's address, Jesse Lemisch, a progressive critic of mainstream history, thought it unfortunate that "no one seems to have noticed the ludicrousness of an admiral wrapping himself in the mantle of objectivity while haranguing his audience on the glories of war and evils of pacifism."[52]

The 1950s McCarthyite purges of academia were followed by the suppression of the New Left in the late 1960s, a campaign that continued into the ensuing decades. Noted mainstream historians such as Oscar Handlin, Samuel Eliot Morison, and Daniel Boorstin vigorously supported the U.S. government's war in Indochina and the repressive measures taken against both student antiwar activists and their more restive colleagues in the history profession.

When it comes to trumpeting a fundamentalist patriotism, celebrating the image of America as God's gift to the world, no historian has been more persistent than Daniel Boorstin. In 1953, before the House Un-American Activities Committee,

Boorstin zealously fingered former friends and teachers as Communist subversives, and heaped praise upon himself as a tireless anti-Communist fighter. In the 1960s he denounced student radicals as "dyspeptics and psychotics," and defended the University of Chicago when it rejected student applicants who came from activist political backgrounds.[53]

During the latter part of the twentieth century, the conservative sway over the history profession was weakened but not broken. The absence of a conservative monopoly is not to be mistaken for leftist dominance—even when left-leaning scholars win election to top professional office. In 1999, Eric Foner, who has written extensively about abolitionism and Reconstruction from a sympathetic viewpoint, and who has been involved in a variety of dissident campus political issues, took office as president of the American Historical Association (membership fifteen thousand). That same year David Montgomery, author of detailed studies of workers' lives and actively involved in labor struggles, became president of the Organization of American Historians (membership nine thousand). The elections of left-leaning scholars like Foner and Montgomery does not gainsay Jon Wiener's observation that of the thousands of AHA and OAH members, "only a small proportion are radicals or activists."[54]

The iconoclasts, the Marxists, and the revisionists remain a minority, ever vulnerable to political retribution by more conservative colleagues and administrators. As Herbert Shapiro notes, "The notion that the U.S. academy is dominated by radicals seeking to impose ideological conformity upon higher education does not conform to reality. Professors with views of the political Right continue to teach and their tenured positions remain undisturbed. Conservatives are a presence in innumerable academic departments, and no university is in the hands of leftists."[55] A study by two mainstream social scientists showed that only 12 percent of the academic historians considered themselves to be "left," and 14 percent "conservative." The rest identify as liberal or middle of the road.[56]

The very structure of U.S. institutions of higher education with their conservative top administrators, boards of trustees dominated by affluent business elites, the growing corporate takeover of university functions, and the dependency on public and private funding militates against anything resembling a radical predominance.

Still, the pockets of dissent found on some campuses represent a departure from the standard ideological conformity found in most institutions in U.S. society. It is enough to incur the wrath of those who treat the mildest signs of heterodoxy as evidence of a leftist takeover.[57] Indeed, what really bothers those who endlessly carp about the campus tyranny of "political correctness" is not the orthodoxy of the politically correct "tyrants" but their *departure* from orthodoxy, their willingness to critically explore gender, ethnic, and class topics in ways that normally are treated as taboo. Leading the fight against radical and multicultural revisionism have been such conservative historians as C. Van Woodward, Gertrude Himmelfarb, Eugene Genovese, Arthur Schlesinger Jr., and Daniel Boorstin. The McCarthyite war they wage to suppress radical dissent is hypocritically portrayed by them as a valiant struggle on behalf of free speech.[58]

The truth is, mainstream academics still predominate on most campuses and control most of the graduate schools, academic journals, foundation funding, and most of what passes for professional research. Such research in recent years has taken a heavy turn toward cliometrics, the analysis of aggregate bodies of numerical data, with a concentration on narrow and often dull topics and a greater reliance on politically safe social-science methodology and concepts.[59]

Historians like Schlesinger and Boorstin walk in Ranke's footsteps, faithfully serving the powers that be and reaping all the rewards, including choice academic appointments, prestigious awards, and high-profile nonacademic posts. Schlesinger served in the Kennedy administration, and Boorstin was appointed Librarian of Congress. Enjoying the benefits of their intensely partisan proestablishment careers, they advise their colleagues to eschew partisan causes that might detract from the professional quality of their scholarship.[60]

Publishing and "Privishing"

Of the left academics who manage to survive within the university system, some are hardly immune to the legitimating constraints of mainstream academe. Being more academic than left, they are primarily concerned with showing themselves to be judicious and restrained, so well attuned to the "nuanced complexities" as to ignore the stark realities. They take pains to present themselves as standing above any "orthodox" left ideology. In this they begin to resemble their more orthodox mainstream colleagues.

In their eagerness to neutralize themselves, scholars tend to neutralize their subject matter. But history is never neutral. And relatively little of it is purely stochastic and accidental. While we need not assume there is a grand design to all that happens, we cannot rule out human agency, human intent, and political interests that are purposive in their actions. Such history does not come off as very "gentlemanly" in the patrician sense, nor very nuanced—if by "nuanced" we mean the academically trained ability to mute and dilute the brute realities of political economy and class power.

Consider Michael Apple, an educator who has produced a number of worthwhile critiques of textbooks and publishing. Apple repeatedly tells us that it is "reductive," "simplistic," and "mechanistic" to see economic dominance as the major determinant of ideological predominance; more "nuanced" and "elegant" are explanations that incorporate other intervening variables. At the same time, he makes the claim that corporate publishers are not ideologically motivated, for they put economic considerations ahead of ideological ones when deciding what to publish: "In the increasingly conglomerate-owned publishing field at large, censorship and ideological control as we commonly think of them are less of a problem than might be anticipated. It is not ideological uniformity or some political agenda that accounts for many of the ideas that are ultimately made or not made available to the larger public. Rather, it is the infamous 'bottom line' that counts."[61] The corporate publishing conglomerates, then, do not exercise political censorship; they merely respond to the market, to what the public wants.

Apple offers no evidence to support this conclusion, nor does he explain why seeing profitability as the sole determinant of what gets published is not the kind of "economistically reductive" perspective he so abhors. Doubtless, books that do not raise ideological problems are measured primarily by their sales potential. But a truly nuanced analysis would allow us to search for additional cases in which, *irrespective of profitability,* ideological considerations might be operative. Instead of mechanistically dismissing such a possibility out of hand, we should stay alert for titles that promise good sales and healthy profits but still do not win publication or proper distribution because they are politically beyond the pale, including works by practiced and gifted authors. We might also want to look for cases in which profitability and ideology interplay upon each other in a causal manner, rather than treating them as mutually exclusive.

In any case, whether one explanatory model is more nuanced than another does not perforce make it more grounded in reality. Such would have to be determined by empirical investigation. Interestingly enough, on the rare occasions Apple tenders specific examples from the real world, they seem to support the straightforward "vulgar" model he bemoans in theory, as when he relates how the National Association of Manufacturers and other business and reactionary political groups succeeded in suppressing a history textbook series by Harold Rugg because of its progressive orientation.[62]

As we enter the twenty-first century, we find the publishing industry dominated by eight or so multibillion-dollar media conglomerates.[63] These giants are not noted for their willingness to support the efforts of progressive authors, even ones that might win a substantial audience. This is demonstrated by the difficulty such writers have finding a mainstream publisher and the frequency with which they must turn to self-publishing or to smaller houses that have only limited access to markets and few promotional resources.

In 1888, Osborne Ward finished his two-volume study of the struggles of working people in the ancient world, a subject largely neglected by the historians of his day. The first edition of this work was circulated privately. For almost twenty years Ward was unable to find a publisher because, as Charles H. Kerr explained, "no capitalist publishing house would take the responsibility for so revolutionary a book, and no socialist publishing house existed."[64] In 1907 Ward's work was published by Kerr's socialist collective and received an enthusiastic reception among those who heard of its existence.

In 1920, American socialist Upton Sinclair wrote a scathing critique of the business-owned press, *The Brass Check,* in which he portrayed the U.S. press as little more than a class institution that served the rich and spurned the poor. One acquaintance told him it was inconceivable that publication of this book would be permitted in America. After exasperating experiences with Doubleday and Macmillan, Sinclair decided to publish it himself. The book enjoyed six printings and sold 100,000 copies within a half-year, though it is difficult to find today.[65]

As noted in chapter one, labor's story is still largely missing from U.S. history textbooks. So Richard Boyer and Herbert Morais collaborated in writing *Labor's Untold Story,* an account of industrial struggles from the 1860s to the 1950s. The book is kept in print and distributed by the United Electrical, Radio and Machine Workers of America, a labor union with an honest and dedicatedly radical leadership. While well researched, interesting in content, accessible in style, and widely translated and read abroad, the Boyer and Morais book remains largely unknown among the U.S. public and is rarely referenced by academic historians and other writers.[66]

Today, self-published books or books published by leftist labor unions do not get the benefit of the Library of Congress's Cataloging-in-Publication (CIP) program, a tax-supported public service.[67] And without cataloging, most libraries will not even consider stocking a book, thereby denying it a wider reading audience. Judy McDermott, chief of the Library of Congress's CIP division, dismissed self-published books as generally lacking in professional quality and professional marketing, and dealing with materials that appeal only to a limited audience. Of course, many commercially published books are poorly written and appeal only to a limited audience, yet they are cataloged, stocked, and circulated by libraries.[68] As dissidents within the American Library Association note, the procurement policies of most public and academic libraries tend to exclude labor and Marxist studies and critical historical works. "Complaints that skewed [book] collections mislead users and distort history are seldom addressed by library administrators."[69]

Publishers think twice before incurring the ire of a powerful multinational corporation, especially when the publisher is owned by the corporate conglomerate, as almost all the big houses are. Many worthy but controversial titles are simply rejected for publication and denied a contract. "Less frequently, manuscripts that have been copyedited and announced in the publisher's catalogue can be yanked almost literally from the presses."[70] Sometimes, when publishers belatedly ascertain that they have signed up a leftist or otherwise troublesome book, the contract will be abrogated before publication, or if the book has already come out, the publisher—without regard for the "infamous bottom line"—will cut off all promotional efforts, withhold distribution, and shred the copies in stock. This process is known among publishers as "privishing" but seldom talked about by them publicly. An inquiry of senior editors throughout New York found that all of them were familiar with the term "privishing" and agreed upon its meaning. None of them were inclined to use it in front of authors. As one remarked, "Authors don't know the word. And I'm not going to let them know it's in my vocabulary either."[71]

A book by Edward Herman and Noam Chomsky, dealing with the violent repression committed throughout much of the world by the U.S. national security state, was first contracted by Warner Modular Publications. The publisher and editors were enthusiastically committed to promoting it. But just prior to publication in 1973, officials of the parent Warner corporation took notice of the work, were pained by its "unpatriotic" content, and decided that it would not see the light of day. Although twenty thousand copies had been printed and an advertisement placed in the *New York Review of Books*, Warner corporation refused to allow distribution—in violation of its contractual obligations. All further media advertising was canceled, and thousands of flyers that listed the book were destroyed. Warner Modular executives were warned that distribution of the Herman-Chomsky book would result in their immediate dismissal.

Warner Modular editors sought to salvage the book by offering to publish, as a counterbalance, a work that vigorously supported U.S. interventionist policies abroad. At first the parent company grudgingly accepted the idea, then decided to close down Warner Modular altogether, selling its backlists and contracts to a small unknown company that did nothing to promote the book. Meanwhile the Herman-Chomsky book was enjoying lively sales abroad, having been translated into several languages. The authors concluded that the corporate censorship they encountered was a function of the book's political content and had nothing to do with market considerations. The suppressed work eventually was reissued by South End Press, a small independent publisher of progressive titles, with very limited promotional resources.[72]

In 1974, Gerald Colby finished work on a critical history of the Du Pont family business, covering the period from 1771 to modern times. Colby had every indication that his book would be a bestseller. It was optioned to a subsidiary of the Book of the Month Club; it received favorable reviews in the *New York Times, Los Angeles Times,* and elsewhere; and it enjoyed brisk early sales. But a Du Pont executive informed an editor at the Book of the Month Club that Du Pont found the book offensive and "actionable." Fearing legal action, the book club dropped the title from its list.[73]

Colby's book outlined Du Pont's extremely unflattering history: its record of strikebreaking, its search for cheap nonunion white labor, its support of right-wing causes, its role in the rearmament of Nazi Germany in violation of the Versailles Treaty, and the like. But was the book "actionable"? William J. Daly, general counsel for Prentice-Hall, Colby's publisher, ruled that aside from four minor factual errors and one or two questionable adjectives, it was fit for publication. Daly's suggested revisions were adopted before publication. Still, Prentice-Hall cut the book's print run and slashed its advertising budget. Though there continued to be a heavy demand, there were no copies in stock.

Colby sued Du Pont and Prentice-Hall for breach of contract. The case made its way through the courts until a three-judge appeals panel ruled against him, labeling his book "a Marxist view of history" and therefore predestined for a small market and not worthy of vigorous promotion—a decision that superimposed a political judgment upon the facts of the case.[74]

Some publishers retain the illusion that they operate independently. Writing in the *New York Times,* Edwin McDowell quotes a Macmillan official who claims, "We have published books lately that we don't necessarily agree with, politically or philosophically, and we have supported them to the fullest." If there are relatively few titles of a radical nature on trade lists, it is not because of censorship but because of the publisher's perception of "what will sell and the quality of the arguments," maintains a senior editor at Morrow—without the slightest awareness that an editor's sense of the "quality of the arguments" itself might be ideologically influenced.[75]

McDowell challenges the belief that publishers will shy away from books that might offend their corporate owners. "Several prominent examples point in the other direction," he claims. But he offers only one instance, quoting Richard E. Snyder, chair of Simon & Schuster: "Shortly after we were bought by Gulf & Western, we published *Global Reach,* parts of which are critical of Gulf & Western. I never thought to discuss the book with corporate officials, and they never thought to discuss it with me. I learned months later they weren't fond of that book, but that showed me there would never be any interference with the book operation, and there never has been."[76]

Even if Snyder's bosses never discussed the book with him, somehow he did learn that they were not pleased with its publication. One wonders whether that would not give him pause the next time a radical critique of multinational corporations came across his desk. In any case, one of the authors of *Global Reach,* Richard Barnet, remembers it somewhat differently, noting that his book was published by Simon & Schuster in 1974 just *before* the house was taken over by Gulf & Western. At about the time of the takeover, Snyder asked Barnet if he would like to meet the Gulf & Western president and visit Brazil to see all the good things the corporation was doing there.[77]

Five years later, Simon & Schuster killed a book entitled *Corporate Murder* by Mark Dowie, the investigative reporter who discovered that Ford Motor Company had designed the Pinto car with dangerous gas tanks, then knowingly continued to market it. The book's editor, Nan Talese, told Dowie that Simon & Schuster president Richard Snyder "was vehemently opposed to the manuscript because, among other reasons, he felt it made all corporations look bad."[78] Living under the shadow of a giant conglomerate seems to have a chilling effect even upon ostensibly independent-minded publishing executives like Snyder.

The above examples of censorship only scratch the surface. It is not unreasonable to assume that many more cases go unreported, for ideological suppression in a society that pretends to great freedom of expression is perforce cloaked in all sorts of excuses having to do with sales anticipation and product quality.

Marketing the Right Stuff

"The increase in the number of books on historiography and historical methodology is proportionally far greater than the increase in the number of historians," writes a member of the profession.[79] Yet, if one were to rely solely upon what mainstream professional historians have to say about their discipline, one would never know that ideas and information are not disseminated democratically. Historians will go on at length about the historical method; how history relates to other social sciences; how historians must grapple with philosophical and research problems, guard against pitfalls and fallacies when sifting through the evidence, accepting little on faith and letting the chips fall where they may; how they must immerse themselves in the historical context of their subject yet keep their perspective and detachment, while showing imagination and resourcefulness, skill and sagacity, and other such sterling qualities of creative scholarship.[80]

Such books seem to assume that any one historian's work has about the same chance of reaching interested audiences as another's. Hardly a word can be found in all this literature about the marketing of history and the ideological forces within the corporate economy that help determine the distribution of historical studies. Little is said about why certain books win foundation funding, are elaborately promoted and widely reviewed, earn awards and book club adoptions, and are kept in print for long periods, while other volumes never emerge from an obscurity that seems no more deserved than the formers' celebrity. Why does some history become official and even popular while some never even makes it into the library? Surely, ideological factors cannot be ruled out.

Big publishers, big distributors, and chain retailers largely determine which books are carried in bookstores and how they are displayed, which ones are highlighted at a front table or hidden away on an obscure shelf. Independent bookstores—more likely to feature serious progressive writers and keep politically and culturally diverse backlist titles in stock—are being squeezed out by giant chains like Borders and Barnes & Noble. To maximize profits, the big chains devote proportionately larger amounts of space to the well-hyped, faster selling "blockbuster" titles. They gather substantial profits by selling display and advertising space in their hundreds of outlets, and by exacting a higher discount rate from publishers than small bookstores are able to do. The preferential discount rate that the chains get from the big commercial publishing houses makes them less willing to carry books by smaller alternative publishers who cannot provide such lucrative deals and cannot afford to buy prime display space for their new titles.[81]

Many bookstores are reducing the number of titles they stock, cutting the slower selling ones in an attempt to lower inventory costs. Serious nonfiction and other "midlist" books are among the prime casualties. Keeping books with a left perspective off the shelves now has a ready financial justification but also "fits comfortably with the political conservatism of the corporate owners of the major publishing houses."[82] Determined readers may still be able to procure titles that are highly critical of the standard version of U.S. history and politics but they will have to look harder as more and more independent stores get pushed out of business.

Ideological bias comes through clearly in which books get reviewed in the major media. Critical progressive titles are less likely than ever to receive any attention, except perhaps to be savaged. A regular reviewer for the *Boston Globe,* a reputedly liberal newspaper, told a South End Press editor that she "would be fired" if she ran reviews of writers with a radical perspective.[83] Publications like *Choice, Kirkus, Library Journal,* and *Publishers Weekly,* used by libraries and bookstores to determine adoptions, are also biased in what they review, tending to ignore—or denounce—titles that stray beyond the ideological norm.

"Reviews necessarily reflect the points of view of the reviewers, who are products of the American educational system, which promotes moderates and conservatives while weeding out radicals. Reviewers usually are employed in the orthodox environment of universities or commercial publishing," argues librarian Charles Willet. Titles acquired by both school and public libraries, he adds, are slanted toward a conventional view of past and present, selected by librarians and faculty "who tend to accept large corporate and university press publishers as objective and trustworthy, while rejecting small nonprofit publishers as 'political' and unreliable." If any change has occurred, it is in a more regressive direction as public and university libraries, faced with declining revenues, acquire even fewer alternative titles.[84]

The distribution and exposure that authors receive varies roughly in accordance with their proximity to the political mainstream. Books by ex-presidents, famous military leaders, or other highly prestigious establishment figures are contracted with big houses for million-dollar advances that are seldom earned back in sales. In an attempt to recoup an enormous advance, the publisher is likely to invest additionally large sums for promotion, often throwing good money after bad. Costly celebrity contracts are pursued despite their dubious profitability because the prestige of the author is thought to redound on the publishing house itself, or as a preemptive measure to prevent another house from getting a potential "blockbuster," or perhaps because many editors, like other unimaginative people, have a knee-jerk inclination to follow the celebrity trail.

Celebrities aside, who are the other writers whose books win special promotion? In some important cases, they are the keepers of the ideological orthodoxy. Consider the historic investigations conducted around the John F. Kennedy assassination. As president, Kennedy was heartily hated by right-wing forces in this country, including many powerful people in secret operations who saw him as "messing with the intelligence community."[85] He had betrayed the national interest as they defined it, by refusing to go all out against Cuba, making overtures of rapprochment with Castro, and refusing to escalate the ground war in Vietnam. They also saw him as an antibusiness pinko liberal or closet Marxist who was taking the country down the wrong path.[86]

For over thirty years the corporate-owned press and other mainstream opinion makers have ignored the many unsettling revelations about the Kennedy assassination unearthed by independent investigators. Such research points to a conspiracy to assassinate the president and a conspiracy to hide the crime. At the very least, the investigators raise enough serious questions as to leave us unwilling to accept the Warren Commission's official version of blaming Lee Harvey Oswald for the killing of President Kennedy.[87]

An end run around the media blackout was achieved by Oliver Stone's film *JFK*. Released in late 1991, the movie exposed millions of viewers to the many disturbing aspects of the assassination. *JFK* was repeatedly attacked seven months *before* it was released, in just about every major print and broadcast outlet, usually in the most caustic and general terms. The media's ideological gatekeepers poured invective upon Stone, while avoiding the more difficult task of rebutting the substantive points made in his film, and without ever coming to grips with the critical historical literature upon which the movie drew. A full exposure of the assassination conspiracy, that might unearth CIA or military intelligence involvement, would cast serious discredit upon the nation's major institutions.[88]

Oliver Stone's *JFK* continued to be attacked years after its initial run. Stone was pilloried as a "ranting maniac" and a "dangerous fellow," guilty of "near-pathological monkeying with history." The idea of a conspiracy in high places was ridiculed as a fanciful scenario that sprang from the imagination of a filmmaker. Like the Warren Commission, the press assumed a priori that Oswald was the lone killer. In 1978, when a House Select Committee concluded that there was more than one assassin involved in the Kennedy shooting, the *Washington Post* editorialized that there still probably was no conspiracy, but possibly "three or four societal outcasts" who acted independently of each other spontaneously and simultaneously to shoot the president.[89] Instead of a conspiracy theory the *Post* created a coincidence theory that might be the most fanciful explanation of all.

Meanwhile, in answer to the question, Did Oswald act alone? most independent investigators concluded that he did not act at all. He was not one of the people who shot Kennedy, although he was involved in another way, in his own words as "a patsy," concluded the critics.

In the wake of the public's renewed interest in the Kennedy assassination, the media bestowed fulsome publicity on one Gerald Posner, a little-known New York lawyer and writer, helping to catapult his book, *Case Closed*, onto the national bestseller list. Posner's book ignored the abundant evidence of conspiracy and coverup and used outright untruths to conclude that Lee Harvey Oswald was a disturbed lone leftist who killed Kennedy.[90] Neither before nor since has a writer about the Kennedy assassination been accorded such lavish fanfare. Posner's book was featured in prime display spaces at major bookstores around the nation. It was quickly adopted for book-club distribution. Posner himself enjoyed ubiquitous major media exposure, being treated as the premier authority on the case.[91] He was granted guest columns and lead letters, lead articles, and adulatory reviews in just about every major publication in the United States. A review of his book in the *Journal of American History* reads more like a promotional piece than an evaluation of a historical investigation.[92] *Case Closed* was hailed as "brilliantly illuminating" and "lucid and compelling" by *New York Times* reviewers who knew all along that conspiracies to murder the president do not happen in a nice country like the United States.[93]

The gaping deficiencies in *Case Closed* went unnoticed in the major media. None of the pundits or reviewers remarked on Posner's bad habit of referring to sources as supporting his position, when in fact they did not. Thus, he very selectively cited as new scientific "proof" the computer-enhanced studies by Failure Analysis Associates, without mentioning that the company had produced evidence for *both sides* in an American Bar Association mock trial of Lee Harvey Oswald. In a sworn affidavit, the CEO of Failure Analysis, Roger L. McCarthy, pointed out that "one Gerald Posner" consulted only the prosecution materials without acknowledging "that there was additional material prepared by FaAA for the defense. Incredibly, Mr. Posner makes no mention of the fact that the mock jury that heard and saw the technical material that he believes is so persuasive and 'closed' the case . . . also saw the FaAA material prepared for the defense, [and] could not reach a verdict."[94]

Posner has another bad habit. He cites interviews with people whom he never actually interviewed and who repudiate the representations he made about their views. Thus, before the House Committee on Government Operations in November 1993, he claimed to have interviewed two of Kennedy's pathologists, James Humes, M.D., and J. Thornton Boswell, M.D., who supposedly admitted to him that they had erred in their original judgment about the location of Kennedy's skull wound, opting for a higher entrance wound that would better fit the theory that the shot came from the book depository where Oswald was supposedly perched.[95] But Gary Aguilar, M.D., an expert on the medical evidence relating to the assassination, telephoned Humes and Boswell: "Both physicians told me that they had not changed their minds about Kennedy's wounds at all. They stood by their statements in *JAMA [Journal of the American Medical Association]*, which contradict Posner. Startlingly, Dr. Boswell told me that he has never spoken to Posner."[96]

Are we to believe, asks Aguilar, that Boswell admitted to Posner he saw a high skull wound at very nearly the same time he was claiming he saw a low wound to a fellow pathologist, the editor of *JAMA*, in a published interview in that journal (May 27, 1992)? Are we to believe that Boswell would forget that he had repudiated his own sworn testimony and autopsy report in a conversation with Posner? Furthermore, such a retraction by Humes and Boswell would have had enormous forensic significance. Why then did Posner fail to mention this "case-closing" news anywhere in either edition of his book? So many inconsistencies in Posner's account exist that only a full release of his research materials could establish that Humes and Boswell have recanted. But despite repeated requests, Posner refuses to release his unedited notes, records, and recordings.[97]

In *Case Closed,* Posner maintains that James Tague, a bystander at the assassination, was hit by a fragment from the first of three shots.[98] Tague maintains that he was not hit by the first shot, which means there must have been a fourth bullet from someone other than Posner's lone assassin.[99] In an April 1994 telephone conversation, Tague told Gary Aguilar the same thing he had told the Warren Commission, thereby flatly contradicting Posner's reconstruction of his testimony. Even more unsettling, in *Case Closed,* Posner cites two interviews with Tague to support his version of Tague's testmony. But Tague informed Aguilar that he has never spoken to Posner.[100]

Posner "picks and chooses his witnesses on the basis of their consistency with the thesis he wants to prove," comments G. Robert Blakey, chief counsel to the House Select Committee on Assassinations. "All through his book, Posner uses our investigation when it serves his purpose but disregards it when it runs counter to his thesis." One example: Secret Service agent Paul Landis, who was riding the running board of the follow-up car, heard shots that came from both the grassy knoll and the book depository. Posner knows about Landis; he quotes him as a credible witness on the timing of the first shot but ignores his testimony about the direction of the third shot, just as he ignores the testimony of others who reported gunfire from the grassy knoll.[101]

There are many questions Posner does not address: What of the witnesses who saw something different from what the Warren Commission—and Posner—say they saw? What of Oswald's links to right-wing groups and the intelligence community? And what of the various operatives who have emerged as participants in the plot?[102] Posner simply ignores the evidence unearthed by investigators or "often presents the opposite of what the evidence says," charges David Wrone in the *Journal of Southern History.*[103]

Those who tried to expose the seemingly purposive distortions in Posner's work have seldom been accorded any air time or print space in the major media.[104] Space does not allow a full exposition and rebuttal, but certainly the unanswered questions and unclassified or disappeared materials are enough to leave any responsible historian unwilling to say that Posner has closed the case and given us the final word.

Nor should our minds be swayed by such buzzwords as "conspiracy," which cause us to reject out-of-hand the idea that ruling elites operate with self-interested intent and sometimes with unprincipled and lethal effect. Furthermore, if the author of *Case Closed* is guiding us away from conspiracy hysteria, "what then are we to make of Posner's claim that his critics have threatened to assassinate him?"[105]

To return to the question asked earlier: Why is it that different authors, addressing the same historical subject from different orientations, enjoy such diametrically contrasting receptions? Why is it that some are put forth as stars while others—whose efforts are at least as commanding and accomplished—languish in relative obscurity? The distinguishing characteristic between the two often is a political one. Posner has given the system's guardians the answer they wanted: the assassination was only an isolated aberration that reveals nothing sinister about the national security state.

To conclude, history is not just what the historians say it is, but what government agencies, corporate publishing conglomerates, chain store distributors, mass media pundits, editors, reviewers, and other ideological gatekeepers want to put into circulation. Not surprisingly, the deck is stacked to favor those who deal the cards.

NOTES:

1. W. Stull Holt, *Historical Scholarship in the United States and Other Essays* (Seattle: University of Washington Press, 1967), 4 and 15; and Theodore S. Hamerow, *Reflections on History and Historians* (Madison, Wisc.: University of Wisconsin Press, 1987), 4.
2. Hamerow, *Reflections on History and Historians*, 4.
3. See his essay "A Dialogue on Politics," in Leopold von Ranke, *The Theory and Practice of History*, (Indianapolis/New York: Bobbs-Merrill, 1973), 102–103. For details on Ranke's life, politics, and scholarship, see the introduction by Geog Iggers and Konrad von Moltke, especially xxviii–xxix and xxx–xxxv; and Felix Gilbert, *History: Politics or Culture, Reflections on Ranke and Burckhardt* (Princeton, N.J.: Princeton University Press, 1990), 11–45.
4. John Emerich Edward Dalberg-Acton, *Essays in the Study and Writing of History*, vol. 2 of *Selected Writings of Lord Acton*, edited by J. Rufus Fears (Indianapolis: Liberty Fund, 1986), 165–172. According to Acton, Ranke was unwilling to acknowledge that those who picked through archives he himself had already consulted would have anything new to contribute.
5. Introduction by Iggers and Moltke to Ranke, *The Theory and Practice of History*, xxxiv–xxxv.
6. Holt, *Historical Scholarship in the United States*, 20.
7. Dero A. Saunders and John H. Collins, introduction to Theodore Mommsen, *The History of Rome* (Clinton, Mass.: Meridian Books, 1958), 5.
8. Saunders and Collins, introduction to Mommsen, *The History of Rome*, 11.
9. On Zimmermann, see Bob Scribner, "Revolutionary Heritage: The German Peasant War of 1525," in Raphael Samuel (ed.), *People's History and Socialist Theory* (London: Routledge & Kegan Paul, 1981), 242–244.
10. David McLellan, *Karl Marx, His Life and Thought* (Frogmore, St. Albans, England: Paladin, 1976), 31.
11. Quoted in McLellan, *Karl Marx, His Life and Thought*, 41.
12. McLellan, *Karl Marx, His Life and Thought*, 41–45.
13. Gordon K. Lewis, *Slavery, Imperialism, and Freedom: Studies in English Radical Thought* (New York: Monthly Review Press, 1978), 267.
14. James E. Thorold Rogers, *Six Centuries of Work and Wages* (London: George Allen & Unwin Ltd., 1884), with frequent reprintings through 1923, and a new edition in 1949. The original seven-volume work had the daunting title, *History of Agriculture and Prices,* the first volume of which came out in 1864 and was given favorable mention by Marx in volume 1 of *Capital*.

15. For comments on Rogers's career, see Raphael Samuel, "People's History," in Samuel, *People's History and Socialist Theory,* xxvi–xxvii.

16. This account is from L. Glen Seretan, *Daniel DeLeon: The Odyssey of an American Marxist* (Cambridge, Mass.: Harvard University Press, 1979), 13–15.

17. Seretan, *Daniel DeLeon,* 14–17.

18. For selections of his writings, see Arnold Petersen, *Daniel DeLeon: Social Architect,* vols. 1 and 2 (New York: New York Labor News, 1941); Daniel DeLeon, *Two Pages from Roman History* (Palo Alto: New York Labor News, 1959); and Daniel DeLeon, *Socialist Reconstruction of Society* (Palo Alto: New York Labor News, 1977).

19. Max Lerner (ed.), *The Portable Veblen* (New York: Viking Press, 1948), 10.

20. Lerner, *The Portable Veblen,* 10–11, 19. See also Thorstein Veblen, *The Higher Learning in America, A Memorandum on the Conduct of Universities by Business Men* (New York: B. W. Huebsch 1918).

21. Quoting Herbert B. Adams in Holt, *Historical Scholarship in the United States,* 50–51.

22. Holt, *Historical Scholarship in the United States,* 51–52.

23. Herbert Aptheker, *The Unfolding Drama: Studies in U.S. History by Herbert Aptheker,* edited by Bettina Aptheker (New York: International Publishers, 1978), 140. Fodor's travel guide describes Samuel Eliot Morison as "the Brahmin historian" who, along with Nelson Rockefeller and George Bush, was one of the "aristocratic" frequenters of the Maine Coast: *Fodor's Maine, Vermont, New Hampshire* (New York: Fodor's Travel Publications, 1995), 15.

24. Quoted in Aptheker, *The Unfolding Drama,* 140.

25. Aptheker, *The Unfolding Drama,* 141.

26. Mark H. Leff, "Revisioning U.S. Political History," *American Historical Review* 100 (June 1995): 832. See also comments in John Higham, *History: Professional Scholarship in America* (New York: Harper, 1973), 8. Many gentlemen historians were endowed with toney Anglo-patrician tri-nomina, befitting their ethno-class background and reminiscent of the cognomen affected by aristocrats of ancient Rome: Frederick Jackson Turner, John Ford Rhodes, Charles Francis Adams, Henry Baxter Adams, James Truslow Adams, Worthington Chauncey Ford, Archer Butler Hurlbert, Wilson Porter Shortridge, John Spencer Bassett, Ulrich Bonnell Phillips, Moses Coit Tyler, Wilbur Fisk Gordy, Albert Bushnell Hart, Harold Underwood Falkner, Henry Eldridge Bourne, Charles Woolsey Cole, Marshall Whithed Baldwin—one could go on. As is said of the patrician class, they own 80 percent of the wealth and 90 percent of the names.

27. Henry Adams, *The Education of Henry Adams* (New York: Random House, 1931, originally 1918), 60.

28. This theme was at least as pronounced in his private correspondence as in his public writings; see Ernest Samuels (ed.), *The Selected Letters of Henry Adams* (Cambridge, Mass.: Harvard University Press, 1992).

29. David Saville Muzzey, *An American History* (1911), quoted in Gary B. Nash, Charlotte Crabtree, and Ross E. Dunn, *History on Trial: Cultural Wars and the Teaching of the Past* (New York: Alfred A. Knopf, 1998), 27.

30. Samuel Eliot Morison and Henry Steele Commager, *The Growth of the American Republic* (first published in 1930), quoted in Nash, Crabtree, and Dunn, *History on Trial*, 60–61.

31. William M. Sloane, "History and Democracy," *American Historical Review*, 1 (October 1895): 9–10, 15–16.

32. Hamerow, *Reflections on History and Historians*, 121–122.

33. Stephen Steinberg, *The Academic Melting Pot* (New York: McGraw-Hill, 1974), 153–166; also Harvey J. Kaye, "Whose History Is It?" *Monthly Review*, November 1996, 30.

34. "Report of the History Department for 1956–57," A. Whitney Griswold Presidential Papers, Yale University, quoted in Peter Novick, *That Noble Dream: The "Objectivity Question" and the American Historical Profession* (New York: Cambridge University Press, 1988), 366.

35. Carl Bridenbaugh, "The Great Mutation," *American Historical Review* 68 (1963): 322–323, quoted in Nash, Crabtree, and Dunn, *History on Trial*, 54.

36. Nash, Crabtree, and Dunn, *History on Trial*, 54.

37. Paul M. Buhle and Edward Rice-Maximin, *William Appleman Williams: The Tragedy of Empire* (New York and London: Routledge, 1995), 1.

38. Morey Rothberg and Jacqueline Goggin, eds., *John Franklin Jameson and the Development of Humanistic Scholarship in America* (Athens, Ga.: University of Georgia Press, 1993), xxx. The comment is Rothberg's.

39. Hamerow, *Reflections on History and Historians*, 122–123.

40. Quoted in Staughton Lynd, "The Bulldog Whitewashed: A Critique of the Investigation of Herbert Aptheker's Nonappointment at Yale University," *Nature, Society, and Thought* 10, nos. 1 and 2 (1997): 119–120.

41. Lynd, "The Bulldog Whitewashed," 121–154.

42. Morris U. Schappes, "Philip S. Foner at City College: Victim of the Rapp-Coudert Committee," in Ronald Kent et al. (eds.), *Culture, Gender, Race, and U.S. Labor History* (Westport, Conn.: Greenwood, 1993), 177–187. Michael Bauman, "400 in N.Y. Mark Achievements of Labor Historian Philip Foner," *The Militant*, February 27, 1995, 7. Another brother also returned to teaching in the mid-sixties. The

two other brothers went on to become labor union officials. For a history of how academia did not oppose the McCarthyite purges but contributed to them, see Ellen Schrecker, *No Ivy Tower: McCarthyism and the Universities* (New York: Oxford University Press, 1986).

43. Sigmund Diamond, *Compromised Campus: The Collaboration of Universities with the Intelligence Community, 1945–1955* (New York: Oxford University Press, 1992), 139–166; see also Jesse Lemisch, *On Active Service in War and Peace: Politics and Ideology in the American Historical Profession* (Toronto: New Hogtown Press, 1975), 43–66; Ellen Schrecker, *No Ivy Tower,* passim; Buhle and Rice-Maximin, *William Appleman Williams,* 45, 70–73.

44. See William Appleman Williams, *The Tragedy of American Diplomacy* (New York: Norton, 1988, originally 1959 and revised 1962 and 1972); and his *Empire as a Way of Life* (New York: Oxford University Press, 1980); and Henry W. Berger, *A William Appleman Williams Reader: Selections from His Major Historical Writings* (Chicago: Ivan Dee, 1992). Williams was not totally oblivious to the issues raised by Marxism, see his *The Great Evasion: An Essay on the Contemporary Relevance of Karl Marx and on the Wisdom of Admitting the Heretic into the Dialogue about America's Future* (Chicago: Quadrangle Books, 1964).

45. For a development of this point, see my *Against Empire* (San Francisco: City Lights Books, 1995).

46. Buhle and Rice-Maximin, *William Appleman Williams,* 69.

47. Buhle and Rice-Maximin, *William Appleman Williams,* 96–101.

48. Buhle and Rice-Maximin, *William Appleman Williams,* 95.

49. Lemisch, *On Active Service in War and Peace,* 111.

50. Buhle and Rice-Maximin, *William Appleman Williams,* 265n.

51. Arthur Schlesinger Jr. quoted in Lemisch, *On Active Service in War and Peace,* 83 and 188.

52. Lemisch, *On Active Service in War and Peace,* 69–70.

53. Lemisch, *On Active Service in War and Peace,* 66–67, 103–105, 109.

54. Jon Wiener, "Scholars on the Left," *Nation,* February 1, 1999, 7.

55. Herbert Shapiro, "'Political Correctness' and the U.S. Historical Profession," *Nature, Society, and Thought* 10, nos. 1 and 2 (1997): 327–328.

56. Everett Carll Ladd Jr. and Seymour Martin Lipset, *The Divided Academy: Professors and Politics* (New York: McGraw-Hill, 1975), 368–369.

57. For examples of well-publicized conservatives who would have us believe that academia has been subverted by multicultural and radical forces, see Martin Anderson, *Imposters in the Temple* (New York: Simon & Schuster, 1992); Allan Bloom, *Closing of the American Mind* (New York: Simon & Schuster, 1987); Roger Kimball, *Tenured Radicals* (New York: Harper & Row, 1990); and Dinesh D'Souza,

Illiberal Education (New York: Free Press, 1991). D'Souza's book was favorably reviewed by C. Van Woodward and even more uncritically by Eugene Genovese; see the latter's "Heresy, Yes—Sensitivity, No: An Argument for Counterterrorism in the Academy," *New Republic,* April 15, 1991: 30–35.

58. See Shapiro, "'Political Correctness' and the U.S. Historical Profession," 309–339; and Leff, "Revisioning U.S. Political History," 840ff; also my *Against Empire,* chapter 10, "The Empire in Academia." For an account of my own experiences with political repression in academia, see my *Dirty Truths* (San Francisco: City Lights Books, 1996), 235–252.

59. See the critique of psychohistory in chapter 7.

60. For only one of many examples, see Arthur Schlesinger Jr., "History as Therapy: A Dangerous Idea," Op-Ed, *New York Times,* May 3, 1996.

61. Michael Apple, "The Culture and Commerce of the Textbook," in Michael Apple and Linda Christian-Smith (eds.), *The Politics of the Textbook* (New York and London: Routledge, 1991), 31. Apple quotes Lewis Coser and his associates: "Ultimately if there is any censorship, it concerns profitability. Books that are not profitable, no matter what their subject, are not viewed favorably": Lewis Coser, Charles Kadushin, and Walter Powell, *Books: The Culture and Commerce of Publishing* (New York: Basic Books, 1982), in ibid., 31.

62. On the suppression of Rugg's series, see the discussion in chapter one.

63. Viacom, Time Warner, News Corporation (Murdoch), Advance Publications (Newhouse), Bertelsmann AG, Hearst, Pearson PLC, and Von Holtzbrinck. For a detailed listing of their various publishing and media subsidiaries, see *Nation,* March 17, 1997: 23–27.

64. Publisher's Note to C. Osborne Ward, *The Ancient Lowly* (Chicago: Charles H. Kerr Cooperative, 1907), v.

65. Upton Sinclair, *The Brass Check: A Study of American Journalism* (Pasadena, Calif.: published by the author, n.d. [c. 1920]); John Ahouse, *Upton Sinclair Bibliography* (Los Angeles: Mercer & Aitchison, 1994), ix; Upton Sinclair, *The Autobiography of Upton Sinclair* (New York: Harcourt, Brace & World, 1962), 223.

66. Richard O. Boyer and Herbert M. Morais, *Labor's Untold Story,* (New York: United Electrical, Radio & Machine Workers of America, 1955, 1972). Earlier editions of the book were put out by small radical houses: Cameron Associates and Marzani and Munsell.

67. The CIP data is found on the page just behind the title page of a book. It gives the author's name and year of birth and the various categories of subjects the book treats, which often determines if a book will be accessed by persons searching for titles relating to a particular topic.

68. "LC's CIP Program Discriminates against Self-Published Books," *Librarians at Liberty* (CRISES Press, Gainesville, Florida), June 1997, 27.

69. Charles Willet, coordinator of the Alternatives in Print Task Force of the Social Responsibilities Round Table, American Library Association, in a letter to me, September 21, 1995.

70. Jon Wiener, "Murdered Ink," *Nation*, May 31, 1993: 743. Wiener discusses six controversial titles by established authors that were suppressed one way or another by corporate pressure. See also Mark Crispin Miller, "The Crushing Power of Big Publishing," *Nation*, March 17, 1997, 11–18.

71. Charlotte Dennett, "Book Industry Refines Old Suppression Tactic," *American Writer*, March 1984: 6.

72. Noam Chomsky and Edward S. Herman, *The Washington Connection and Third World Fascism,* (Boston: South End Press, 1979). This account of corporate suppression is from the book's prefatory note, xiv–xvii, and is based on affidavits supplied to the authors by the publisher and associate publisher of Warner Modular Publications.

73. Dennett, "Book Industry Refines Old Suppression Tactic," 5–6; Elizabeth Bowman, "Corporate Censorship," *Daily World*, October 15, 1981.

74. Gerard Colby, "My Turn," *American Writer*, March 1984: 6; Bowman, "Corporate Censorship"; John Judis, "Book Biz Censors," *In These Times*, October 12–18, 1983: 2. The book in question is by Gerard Colby Zilg, *Du Pont: Behind the Nylon Curtain* (New York: Prentice-Hall, 1974). For his pen name, Colby has since dropped Zilg.

75. Edwin McDowell, "Publishing: Censorship Can Take Indirect Forms," *New York Times*, February 18, 1983.

76. McDowell, "Publishing . . ."; see Richard Barnet and R. E. Müller, *Global Reach: The Power of the Multinational Corporations* (New York: Simon & Schuster, 1974).

77. Richard Barnet, telephone interview with me, February 21, 1999.

78. Wiener, "Murdered Ink," 749. Wiener cites Ben Bagdikian as the source of that story.

79. Joseph Strayer in his introduction to Marc Bloch, *The Historian's Craft* (New York: Random House, 1953): vii.

80. A conclusion I draw from my sampling of the vast historiography literature: Bloch, *The Historian's Craft;* Edward Hallett Carr, *What is History?* (New York: Random House, 1961); R. G. Collingwood, *The Idea of History* (New York: Oxford University Press, 1956); Leopold von Ranke, *The Theory and Practice of History* (Indianapolis/New York: Bobbs-Merrill, 1973); Ernest Scott, *History and Historical Problems* (London: Oxford University Press, 1925); C. Vann Woodward, *Thinking Back: The Perils of Writing History* (Baton

Rouge/London: Louisiana State University Press, 1986); Marie
Collins Swabey, *The Judgment of History* (New York: Philosophical
Library, 1954); Allan Lichtman and Valerie French, *Historians and
the Living Past* (Arlington Heights, Ill.: Harlan Davidson, 1978);
Robin Winks (ed.), *The Historian as Detective: Essays on Evidence*
(New York: Harper & Row, 1968); David Hackett Fischer,
Historians' Fallacies: Toward a Logic of Historical Thought (New York:
Harper & Row, 1970); and James West Davidson and Mark
Hamilton Lytle, *After the Fact: The Art of Historical Detection* (New
York: Alfred Knopf, 1982); this last volume would have been more
accurately subtitled "The Art of Historical Deferment" since the
authors seem unable to come to any conclusions one way or another
on the controversial cases they investigate — which presumably
demonstrates their judicious restraint. Only on the one relatively
noncontroversial and politically safe case (Silas Deane's death) do
they arrive at a definite decision.

81. Sanford Berman, "Three Kinds of Censorship that Librarians
(mostly) Don't Talk About," *Minnesota Library Association Newsletter*
August/September 1996, reprinted in *Librarians at Liberty,* June
1997: 18–19.

82. Craig Gilmore, "Notes on the Book Trade," *Monthly Review
Newsletter,* winter 1997: 2, 4.

83. Ellis Goldberg, "Bookstores Have Their Own Censorship," *Guardian*
(New York), March 15, 1989: 2.

84. Charles Willet, "Librarians as Censors," *Librarians at Liberty*
(CRISES Press, Gainesville Florida), June 1995: 6–7.

85. In 1992, I was listening to a late night call-in show on KGO. The
guest was Mark Lane, noted JFK assassination investigator and
author. A man called in who identified himself only as having been
with army intelligence in Japan when Kennedy was shot. He said
there was a general expectation held by him and other members of
his unit that Kennedy would be assassinated because he was "messing with the intelligence community." The news of his death was
happily received.

86. This was certainly Ronald Reagan's view, shared by other conservatives. After Kennedy won the Democratic nomination for president
in July 1960, Reagan commented, "Shouldn't someone tag Mr.
Kennedy's 'bold new imaginative' program with its proper age?
Under the tousled boyish haircut it's still old Karl Marx — first
launched a century ago. There is nothing new in the idea of a government being Big Brother to us all." Later on, Reagan maintained
that liberals like Kennedy have one thing in common with "socialists
and communists — they all want to settle their problems by government action": Kitty Kelley, *Nancy Reagan, The Unauthorized
Biography* (New York: Simon & Schuster, 1991), 125–126.

87. For a sampling of this literature, see Michael L. Kurtz, *Crime of the Century: The Kennedy Assassination from a Historian's Perspective* (Knoxville, Tenn.: University of Tennessee Press, 1982); Mark Lane, *Rush to Judgment: A Critique of the Warren Commission's Inquiry into the Murders of President John F. Kennedy, Officer J.D. Tippit and Lee Havey Oswald* (New York: Holt, Rinehart & Winston, 1966); Sylvia Meagher, *Accessories After the Fact: The Warren Commission, the Authorities and the Report* (New York: Vintage Books, 1992, originally 1967); Jim Marrs, *Crossfire: The Plot that Killed Kennedy* (New York: Carroll & Graf, 1989); Jim Garrison, *On the Trail of the Assassins: My Investigation and Prosecution of the Murder of President Kennedy* (New York: Sheridan Square Press, 1988); Philip H. Melanson, *Spy Saga: Lee Harvey Oswald and U.S. Intelligence* (New York: Praeger, 1990); James DiEugenio, *Destiny Betrayed: JFK, Cuba, and the Garrison Case* (New York: Sheridan Square Press, 1992); David S. Lifton, *Best Evidence* (New York: Carroll & Graf, 1980); Peter Dale Scott, *Deep Politics and the Death of JFK* (Berkeley, Calif.: University of California Press, 1993); Stewart Galanor, *Cover-Up* (New York: Kestrel Books, 1998); Gaeton Fonzi, *The Last Investigation* (New York: Thunder's Mouth Press, 1993); Charles A. Crenshaw, M.D., *JFK: Conspiracy of Silence* (New York: Signet, 1992); and the two articles I wrote on the JFK assassination in my book *Dirty Truths* (San Francisco: City Lights Books, 1996), 153–191.

88. A point made by columnist Tom Wicker who dismissed Stone's "wild assertions": *New York Times,* December 15, 1991. The *Washington Post* (May 19, 1991) gave George Lardner Jr. the whole front page of its Sunday "Outlook" section to slam Stone for "chasing fiction." Lardner was an interesting choice. He never reviews movies but he was the *Post* reporter who managed to cover the CIA without ever criticizing that agency's record of crime throughout the world.

89. *Washington Post,* January 6, 1979.

90. Gerald Posner, *Case Closed: Lee Harvey Oswald and the Assassination of JFK* (New York: Random House, 1993).

91. Posner's appearance on CNN's "Crossfire" was one of the rare occasions he had to confront a critic of the Warren Commission, Cyril Wecht, M.D., J.D. But he had ample support from the two hosts, Michael Kinsley and John Sununu, both of whom took the official line.

92. Thomas C. Reeves, review of *Case Closed* in *Journal of American History,* 81 (December 1994): 1379–1380.

93. For an incomplete sampling of the exposure given to Posner in the form of favorable reviews, guest editorials, and letters by him, see Geoffrey C. Ward, "The Most Durable Assassination Theory: Oswald Did It Alone," *New York Times Book Review,* November 21, 1993: 15–16; Christopher Lehmann-Haupt, "Kennedy

Assassination Answers," *New York Times,* September 9, 1993; *New York Times,* June 26, 1994, and March 26, 1998; *Washington Post,* August 24, 1993; Gerald Posner, "Who Was Lee Harvey Oswald?" *Penthouse,* November 1993; Gerald Posner, "Cracks in the Wall of Silence," *Newsweek,* October 12, 1998: 49; "New Probe Says Oswald Was JFK's Lone Assassin," *San Francisco Chronicle,* August 23, 1993.

94. Affidavit of Roger L. McCarthy, subscribed and sworn on December 6, 1993, provided to me by Gary Aquilar.

95. *Hearing Before the Legislation and National Security Subcommittee of the Committee on Government Operations,* House of Representatives, 103d Congress, 1st Session, November 17, 1993 (Washington, D.C.: U.S. Government Printing Office), 112–113.

96. Gary L. Aguilar, letter to the editor, *Federal Bar News & Journal,* 41 (June 1994): 388. Posner has since claimed that Boswell "retracted" his denial to Aguilar, yet he refused to produce any evidence of a retraction. Posner claims to have recorded an April 1992 conversation with Boswell in which the latter changed his testimony, yet he refuses to produce that also. When the Assassination Records Review Board (appointed by President Clinton to declassify documents relating to the assassination) asked Posner to donate his notes and any tapes he had of those interviews, Posner failed to do so. "The Review Board's initial contact with Posner produced no result. The Review Board never received a response [from Posner] to a second letter of request for the notes": *Final Report of the Assassination Records Review Board,* John R. Tunheim, chairman (Washington, D.C.: U.S. Government Printing Office, 1998), 134.

97. Gary L. Aguilar, "Gerald Posner and the Evidence—Some Irreconcilable Differences," *Open Secrets,* November 1995: 6–7.

98. Posner, *Case Closed,* 325–326.

99. Harold Weisberg, *Case Open: The Omissions, Distortions, and Falsification of "Case Closed"* (New York: Carroll & Graf, 1994), 159.

100. Aguilar, letter, *Federal Bar News & Journal,* June 1994: 388; and in Posner, *Case Closed,* 553, citation 31 reads: "Interview with James Tague, January 19, 1992"; and notes 32 and 33 also cite interviews with Tague. In his review of Posner's book for the *Journal of Southern History* 6 (February 1995): 186–188, David R. Wrone notes: "Massive numbers of factual errors suffuse the book, which make it a veritable minefield." One of the many errors he enumerates is that Posner has Tague standing under the triple underpass when in fact he was twenty feet east, where he could not have been hit by fragments of the first bullet.

101. G. Robert Blakey, "The Mafia and JFK's Murder," *Washington Post*

Weekly Edition, November 15–21, 1993: 23–24. Blakey received space in the *Post* because, though he rejects the lone assassin theory, he blames the Mafia, not the intelligence community, for Kennedy's death. For a refutation of that thesis, see Carl Oglesvy's "Afterword" in Garrison, *On the Trail of the Assassins,* 295–308.

102. See Mark Lane, *Plausible Denial: Was the CIA Involved in the Assassination of JFK?* (New York: Thunder's Mouth Press, 1991); Robert D. Morrow, *First Hand Knowledge: How I participated in the CIA-Mafia Murder of President Kennedy* (New York: Shapolsky Publishers, 1992); Glen Sample and Mark Collom, *The Men on the Sixth Floor* (Garden Grove, Calif.: Sample Graphics, 1995); Hugh C. McDonald, *Appointment in Dallas* (New York: Hugh McDonald Publishing Group, 1975).

103. Wrone's review of *Case Closed* in *Journal of Southern History* 6 (February 1995): 186.

104. For telling critiques of Posner's research, see Peter Dale Scott, "Gerald Posner and the False Quotation Syndrome," *Prevailing Winds,* premiere issue, 1995: 58–63; also Scott's review of Posner's book in that same issue; George Costello "The Kennedy Assassination: Case Still Open," *Federal Bar News and Journal,* 41 (March/April 1994): 233; Galanor, *Coverup;* Weisberg, *Case Open;* and Aguilar, "Gerald Posner and the Evidence," 6–7;.

105. Charley Shively, letter to the editor, *Journal of History,* 82 (June 1995): 389.

6

THE STRANGE DEATH OF PRESIDENT ZACHARY TAYLOR, A STUDY IN THE MANUFACTURE OF MAINSTREAM HISTORY

What follows is a detailed demonstration of how historical memory is politically constructed, how unsubstantiated, highly questionable, raw speculations are transformed into acceptable history by public officials, academic historians, and the news media. The process is similar to propaganda. Some basic ingredients of propaganda are omission, distortion, and repetition. Regarding repetition, one cannot but be impressed by how mainstream historians, like mainstream journalists, find validation for their images in the images they have already produced, how without benefit of evidence or independent research they revisit each other's unsubstantiated representations again and again, creating an undeserved credibility through a process of repetition. If reiterated often enough by "experts and other reputable sources," the assertion becomes accepted as true. Along with pack journalism we have pack historiography. Indeed, the two often work in tandem to buttress the politically safe conclusion. This seems to be the case regarding the death of the twelfth president of the United States, Zachary Taylor.

On the evening of July 4, 1850, President Taylor suddenly sickened. Five days later, at the age of sixty-five, he died. At the time, there were rumors he had been poisoned. More than 140 years later, an investigation was launched into his death by Clara Rising, a writer. In the course of doing a book about Taylor, she came to suspect that he had been murdered because of his uncompromising stance against the spread of slavery into U.S. territories. After receiving permission from Taylor's descendants to have his remains examined, Rising enlisted the cooperation of the Jefferson County coroner in Louisville, Kentucky. Zachary Taylor's crypt was opened on June 17, 1991. Fingernail, hair, and tissue samples, along with bone scrapings, were removed from his body, and tests were run at three different laboratories.

The exhumation drew immediate and sharp criticism from the press. A *New York Times* editorial chastised Clara Rising for "a cavalier contempt for the dead" and for "tampering with a grave" while having no "serious historical evidence" to support her suspicions.[1] The *New Republic* described the investigation as a "sacrilege" and "grisly exercise."[2] Syndicated columnist Charles Krauthammer likened the interest in Taylor's death to the interest in President Kennedy's assassination and denounced all such "conspiracy theories" for undermining the "constitutional transitions of power" in our political system.[3]

Professional historians were equally critical. Elbert Smith, author of books on the Taylor-Fillmore years, thought the idea of foul play was "sheer nonsense." He explained that historians never suspected Taylor was murdered because "conspiracies and poisoning" were common in ancient Rome and Greece but not in the United States of the 1850s. Civil War historian Shelby Foote thought that even if it were discovered that Taylor had been poisoned, it would be of no significance and would lead only to a pointless engagement in "what-might-have-beens."[4] He was referring to the seemingly useless conjectures about what might have happened had Taylor lived and his antiextensionist policy prevailed.

Foote trivializes the investigation by assuming that any revelation about poisoning would lead only to fruitless speculation rather than to a more accurate grasp of what might be a darker side of American politics. The goal is not to speculate about "what-might-have-beens" but to uncover the more menacing actualities — if there are any to uncover. Is it of any historical significance whether Zachary Taylor was poisoned? Although he is not regarded as an important president, the idea that he met such a fate challenges the notion propagated by the guardians of orthodox history who maintain that U.S. political institutions are above such skulduggery, and America is a uniquely blessed land where such things do not happen. If Taylor was poisoned, this would raise troubling questions about the security of presidents from assassination and the role of conspiratorial murder in high places. It suggests the possibility that powerfully vested interests have been capable of taking extreme measures against top political leaders. And it might cause some of us to wonder about the legitimacy and virtue of what passes for democratic rule.

On June 26, 1991, Kentucky State medical examiner Dr. George Nichols announced at a news conference in Louisville that Zachary Taylor had not been poisoned. Traces of arsenic were found in his body but nowhere near the lethal level. That evening ABC-TV news anchor Peter Jennings announced: "a mystery solved." Taylor "died of natural causes."[5] The next day, the *New York Times* story was headlined: "VERDICT IN: 12TH PRESIDENT WAS NOT ASSASSINATED."[6] A *Washington Post* headline proclaimed: "NO EVIDENCE OF POISONING UNEARTHED IN TAYLOR CASE."[7] A follow-up story in the *Post* reported: "In a setback to conspiracy buffs everywhere, [Clara Rising's] theory of assassination by arsenic-sprinkled cherries was disproved this week."[8] The media stories indicated that Taylor died from consuming cherries and milk.

Examining the Examination

Having never known cherries and milk to be fatal, I decided to examine the matter more closely. When my research assistant Peggy Karp called Dr. Nichols, six weeks after his press conference, to request a copy of the medical report, he said it was still in the computer and had not been printed out. If true, this means all the news stories announcing that Taylor had not been poisoned were filed by journalists who had never seen the actual report and who had uncritically accepted at face value the medical examiner's opinion enunciated at the press conference.

Eleven days later, in response to another inquiry from my assistant, Nichols offered a different excuse for not letting us have the report, saying he was under orders from the county coroner not to release it. Several weeks later, Nichols's secretary offered yet another reason: the report was available only through the person who had requested and funded the autopsy. Peggy Karp contacted Dr. Richard Greathouse, the county coroner in Louisville who had supervised the investigation. He eventually mailed us a copy of what appeared to be the medical examiner's statement.

Entitled "Results of Exhumation of Zachary Taylor," the report is a little over three pages, double-spaced, with no date, location, or letterhead. Though written in the first person, it lists no author. It concludes: "It is my opinion that President Zachary Taylor was not poisoned by arsenic." Arsenic was found in the samples taken from Taylor's remains but the amounts were "within the anticipated baseline concentration of that substance in human tissues." Regarding the symptoms preceding Taylor's death, the report says something interesting:

> The symptoms and duration of Zachary Taylor's disorder are historically and medically compatible with acute arsenic poison-

ing and many natural diseases. Symptoms begin within 30 minutes to 2 hours after ingestion. The symptoms include nausea, vomiting, severe abdominal cramping pain, burning epigastric pain, and bloody diarrhea. Death usually results within 24 hours to 4 days. . . .

It is my opinion that Zachary Taylor died as the result of one of a myriad of natural diseases which would have produced the symptoms of "gastroenteritis."

Lastly, the symptoms which he exhibited and the rapidity of his death are clearly consistent with acute arsenic poisoning.[9]

Taylor's symptoms included abdominal cramps, diarrhea, vomiting, fever, burning epigastric pain, and severe thirst. Though not mentioned in the report, severe thirst is a common symptom of arsenic poisoning. While the report asserts that a "myriad of natural diseases" fit this clinical picture, it names none.

Accompanying the report was a half-page statement entitled "Final Diagnosis" signed by Nichols, who concluded: "Opinion: No anatomic or toxicologic cause of determined by [sic] this examination. The manner of death is natural." He states further: "Historical data consistent with undetermined natural disorder presenting as [sic] clinical 'gastroenteritis.'" If I understand Nichols, Taylor died of an undetermined disorder, the symptoms of which resembled gastroenteritis—a catchall diagnosis given to stomach and intestinal inflammation and other internal distresses, a term so imprecise that even Nichols felt compelled to bracket it repeatedly with distancing quotation marks in his report. Though he referred to "historical data" consistent with his conclusion, he offered none.[10] The report said nothing about what caused the gastroenteritis.

Some months later, when asked if Taylor had died from gastroenteritis, Dr. Greathouse emphasized that such a conclusion was "an opinion, an opinion only, an opinion based on symptoms."[11] It seems the investigators were not as certain of their conclusions about how Taylor died as they—or as the media—

were leading us to believe. Greathouse described gastroenteritis as "a very general term." The cause could be "chemicals or viruses or bacteria, as in food poisoning or allergies."[12]

As already noted, the medical examiner's report states that Taylor's symptoms were consistent with arsenic poisoning but also with "many natural diseases," indeed a "myriad of diseases." When asked what other afflictions displayed these symptoms, Greathouse could not say. He remarked that "they said at the time [Taylor] had cholera morbus. . . . [But] he didn't really have the symptoms of cholera." Cholera morbus is a noninfectious, rarely fatal affliction that brings on diarrhea and cramps. Greathouse also mentioned several varieties of food poisoning but conceded that these do not normally cause death. He conjectured that Taylor could have contracted some kind of bacterial or acute viral infection from the food and water he had consumed that day. He also allowed that "myriad" was "too flowery a word" and that "several" other diseases would have been more accurate.[13]

Judging from Greathouse's own comments, food poisoning seems to be the only malady that fits Taylor's symptoms other than arsenic poisoning. With food poisoning there comes the sudden onset of stomach cramps, vomiting, and diarrhea an hour or so after eating—but not five days of agony and not the raging thirst, peculiar weakness in the legs, and rarely the death that comes with arsenic poisoning.

Exactly how much arsenic was found in Taylor's remains? Since arsenic is present in the atmosphere, anyone tested today would range from 0.2 to 0.6 of a microgram per gram, or parts per million (ppm).[14] The colorimetric spectrophotometry tests done on Taylor's hair and nails, conducted by Michael Ward, a forensic scientist with the Kentucky Department of Health Services, found up to 1.9 micrograms per gram of arsenic in Taylor's hair sample—three to nine times the modern-day rate. His nail sample revealed 3.0 ppm, which is five to fifteen times higher than today's normal range.[15]

Taylor spent his life on his Louisiana and Kentucky plantations, on army bases in Wisconsin, Florida, Missouri, and Louisiana, and his last fifteen months mostly in Washington, D.C. None of these sites had any industrial pollution to speak of. He should have had much less arsenic in him than do people exposed to today's chemicalized environment. In fact, he had substantially more, although apparently not a lethal amount.

Nichols is quoted in the *Washington Post* as saying that the concentration of arsenic would have had to be "hundreds to thousands of times greater" than was found in Taylor to cause death.[16] But the Swedish toxicologist Sten Forshufvud demonstrated that whole-hair samples (that is, the entire length of hair) from an arsenic victim showed amounts not much higher than Taylor's. However, a *sectional* analysis of that same victim's hair (an analysis of specific portions of the hair shaft that grew during the time immediately after poisoning) revealed a value of 10.38 micrograms per gram or seventeen to fifty-one times more than the "normal" modern range.[17] As already noted, Taylor's level, though only of the gross sample, was still three to nine times higher.

Both the *New York Times* and *Washington Post* dismissed the presence of arsenic in Taylor's body, noting that the element was used in early medicines and embalming fluid.[18] Both papers failed to mention that, at the request of his wife, Margaret Taylor, the president was not embalmed. And there is no evidence he was administered any medicine containing arsenic before or during his illness.[19]

Also mentioned as a contaminant was groundwater arsenic, which sometimes seeps into graves. But Taylor was not interred. His crypt was above ground and his lead coffin tightly sealed. The press reported that arsenic was sometimes used in certain products like wallpaper. As far as we know, Taylor was not given to munching on wallpaper, which would have been the only way traceable amounts might enter his digestive tract, his blood-stream, and eventually his nails and hair.

Greathouse contends that the arsenic in Taylor came from pollution. "Do you live in Los Angeles?" he asked when interviewed by my research assistant.[20] Certainly Taylor never lived in a polluted megalopolis like Los Angeles. If the main source of arsenic in our bodies is industrial effluent — of which there was far less in Taylor's time than today — would not the normal levels for 1850 be substantially lower? "Not necessarily," Greathouse insisted, "Arsenic was also present in some medications and in food." He offered no specifics.

Greathouse added an interesting comment: Taylor's symptoms were congruent with *acute* arsenic poisoning, the result of one lethal dosage, as opposed to *chronic* poisoning, involving ingestion of smaller amounts over a protracted period. At the postmortem, Taylor's nails were removed in their entirety and hair samples were extracted in whole shafts. Even if Taylor had been poisoned, most of the hair and nail substance would have been free of high concentrations of arsenic — having been produced long before the poisoning.

As already noted, acute dosages measure fairly low when a gross sample analysis is done but are much higher when a sectional analysis is performed of the specific portion of hair that grew immediately after the poisoning. To test properly for acute poisoning, one would have to test only the base of the nail and root end of the hair, the minute portions that had grown out during Taylor's illness, the last five days of his life. (Contrary to popular belief, hair and nails do not continue growing after death.)

The tests done by Michael Ward were of entire nails and hairs. But whole samples would greatly dilute the concentration of arsenic and mask the presence of an acute poisoning. The 3.0 ppm of arsenic found in Taylor's nail is the ratio of arsenic to the entire substance of the nail or "combination of finger and toe" nails, as Ward's laboratory report states. Almost all that substance would have been relatively free from arsenic whether or not Taylor had been poisoned. Had shavings only from the last five-day growth period been tested—assuming it was solidified enough not to have decomposed entirely—then the concentration might have been dramatically higher.

The same would be true of the hair sample. Since hair grows about one centimeter per month or 4.7 inches a year, then the arsenic content in almost all of Taylor's hair would have been around the "normal" level. The only portion of Taylor's hair that should have been tested is the .166 of a centimeter or slightly more than one-twentieth (.065) of an inch that might have grown in the last five days of his life. Here we are assuming Taylor's hair was growing at an average rate, which may not have been the case given his partial baldness, advanced years, and the mortal struggle his body was undergoing in those final days.

Would not the hair root have shown a much higher concentration of arsenic if not diluted by the whole sample? Dr. Vincent Guinn, forensic consultant at the University of Maryland, thinks so, noting that gross-sample testing is useful in cases of chronic or repeated poisoning, but in regard to acute poisoning "the results would be invalid because you would be averaging the root section concentration with the rest of the hair shaft."[21] What is needed is a sectional analysis—with special attention given to the root.

One of the pioneers of sectional hair testing, Dr. Hamilton Smith of Glasgow University's School of Forensic Medicine in Scotland demonstrated the masking effect of whole-hair analysis. Using neutron activation analysis, Smith tested a whole-hair sample (30 cm) taken from a modern-day arsenic victim and found an arsenic content of 0.86 ppm (substantially less than in Taylor's hair). But when the root and first centimeter were tested as a separate section it revealed a value of 9.40 ppm, or 10.9 times the level in the whole hair.[22]

Test results are only as good as the samples tested. Samples from a cadaver that is over 140 years old have less reliability than samples from recent victims. Both Dr. Greathouse and Dr. William Maples, a forensic pathologist who attended the postmortem, mentioned that Taylor's nails and hair were loose and, in Maples's words, "came out easily." Maples conceded that this might have been due to decomposition at the base.[23] According to Dr. Richard Bisbing, senior research microscopist at McCrone Laboratory in Chicago, if the hair root had decomposed entirely or in part, this would call into question the reliability of any test.[24]

There is the additional problem of how the samples were extracted from Taylor's remains. Dr. Guinn notes that hairs removed from a body should be placed on a clean piece of paper, with the paper folded over the root end, "a procedure that sometimes is not followed because people do not know about it."[25] It was not followed in the Taylor autopsy.

Along with the work done at the Kentucky Department of Health Services, two other laboratories tested the Taylor samples. There appears to be no final report from the Analytical Electronic Microscope Laboratory at the University of Louisville. Laboratory manager Beverly Giammara spent a day working alongside Nichols and several assistants on the samples. Nichols then took all the materials with him. Giammara is not a pathologist and did not know the significance of the arsenic levels but she kindly made available the raw data from the tests.

In his "Final Diagnosis," Nichols refers to a finding "received and reported" from "Ms. Barbara [sic] Giammara" showing an arsenic elemented weight percentage of "up to 1.80." Reviewing the same data, I found one nail sample test at 1.80 but another at 2.229. The test on one hair sample revealed an even higher arsenic elemented weight percentage of 3.84, which Nichols did not mention.[26] According to Dr. Bisbing of McCrone Laboratory, the figures from electron microscopy tests ignore carbon and nitrogen, which make up over 99 percent of the hair, so they are of little significance.[27]

A more accurate test is neutron activation analysis. This was the method used at the Oakridge National Laboratory by Drs. Frank Dyer and Larry Robinson, who found 2.0 ppm of arsenic, a measure that is above average but not considered lethal.[28] Dyer himself raised questions about the procedure. He recognized the possibility that when Taylor's hair was extracted it could have broken off at the root because of decomposition. He would not be part of any further investigation unless he could participate in taking the samples. "I'm becoming more and more appreciative of the importance of quality assurance."[29] Dyer added, "I was very dependent on George Nichols to give me what I needed. I asked Nichols if he could see which ends were the root ends. He didn't seem too interested in talking about it. I feel now that Nichols didn't really understand it was the roots that needed to be measured."[30]

Dyer was not certain he had tested the roots. He did not check the ends under a microscope. In any case, he was not sure how roots ought to look "after sitting around for a hundred years." With one selection of hairs he cut a little off both ends, mixed them together, and tested. In another sample, hairs were stuck together with what he thought was blood. He allowed that the blood could add to the weight and reduce the arsenic measurement by about a factor of two.

Dyer volunteered that he knew very little about the morphology of hair, yet he seemed to know more than anyone else involved in the investigation. He pointed out that at any one time some of the hairs on one's head are growing, some are not growing, and some are in an intermediate state. "So if a hair was not growing, it would not have picked up the arsenic" even with its root intact.[31] If nongrowing hairs do not take up arsenic, then their presence would further dilute the ratio of arsenic found in the gross sample.

Of more than passing significance, Dyer found a suspiciously high level of antimony, 8.0 ppm, in the hair samples and 10.0 ppm in what he took to be the root ends. Antimony, a heavy metal element, has been used as a poison. It has a clinical picture similar to arsenic poisoning, with symptoms of nausea, frequent vomiting, dehydration, and severe diarrhea.[32] It has a higher toxicity level than arsenic; an antimony value of 10.0 ppm is equivalent in toxicity to 12.0 ppm of arsenic. Considering that the root probably was partly or largely decomposed, such a toxic level seems significant. Dyer was disturbed enough about the antimony to inform Nichols, who said he would look into it. But Nichols never called back.[33]

The materials taken from Taylor's body were deposited with the Filson Club, a Kentucky historical society. To conduct further tests, my assistant and I requested hair samples from the club, representing our investigation as a serious, scholarly undertaking. We informed the club that we had contacted a forensic consultant who agreed to do a nuclear activation sectional analysis and that we would pay for the tests. The Filson Club denied our request, concluding that "thorough testing of these samples has already been accomplished and [additional tests] would be considered a duplication of previous effort."[34]

Confrontation with the Slavocracy

Certain of the events surrounding Taylor's presidency raise suspicions about his death. Capitalizing on Taylor's popularity as the hero of the Mexican War, the Whig Party nominated him as its presidential candidate in 1848. There was much interest in the candidate's views regarding what one contemporary called "the all-absorbing and most embarrassing subject of slavery."[35] Some northerners feared that, being a southerner, Taylor would support its extension into the newly acquired territories. Others were aware that Taylor, though himself a slaveholder and not an abolitionist, considered slavery "a social and political

220

evil," and wanted it contained.[36] Once in office, the new president left no doubts in anyone's mind. He sent representatives to urge California and New Mexico to apply for entry into the Union as free states—initiatives that greatly agitated both slaveholders and Whig "compromisers" like Senators Henry Clay and Daniel Webster, who were willing to make major concessions to the slavocracy.

Taylor entered the White House in apparently excellent health. A visitor to his Mexican camp sometime the year before described him as a "hearty-looking old gentleman" whose visage was "remarkable for a bright, flashing eye, a high forehead, a farmer look and 'rough-and-ready' appearance."[37] In the fifth month of his administration, on August 9, 1849, the president embarked on a trip through a number of northern states. His first stop was Pennsylvania. In Mercer, he made a bold public assertion: "The people of the North need have no apprehension of the further extension of slavery."[38] Taylor was assuming an unambiguously antiextentionist position.

A fortnight after he began expressing his strong position against the extension of slavery, Taylor mysteriously fell ill. On August 24, at Waterford, he suddenly was stricken by vomiting and diarrhea. He continued on to Erie where his physician, Dr. Robert Wood, put him to bed with the "shakes." After a sleepless night, the president worsened and ran a fever. Dr. Wood now feared for his patient's life. Not until the fifth day did he throw off the illness.[39] After a week of convalescence, the president was much improved but still suffered from a weakness in his legs that made it difficult to walk.[40]

Taylor's illness alarmed members of his administration. "You have been so long accustomed to look danger in the face, that you do not fear it," wrote Secretary of State John Clayton on behalf of the entire cabinet, "but we think that you have been sick so much since you left Washington, that it is evident your journey cannot be continued without peril."[41] Yielding to his cabinet's entreaties, Taylor returned to the capital in early September. He did not recuperate until several weeks later.

What was the malady that so mysteriously seized the president on his journey north? Neither contemporaries nor historians tell us. Dr. Sten Forshufvud, the toxicologist who conducted an interesting study of the death of Napoleon, observes: "If someone in apparently perfect health is suddenly attacked by violent symptoms of illness, without anything to announce their approach, we are, first and foremost, led to think of poisoning. Generally speaking, a natural, normal sickness gives a number of warning signals before entering its pronounced phase."[42] While the reaction to poisoning comes abruptly, the recovery is slow. The prolonged effects of arsenic poisoning, for instance, include a weakness in the legs that can linger for some time after.[43] This was one of Taylor's symptoms.

If Taylor was poisoned in Pennsylvania, this might explain the above-average arsenic levels in the gross sample tests of his nails and bone tissue and the very high level of antimony in his hair.

In November 1849, as debates raged in Congress regarding the slavery issue, Taylor's health was once more deemed "excellent" by his doctor. By December, "he gave the impression of being robust."[44] The following spring found a fully restored president on a collision course with the slavocracy. Henry Clay wrote an associate, "The all-engrossing subject of slavery continues to agitate us, and to paralyze almost all legislation."[45] On January 29, 1850, Clay put together an omnibus bill, later known as the Compromise of 1850. It contained the following proposals: (a) A stronger fugitive slave law for the "restitution and delivery" of runaway slaves. (b) In regard to the slave trade, Congress would relinquish its constitutional power to regulate interstate commerce. There would be no restrictions against slavery in the territories. (c) New Mexico would remain as a territory with no decision on slavery. (d) Texas would relinquish its claim to New Mexico. As compensation, the federal government would assume Texas's entire public debt.

Clay's package contained much of what the slave interests wanted. It also offered substantial economic benefits to the moneyed creditors of Texas, whose notes would now enlist the "full faith and credit" of the U.S. government. Clay's bill earned the name of "compromise" because it offered a couple of concessions to the North: California was to be admitted as a free state and the slave trade would be abolished in the nation's capital. But slavery itself would continue in that city unless slaveholders agreed to its abolition — in which case they would receive full compensation.

Taylor adamantly opposed the bill. On May 20, Clay excoriated the president on the Senate floor for pursuing a dangerously uncompromising antiextensionist policy. The slaveholding president was taking a surprisingly tough stance against the slaveholding interests. When threats of secession filled the air, Taylor let it be known that he personally would lead troops against any "traitors," and hang secessionists "with less reluctance than I hanged spies and deserters in Mexico."[46] On June 17, 1850, he informed Congress that Texas was threatening to use force to incorporate about half of New Mexico within its jurisdiction and that he was ready to send federal troops to crush such a move.

The slaveholders believed that their class system was doomed if it remained an isolated southeastern enclave while free states spread across the entire continent. Slavery would have to extend itself into a good portion of the newly acquired territories if it was to survive. In the crisis over how the territorial spoils of the imperialist war against Mexico were to be apportioned, Taylor was emerging as a pivotal player. The slaveholders must have viewed the president as a particularly threatening figure: a war hero, himself a southerner and a slaveholder, who thereby lent additional credibility to the antiextensionist position even within the South, a president who would veto any extensionist bill and would not hesitate to apply the full force of the U.S. military to suppress secession and even contain extensionism.

Here we might note the significance of Vice President Millard Fillmore's views. A devoted friend and admirer of Henry Clay, Fillmore informed Taylor that in the event of a tie in the Senate on Clay's compromise package, the vice president, as presiding officer, would cast the deciding vote in favor of it.[47] It must have been a discouragement to the chief executive to know that his vice president would line up against him.

Clay's omnibus bill, in the words of one historian, "was doomed as long as Zachary Taylor lived."[48] It was no secret that if Taylor died and Fillmore became president, there would be a dramatic shift in policy on the slavery question.

A Lethal Dose of Cherries and Milk?

On July 4, 1850, Zachary Taylor attended the laying of the cornerstone of the Washington Monument. That evening after dinner, he suddenly took ill. Five days later he was dead. Trying to explain the suspicious affliction, historians repeatedly note that Taylor spent much of that afternoon walking around or sitting in the hot sun and humidity, thereby weakening himself. But Taylor evidenced none of the symptoms of excessive heat exposure, neither during that day nor throughout his ensuing illness.

"Rough and Ready," as he was affectionately known, had spent much of his life exposed to the elements at army camps around the country and on battlefields under the blazing sun. In any case, on July 4, he was not "walking around" but took a carriage to the site of the monument where he participated in the ceremony.[49] The *Philadelphia Bulletin* correspondent who attended the event described the president as "to all appearances, sound in health and in excellent spirits . . . and even up to five o'clock, exhibit[ed] no symptoms of illness."[50] The

National Intelligencer reported that he appeared "in the full enjoyment of health and strength participating in the patriotic ceremonies."[51] Arriving at the Executive Mansion, Taylor remarked to his physician Dr. Alexander Wotherspoon that he was "very hungry."[52] A hearty appetite is not symptomatic of someone debilitated by heat or impending illness.

Taylor's major biographer, Holman Hamilton, writes that the president seemed, "slightly under par" on July 3. But others, including the reporters quoted above and the president's physician, said he seemed quite fit on July 4. Hamilton tells us that earlier in the day, Taylor "may have munched green apples immediately before or after attending a Sunday school recital." If he did, he made no complaint of indigestion for the entire day. And green apples are not known to be fatal.

Hamilton asserts that during the ceremony, Taylor "sat two hours in the broiling sun" as it beat on "his head which was probably bare most of the time."[53] Hamilton does not explain why the president would deny himself the protection of his hat while exposed to the broiling sun nor why he would remain bareheaded when the proper style was to keep one's hat on during formal outdoor ceremonies. Samuel Eliot Morison claims that Taylor was "subjected to two hours' oratory by Senator Foote in the broiling sun."[54] Similar assertions are repeated by other historians—none of whom thought it odd that no provision was made for the comfort of the president and the numerous other dignitaries.

Two eyewitness reports I unearthed offer a different picture. According to a *National Intelligencer* reporter who was present, there was shade aplenty as "one to two thousand ladies and gentlemen assembled under the broad awning."[55] Provision *was* made to protect the audience from the sun. Another participant, Senator Henry Foote, who exchanged friendly words with the president after delivering his oration, wrote, "Never had I seen him look more robust and healthful than while seated under the canopy which sheltered the speaker and the assembled concourse from the burning rays. . . ."[56] In sum, the image of Taylor sitting for hours under a "broiling sun" is a fabrication introduced by historians, made no less imaginary by repeated assertion.

Hamilton alludes to typhoid and cholera, observing that the District of Columbia had a "primitive water supply and arrangements for sewage disposal invited the worst from flies and insects." He reports that "Asiatic cholera was still abroad in the land," but admits "there is no proof that this scourge invaded Washington in 1850." And "in diagnosing Taylor's case, Asiatic cholera can be dismissed." Likewise, "typhoid fever is out of the question; his symptoms simply were not those of typhoid."[57]

What then killed Taylor? Most historians who have dealt with the question say he consumed something that attacked his digestive tract. They repeatedly ascribed the fatal results to seemingly innocuous food and drink: "cherries, and cabbage," "a glass of milk," "bread and milk and cherries," "ice water," "mush and milk," "raw fruit or vegetables or both."[58] Samuel Eliot Morison decided the fatality was caused by "an excessive quantity of cucumbers."[59] Elbert Smith opts for "raw fruit . . . various raw vegetables as well, which he washed down with large quantitites of iced milk."[60] Paul Wellman combines the weather and the food: "Zachary Taylor died very suddenly of indigestion contracted from too much iced water and milk and too many cherries, after he returned hot and tired from Fourth of July ceremonies."[61] Henry William Elson weaves together the entire string of causalities—and improves upon them: the two hours in the sun is expanded to "several hours in the boiling sun"; the milk and cherries become "large draughts of iced milk and iced fruit"; and the president's affliction is "cholera morbus" merging in a few days "into typhoid fever" and death.[62]

Where did these historians get their peculiar information

about what Taylor supposedly consumed? They do not tell us. Neither contemporary news reports nor latter-day historians offer any source for their widely varied and conflicting accounts regarding the president's ingestions that day.

Taylor had no history of chronic indigestion or delicate stomach. Quite the contrary, Hamilton reports that Old Zach was known to be a trencherman who could digest anything.[63] Yet, in the next breath Hamilton describes Taylor as an infirm old man who "had led a hard life," who was "in less than the best of health," and who "ate raw stuff and drank cold liquids" on July 4th.[64]

Taylor's physicians would not have agreed with that portrait, having reported months earlier that the president was fully recovered from the Erie attack and in "excellent" health and of "robust" appearance—as Hamilton himself reports.[65] During the early phase of Taylor's fatal illness, his physicians believed "his strong constitution and superb physique would overcome the temporary disability."[66] Another contemporary, Montgomery, also talks about Taylor's "naturally strong constitution."[67]

According to Taylor's physician, Dr. Wotherspoon, Taylor developed severe cramps about an hour after his evening meal. Later he suffered attacks of nausea and diarrhea and spent an uncomfortable night. The following day, Friday, July 5, the president's discomfort worsened, as he continued to suffer diarrhea and some vomiting. On Saturday, Taylor's family grew increasingly concerned. Summoned to the White House, Dr. Wotherspoon diagnosed the ailment as "cholera morbus"—which, despite its awesome name, has no relation to the dread scourge of Asiatic cholera. As already noted, cholera morbus was a flexible mid-nineteenth-century term applied to diarrhea and other such intestinal ailments. Wotherspoon prescribed calomel, opium, and quinine, which appeared to produce an immediate improvement.[68]

On Sunday other physicians were called in. The diarrhea

subsided but the vomiting continued and an intermittent fever ensued. Taylor also experienced severe pain on the side of his chest and a raging thirst. He drank constantly until his stomach rejected the fluid. Dr. Robert Wood, who had attended to Taylor when he journeyed north the year before, arrived on Monday. He observed that the sudden illness "was very like" Taylor's "attack at Erie."[69] There is no indication that Taylor sickened in Erie because of heat exposure or raw foods and iced drink.

By Monday the president was despondent. He commented to his medical attendant: "I should not be surprised if this were to terminate in my death. I did not expect to encounter what has beset me since my elevation to the Presidency. God knows I have endeavored to fulfill what I conceived to be an honest duty. But I have been mistaken. My motives have been misconstrued, and my feelings most grossly outraged." This comment was reported in a number of newspapers of that day but has been ignored by every latter-day historian.[70] One might wonder whether Taylor himself was not entertaining suspicions of foul play.

By Tuesday, July 9, the physicians refused to administer any more medication, considering it a lost cause. That afternoon, Taylor was vomiting green matter from his stomach.[71] He died that night at 10:35 P.M.[72] Hamilton records the cause of death as "acute gastroenteritis, the inflammation of the lining membrane of his stomach and intestines."[73]

If gastroenteritis caused Taylor's death, what caused the gastroenteritis? Could his intestinal passage have been so fatally assaulted by the seemingly wholesome food and drink he is said to have consumed? That remains to this day the acceptable view. Thus on June 27, 1991, the *New York Times* misinformed its readers that Taylor fell ill "after consuming large quantities of iced cherries and milk at the dedication of the Washington Monument on July 4." There is no evidence that Taylor consumed cherries and milk at the ceremony. In fact, he took sick after his evening meal.

On June 28, 1991, the *Washington Post* told its readers: "A too-active, too-hot Fourth of July celebration, too many cherries and bad medicine were indeed responsible for killing off the 12th president." A *Post* article from the previous day reported that his gastroenteritis worsened when doctors "bled the president."[74] But the bleeding did not come until the fifth and last day, well after his illness had reached a critical stage.[75]

Newsweek offered the view "advanced by many mainstream historians, that Taylor died of the mercury and other poisons used in the medicines."[76] In fact, the "mercury" was calomel, a mercurous chloride used as a cathartic. The electron microscope scanning shows no mercury in Taylor's nails and a percentage level in his hair (0.70) lower than the arsenic level (1.42). It might be important to note that one effect of calomel is to mask the traces of arsenic in a victim's body.[77] The "other poisons" were quinine and opium. None of the medicines were administered until Saturday afternoon, the third day of illness, well after the extreme thirst, bloody diarrhea, and vomiting had begun.

Honorable Men and Official History

Taylor's death marked a dramatic turning point in policy. Immediately after his demise, the policy of containment against the spread of slavery was reversed. On July 11, 1850, with Taylor not yet entombed, Daniel Webster wrote to an associate that Fillmore's "coming to power is a heavy blow" to the "half abolition Gentlemen. I believe Mr. Fillmore favors the compromise, & there is no doubt that recent events [the president's death] have increased the probability of the passage of that measure."[78] Later, Webster wrote, "I think the country has had a providential escape from very considerable dangers."[79] Clay was of like mind, writing to his daughter-in-law: "I think the event which has happened [Taylor's death] will favor the passage of the Compromise bill."[80]

The two old rivals, Clay and Webster, joined forces with Clay's friend and admirer, the newly installed President Fillmore, who put the power of his office, including its ample patronage resources, behind the compromise package.[81] Within a month after Taylor's death, many of the issues that fervently concerned the slaveholders were settled to their satisfaction. The Texas boundary was set at expanded limits of 33,000 square miles above even what Clay had proposed. California was made a state but New Mexico remained a territory. The interstate slave trade continued without federal interference, and a strong fugitive slave bill was passed. Fillmore's vigorous enforcement produced "an era of slave hunting and kidnapping."[82] People who harbored runaways, and even persons who had knowledge of such activity but failed to report it, now risked fine and imprisonment.

Both Clay and Webster went to their graves not long after Taylor thinking that the president's death and their compromise efforts had averted war. At least one contemporary, Congressman Abraham Lincoln, was of a different opinion: Zachary Taylor's death meant a loss in confidence that the people had, "which will not soon pertain to any successor. . . . I fear the one *great* question of the day [slavery], is not now so likely to be partially acquiesced in by the different sections of the Union, as it would have been, could General Taylor have been spared to us."[83]

If someone had wanted to poison Taylor, it would not have been too difficult a task to accomplish. There was no Secret Service in those days. Security in the White House was poor and in the White House kitchen nonexistent. Uninvited guests wandered about upstairs.[84] A would-be assassin who gained employment on the White House staff or perhaps a well-bribed southern sympathizer or an interloper on familiar terms with the staff could have done the deed.

Ten years after Taylor's death, some people still entertained misgivings. In 1860, numerous letters from private citizens to

President-elect Abraham Lincoln expressed the suspicion that Zachary Taylor had been poisoned and urged Lincoln to be aware of his enemies and exercise the utmost caution in what he ate and drank.[85]

As far as I know, no political leader of Taylor's day publicly questioned the sudden, suspicious nature of his death. Nor did the press. A discovery of assassination might have brought the nation to the brink of sectional war. There was no investigation into Taylor's death. No one examined the food or drink at his table nor the plates and cups he used. There was no interrogation of the staff, no autopsy, no tests for poison.

Would any political protagonist in the United States of 1850 be capable of such a deed? Historian Eugene Genovese thinks not. While granting that the political circumstances of the era suggest that an assassin would likely be a pro-slavery southerner, he concludes, "I can't imagine any Southern personalities who would have been involved in such a conspiracy. But there is always the possibility that there were some nuts who had access to him and did it."[86]

History shows us that "nuts" are not the only ones capable of evil deeds. Gentlemen of principle and power, of genteel manner, can arrive at grim decisions. We should recall how the slavery question dwarfed all other issues during the antebellum period, filling the air with dire misgivings about secession and civil war. Leaders facing a crisis of such magnitude will often contemplate drastic options. If they commit crimes, it is not because they harbor murky and perverse impulses but because they feel compelled to deal with the dangers posed to their way of life. This does not mean they are motivated merely by pocketbook concerns. They equate their vital personal interests with the well-being of their society and nation, or, in this case, with "the cause of Southern rights."

Far from being immoral or unscrupulous, they are persons of principles so lofty as to elevate them above the restraints of ordinary morality. They do not act on sudden impulse. But, confronting inescapable urgencies, they soon find themselves no longer shocked by the extreme measures they are willing to employ. The execution of the unsavory deed is made all the easier by delegating its commission to lower-level operatives. Most of the evil in history is perpetrated not by lunatics or monsters but by individuals of responsibility and commitment, whose most unsettling aspect is the apparent normality of their deportment.

In any case, the men whom Genovese refers to as "Southern personalities" had few scruples when dealing with those who challenged their slavocracy. They presided over their huge estates as heartless aristocrats, each owning hundreds of hapless slaves over whom they exercised the unrestrained law of the whip and the gun. They were colonels of militia regiments that hunted down runaways. "They openly carried pistols and Bowie knives. Alternately courtly and dangerously belligerent, they interpreted political opposition as a slight upon their honor. Abolitionism they looked upon as simple robbery."[87] They would as soon kill an abolitionist or opponent of extensionism as look at him. They spent decades before the Civil War threatening to secede from the Union and secure their slaveholders' "way of life" with force and violence. The "Southern gentlemen" who led this slavocracy happened to compose one of the most brutal and vicious ruling circles ever to exist on the North American continent.

What I have tried to demonstrate with the Zachary Taylor case is how self-legitimating history is fabricated before our very eyes through a ready tendency of past and present opinion-makers to find unsuspicious causes in the face of suspicious symptoms. Once science, in the guise of the Kentucky medical examiner, joined the mainstream press and academic historians to put an imprimatur on a particular interpretation of events, haphazard opinions were transformed into official truth. Thus, in 1992, *Life* magazine could report with false finality that Taylor died "after eating cherries and cream on a steamy July Fourth. . . . Last year amid speculation he'd been poisoned, his body was exhumed, but no arsenic was found."[88] In 1994, in an article on how "high-tech tests" were inspiring new investigations into the deaths of famous people, the Associated Press referred to the "conclusive results . . . obtained from the 1991 exhumation of President Taylor in Kentucky. Dr. George Nichols, the state's medical examiner, determined that the president died of natural causes, not arsenic poisoning as a writer speculated."[89]

In 1996, five years after the exhumation, the mythology continued in full force, as *Time* magazine announced that Taylor died a few days after "he ate a bowl of cherries and downed a glass of buttermilk." But after "his tissue samples were assailed with neutrons . . . the forensic conclusion was that he had not been poisoned after all."[90] By 1996, the misrepresentation had passed back into the history books. Even an exceptionally cogent and insightful historian like Paul Finkelman—who swims against the mythic tide on issues such as Jefferson and slavery—can get caught in the current of another myth: "Scientists recently exhumed the remains of President Zachary Taylor to determine if he was murdered. The tests proved negative."[91]

Contrary to what has been widely publicized by historians, scientists, and media, nothing conclusive has been offered to demonstrate that President Taylor died a natural death. The official explanations for his death remain no less incredible for being tirelessly repeated. Through a process of uncritical reiteration, historians and media have reinforced each other's implausible speculations about fatal sun exposure and lethal ingestions of cherries and milk. Historians and media, joined by forensic investigators, offered the imprecise diagnoses of "gastroenteritis," wrongly treating a set of *symptoms* as the *cause* of death. The chief medical examiner's investigation pretended to a precision and thoroughness it never attained. And the press eagerly cloaked the inquest with an undeserved conclusiveness.

A closer examination of the postmortem investigation and the historical record should leave us more discomfited than ever. The presence of arsenic was never satisfactorily explained, and the levels were sometimes inaccurately reported. The suspiciously high antimony level went unreported. The samples themselves were of dubious reliability. No precise sectional hair analysis was performed. The symptoms were distinctly those of poisoning. The ludicrous cherries-and-milk, cucumbers-and-cabbage, sunstroke-and-sickness explanations for Taylor's death conjured by historians are without a shred of supporting evidence and cannot be taken seriously—yet they are. If we cannot say for sure that Zachary Taylor was poisoned, we *can* say with certainty that he did not die from sunstroke or cherries and milk. Yet these latter imaginings remain the acceptable explanation, the one that puts to rest any thoughts about an ugly side to U.S. history. The case of Zachary Taylor's death demonstrates how ideological gatekeepers close ranks against any issue that challenges their expertise or suggests conspiracy in high places.

Historians and journalists may not consciously plan to legitimize the more reassuring, less controversial finding. But to move in a contrary direction would definitely require swimming against the ideological tide, a special effort inviting possible risks to one's credibility. Those who hasten to assure us that Taylor was not poisoned are reassuring us that, unlike other lands, such things do not happen in this country. So "our" institutions remain untouched by crime, conspiracy, and covert action. The legitimacy that sustains these institutions would be open to question were it shown that a president can be exterminated without anyone knowing it. What would such an assassination say about assassination controversies of more recent times, like the ones surrounding John F. Kennedy and Martin

Luther King Jr.? What would such an assassination say about our nation and the people who rule it? What would it say about our history and the historians who write it?

In regard to poisoning, the absence of conclusive proof is not conclusive proof of absence. In this case the absence of proof may be more the result of sloppy and superficial investigative procedures, fuzzy and far-fetched speculations by academics, and the heraldry of a press that reassures us that all is basically well with political life in America, past and present. Inconclusive and highly questionable results are now treated as settled fact. Through a process of unexamined reiteration these findings come to occupy a secure place in the manufactured history whose function is to legitimize existing institutions. In the face of such ideological forces, an empirical investigation of the actual facts does not stand a chance.

NOTES:

1. *New York Times*, editorial, June 20, 1991.
2. Alex Heard, "Exhumed Innocent," *New Republic*, August 5, 1991.
3. Charles Krauthammer in *Washington Post*, July 5, 1991.
4. Both Smith and Foote are quoted in *Newsweek*, July 1, 1991, 64–65.
5. ABC-TV evening news report, June 26, 1991.
6. *New York Times*, June 27, 1991.
7. *Washington Post*, June 27, 1991.
8. *Washington Post*, June 28, 1991. Rising never expressed a theory about "arsenic-sprinkled cherries."
9. "Results of Exhumation of Zachary Taylor," released by the Office of the Coroner, Jefferson County, Kentucky, September 1991.
10. "Final Diagnosis: Taylor, Zachary," n.d., signed by George Nichols, attached to a brief statement entitled "Post Mortem Examination of the Body of Taylor, Zachary ME-91–514," no date, location, letter-head, or author.
11. Greathouse interview, May 5, 1992. All interviews were conducted by telephone by Peggy Karp.
12. Greathouse interview, May 5, 1992.
13. Greathouse interview, February 17, 1992.
14. Oak Ridge National Laboratory researcher Frank Dryer quoted in the *Atlantic Constitution*, June 27, 1991.

15. Report filed by Michael Ward, June 29, 1991, Department of Health Services, Division of Laboratory Services, Frankfort, Kentucky. This report was sent to my assistant Peggy Karp by Dr. Greathouse.

16. *Washington Post,* June 27, 1991. The quotation is the *Post*'s paraphrase of Nichols's statement.

17. Forshufvud was dealing with the chronic poisoning of Napoleon: Ben Weider and David Hapgood, *The Murder of Napoleon* (New York: Congdon and Lattes, 1982), 75; also Sten Forshufvud, *Who Killed Napoleon?* (London: Hutchinson, 1961). To be sure, a chronic poisoning would not have the single concentrated dosage of an acute poisoning, but over the entire shaft of hair, the smaller successive dosages might register as much or more than the acute dosage.

In 1993, the body of General Asif Nawaz, Pakistani Army Chief of Staff, was exhumed because his widow believed he "was poisoned to death by certain persons who perceived him to be a threat to their power and ambitions." The National Medical Services of Pennsylvania analyzed hair that Mrs. Nawaz retrieved from the general's hairbrush and found that it contained more than sixteen times the normal level of arsenic. The results led the police to order the exhumation: *New York Times,* October 2, 1993.

18. *New York Times,* June 15 and June 20, 1991; *Washington Post,* June 27, 1991.

19. Dr. William Maples, forensic anthropologist, interview, March 10, 1922; also *Newsweek,* July 1, 1991: 65.

20. Greathouse interview, September 23, 1991.

21. Guinn interview, July 13, 1992.

22. Hamilton Smith, "The Interpretation of the Arsenic Content of Human Hair," *Journal of the Forensic Science Society,* vol. 4, summarized in Sten Forshufvud and Ben Weider, *Assassination at St. Helena* (Vancouver, Canada: Mitchell Press, 1978), 488–489. See also V. P. Guinn, M. Gavrilas-Guinn, and R. Demiralp, "Measurement of Arsenic in Sectioned Hair Samples by Instrumental Neutron Activation Analysis," paper presented at NAC-II conference, Toronto, June 3–5, 1992, for a sectional analysis of a case of present-day arsenic poisoning. The arsenic levels found in the base sections were up to 40ppm and 100ppm, demonstrating the importance of having the entire root section, something that is more easily accomplished with a fresh hair shaft than one that is 140 years old.

23. Greathouse interview, September 23, 1991; Maples interview, April 30, 1992.

24. Bisbing interview, April 29, 1992.

25. Guinn interview, July 13, 1992.

26. Data with handwritten title "U of L scanning electron microscope EDAX," n.d., from Beverly Giammara and David Birch, Analytical Electron Microscope Laboratory, University of Louisville.

27. Bisbing interview, June 5, 1992.
28. Dyer and Robinson to Nichols, letter, June 24, 1991, a copy of which Dyer provided.
29. Dyer interview, February 17, 1993.
30. Dyer interview, November 4, 1992.
31. Dyer interview, November 4, 1992.
32. Serita Deborah Stevens and Anne Klarner, *Deadly Doses, A Writer's Guide to Poisons* (Cincinnati: Writer's Digest Books, 1990), 203–204.
33. Dyer interview, June 12, 1992.
34. R. R. Van Stockum, interim director, The Filson Club, letter to Peggy Karp, August 18, 1992.
35. Henry Montgomery, *The Life of Major-General Zachary Taylor* (Philadelphia: Porter and Coates, c. 1851), 412.
36. Taylor quoted in Paul Wellman, *The House Divides* (Garden City, N.Y.: Doubleday, 1966), 332. In fact, Taylor was on good terms with such notable abolitionist families in the North as the Adamses. Henry Adams recalls the warm reception he and his father received when visiting Taylor in the White House. He opined that "President Taylor owed his election to Martin Van Buren and the Free Soil Party": *The Education of Henry Adams* (New York: Random House, 1931, originally published 1918), 46.
37. Newsclip (undated) in the Zachary Taylor papers, series 4, manuscript division, Library of Congress. From the newsclip's content, it is clear that the visit occurred after the war.
38. Holman Hamilton, *Zachary Taylor, Soldier in the White House,* vol. 2 (Hamden, Conn.: Anchor Books, 1966), 225.
39. Jack Bauer, *Zachary Taylor, Soldier, Planter, Statesman of the Old Southwest* (Baton Rouge, La.: Louisiana State University Press, 1983), 269.
40. Brainerd Dyer, *Zachary Taylor* (New York: Barnes and Noble, 1946), 402–403.
41. Clayton to Taylor, August 29, 1849. Zachary Taylor papers, manuscript division, Library of Congress.
42. Forshufvud, *Who Killed Napoleon?* 213.
43. Forshufvud, *Who Killed Napoleon?* 227. Despite the continued weakness in his legs, Taylor was writing to Secretary of State John Clayton about a matter of state five days after the attack in a handwriting that was firm and intact: Taylor to Clayton, August 29, 1849, John Middleton Clayton papers, manuscript division, Library of Congress.
44. Hamilton, *Zachary Taylor,* vol. 2, 227, 255.
45. Henry Clay to James Harlan, March 16, 1850, in Calvin Colton (ed.), *Private Correspondence of Henry Clay* (Freeport, N.Y.: Books for Libraries Press, 1971, originally published 1855), 603.
46. Paul Wellman, *The House Divides* (Garden City, N.Y.: Doubleday, 1966), 332.

47. Wellman, *The House Divides*, 333.
48. Hamilton, *Zachary Taylor*, vol. 2, 383.
49. *Daily National Intelligencer* (Washington, D.C.), July 12, 1850.
50. *Philadelphia Bulletin*, correspondence datelined July 10, 1850; reprinted in *New York Daily Tribune*, July 12, 1850.
51. *Daily National Intelligencer*, July 10, 1850.
52. *Philadelphia Bulletin*, July 11, 1850; *New York Daily Tribune*, July 12, 1850.
53. Hamilton, *Zachary Taylor*, vol. 2, 389.
54. Samuel Eliot Morison, *The Oxford History of the American People* (New York: Oxford University Press, 1965), 573. In fact, Foote spoke for only one hour, which was probably long enough.
55. *Daily National Intelligencer*, July 6, 1850.
56. Henry S. Foote, *War of the Rebellion* (New York: Harper & Brothers, 1866), 149.
57. Hamilton, *Zachary Taylor*, 388–389.
58. Hamilton lists the various offerings, *Zachary Taylor*, vol. 2, 388.
59. Morison, *The Oxford History of the American People*, 573.
60. Elbert Smith, *The Presidencies of Zachary Taylor and Millard Fillmore* (University of Kansas Press: Lawrence, Kansas, 1988), 156.
61. Wellman, *The House Divides*, 333.
62. Henry William Elson, *History of the United States of America* (New York: Macmillan, 1923), 545.
63. Hamilton, *Zachary Taylor*, vol. 2, 389.
64. Hamilton, *Zachary Taylor*, vol. 2, 389.
65. Hamilton, *Zachary Taylor*, vol. 2, 227, 255.
66. Oliver Otis Howard, *General Taylor* (New York: D. Appleton, 1892), 370.
67. Montgomery, *The Life of Major-General Zachary Taylor*, 426.
68. Bauer, *Zachary Taylor, Soldier, Planter* 315.
69. Bauer, *Zachary Taylor, Soldier, Planter* 315 and Hamilton, *Zachary Taylor*, vol. 2, 390.
70. *Philadelphia Bulletin*, July 11, 1850; *New York Daily Tribune*, July 12, 1850; *Daily Evening Transcript* (Boston), July 12, 1850 and various other publications. I found only one historical account, published soon after Taylor's death, that carried the quotation: Montgomery, *The Life of Major-General Zachary Taylor*, 426.
71. Montgomery, *The Life of Major-General Zachary Taylor*, 428.
72. Frequent telegraphic bulletins covering the last two days of Taylor's life were reprinted in the *New York Herald*, July 10, 1850.
73. Hamilton, *Zachary Taylor*, vol. 2, 389.
74. *Washington Post*, June 27, 1991.
75. Hamilton, *Zachary Taylor*, vol. 2, 392.
76. *Newsweek*, July 1, 1991, 66.
77. Weider and Hapgood, *The Murder of Napoleon*, 20.

78. Webster to Franklin Haven, July 11, 1850, in Charles Wiltse and Michael Birkner (eds.), *The Papers of Daniel Webster,* correspondence, vol. 7 (Hanover, N.H.: University Press of New England, 1986), 123.

79. Webster to Franklin Haven, September 12, 1850, *The Papers of Daniel Webster,* 144.

80. Clay to Mrs. Thomas Clay, July 13, 1950, *Private Correspondence of Henry Clay,* 610–611.

81. On Fillmore's efforts, see Benson Lee Grayson, *The Unknown President: The Administration of Millard Fillmore* (Washington, D.C.: University Press of America, 1981).

82. Hamilton, *Zachary Taylor,* vol. 2, 404.

83. Hamilton, *Zachary Taylor,* vol. 2, 411. When I submitted a slightly modified earlier version of this chapter as an article to *Radical History,* the editor of that academic journal wrote back that all three of the anonymous reviewers were impressed by the forensic critique but rejected the piece because I "impose the corollary conclusions of assassination, conspiracy, and a fundamental altering of the course of American history." In fact, I conclude no such thing. The closest I come to that is in the above quotation by Lincoln conjecturing that the different sections of the Union would have more likely "partially acquiesced" on the slavery question had Taylor lived—a view I do not share at all. Had Taylor survived in office, I cannot imagine that the course of sectional conflict would have been dramatically different. The conclusions the academic reviewers leap to is yet another example of the knee-jerk response of those who live in fear that someone somewhere is trying to explain the "fundamental" course of history as a series of conspiracies. As history shows us, excessive vigilance often leads to imaginary perceptions. If true of some conspiracy theorists, it is at least equally true of conspiracy phobics.

84. Interview with Clara Rising, September 23, 1991. Even fifty years later, during the McKinley administration, there was only one White House guard on duty at night.

85. David Chambers Mearns (ed.), *The Lincoln Papers, The Story of the Collection,* vol. 1 (Garden City, N.Y.: Doubleday, 1948), 292–294, 301–302, 306, 318–319.

86. As quoted in *New York Times,* June 15, 1991.

87. Gene Smith, *High Crimes and Misdemeanors, The Impeachment and Trial of Andrew Johnson* (New York: McGraw-Hill, 1976), 13.

88. *Life,* October 30, 1992.

89. Associated Press report, *San Francisco Chronicle,* October 27, 1994.

90. Roger Rosenblatt, "Dig, Must We?" *Time,* July 8, 1996.

91. Paul Finkelman, *Slavery and the Founders: Race and Liberty in the Age of Jefferson* (Armonk, N.Y.: M. E. Sharpe, 1996), 204, n17. In every other way, this is a superb book.

7

AGAINST PSYCHOPOLITICS

In recent times, a considerable number of historians, political scientists, psychologists, and others have begun to rely on psychology to explain political phenomena. These academic subfields of "psychopolitics" and "psychohistory" treat leaders and masses as driven by covert, personal emotions having little to do with the manifest content of public issues. Here I want to argue that psychoanalytic precepts and "depth" psychology theories tend to distort our understanding of political life and trivialize the political significance of history.

Depoliticizing the Political

"Many great public issues" C. Wright Mills once wrote, "as well as many private troubles are described in terms of the 'psychiatric'—often, it seems in a pathetic attempt to avoid the large issues and problems of modern society."[1] The psychologistic approach often serves as a means of avoiding the realities of political economy. This might help explain why psychopolitics and psychohistory have enjoyed generous funding and a ready reception as respectable academic subfields.[2] This is in marked contrast to the relentless attacks and outright exclusion long endured by scholarship that deals explicitly with class exploitation and class power. The controversies that a psychopolitical analysis might stir up are not too controversial, since "the large issues" Mills mentioned are painlessly avoided or reduced to problems of personal mindset.

Among the foremost pioneers in psychopolitics was Harold Lasswell, a political scientist by training but heavily influenced by Freudianism, and himself a lay analyst. Over sixty years ago Lasswell postulated the following formula to explain "political man": $p \} d \} r = P$. The private motives of the individual (p), "nurtured and organized in relation to the family constellation and the early self," are displaced (d) onto public objects. The displacement is then rationalized (r) in terms of public interests to produce political man (P).[3]

Regarding political displacement Lasswell writes: "The prominence of hate in politics suggests that we may find that the most important private motive is a repressed and powerful hatred of authority, a hatred which has come to partial expression and repression in relation to the father." And "the repressed father hatred may be turned against kings or capitalists." Individuals who condemn "the merciless exploitation of the tool-less proletariat by the capitalists" may be just voicing "the rational justification" of earlier unresolved family animosities.[4] Not just individuals but whole "political movements derive their vitality from the displacement of private affects upon public objects."[5]

Consider some examples of how this displacement-rationalization model has been applied. In 1969, the noted psychologist Bruno Bettelheim ascribed the student antiwar protests that were sweeping the nation's campuses to the influence of a permissive society and to the "guilt" the students suffered because they had avoided military service. As Bettelheim explained to a special House Education Subcommittee: the guilt-ridden students, having evaded military service, "feel like parasites of society and hence come to hate a society which they think makes them feel this way."[6] In a word, the students were not bothered by the Vietnam War as such but by the fact that they were able to evade their moral obligation to fight in it.

Reaching beyond Bettelheim, Lewis Feuer diagnosed practically every student rebellion in the twentieth century as suffering from irrational hostility toward surrogate parental figures. He maintains that Fidel Castro, who developed his rebellious ways during his student days, "repeatedly blamed others, that is, his father, for his own entry into legal study" a field he did not really wish to pursue. This "suggests some of the roots of Castro's own generational conflict and indirectly his anti-Americanism. In his blaming of others for having misled him, the United States became a surrogate father to be blamed."[7]

However, not all student uprisings have pursued such "pseudo-goals," according to Feuer. University rebels in Communist countries—whose efforts he applauds—were the exception; they were not acting out their filial resentments, rather they were engaged in a "quest for real freedom."[8]

For a group of social scientists, including Ernest Van den Haag, Nathan Glazar, and Stanley Rothman, who believe that capitalism is the finest economic system ever devised, the continued opposition to it from intellectuals and others defies logic. Such hostility, they reason, can be understood only by putting aside economic arguments and concentrating on the psychological disturbances of the anticapitalist critics: the "emotional and irrational causes" that leave consumers frightened by the very freedom the free market breeds, the guilt feelings some have about their good life, the envy that others feel toward the more affluent, and so forth.[9]

Historians Henderson and Chaloner describe Frederick Engels, Marx's collaborator, as driven by a personal fury against the English bourgeoisie and factory owners in particular. His "extreme political views . . . represented a violent reaction against the whole way of life of the highly respectable [capitalist] household in which he had been reared." Engels was "a young man in a bad temper who vented his spleen in a passionate denunciation of the factory system." This explained "the unrestrained violence of his language." Henderson and Chaloner were referring to Engels's book, *The Condition of the Working Class in England* (which I would not at all describe as written in a language of "unrestrained violence"), whose content convinces them that "Engels was suffering from an overwhelming sense of frustration."[10]

Psychologizing about the disturbed psyches of protestors and dissidents is not the exclusive province of political psychologists and psychohistorians. In 1972, acts of insubordination and minor sabotage, along with a growing antiwar sentiment and increasing numbers of desertions, were becoming a serious concern to the U.S. Navy. Admiral Charles Duncan publicly labeled the resisters in the enlisted ranks as "those few with mental aberrations," "anti-social, anti-military" individuals.[11]

The voluminous file that the CIA kept on the revolutionary leader Che Guevara contains reports telling us that Che "hates to wash and will never do so," "is fairly intellectual for a 'Latino,'" and his "attitude towards the U.S. is dictated . . . by somewhat childish emotionalism and jealousy and resentment."[12] After Philip Agee defected from the CIA and publicized some of its worst practices abroad, the agency produced a psychiatrist who announced that Agee was "sick and unstable."[13] (As one who knows Agee personally, I find him to be healthy and stable.)

As these illustrations suggest, psychopathological explanations tend to ignore the political content of things and conjure a latent predetermining apolitical need. Thus Lasswell does not deal with the seemingly more evident possibility that people hate kings or capitalists not because of filial conflicts but because they often find the social conditions imposed by autocracy and plutocracy to be insufferable.

Likewise, Van den Haag and his associates do not consider the idea that hostility toward capitalism might stem from justifiable grievances relating to economic deprivation, job insecurity, poor work conditions, low pay, high rents, environmental devastation, undemocratic concentrations of political power by moneyed interests, and many other such things.

And the historians who see Engels as venting only a personal frustration in his exposé of the factory system do not entertain the possibility that he might have felt outraged by the sight of battered children working twelve-hour days for near-starvation wages under the most horrific conditions.

So with Feuer. In a Cuba ruled by a much-hated American-backed tyrant like Fulgencio Batista, where the major industries, markets, land, labor, and capital were in the profiteering grip of U.S. corporations while a large segment of the populace lived in poverty, are we to believe that a Cuban's grievances toward the detested "Yanquis" were primarily a displacement of filial hostility anchored in a resentment at being required to go to law school? And what of the many thousands of others who joined revolutionary ranks? Were they all bestirred principally by unresolved familial antagonisms — as Feuer claims was the case with the Chinese students who joined Mao? If so, history owes a remarkable debt to the deficiencies in father-son relationships.[14]

Psychologistic investigators presume that the filial relationship not only precedes but supersedes the experiences of later life and the influences of the wider social sphere. But that premise remains unexamined; it is a self-determining psychologism. It not only *fosters* political ignorance, it *relies* on political ignorance for its credibility. By ignoring important political data, psychological speculation gains plausibility.

To illustrate: anyone who listened to the outrage that students expressed against the Vietnam War, who witnessed what they were actually saying, reading, writing, and doing, can be forgiven for rejecting Bettelheim's contention that they were motivated by guilt about not fighting in the very war they detested. The *observable evidence* of their words and deeds suggests that they opposed the war because they believed it unjust and destructive of innocent lives. What is missing from Bettelheim's view is just such observable evidence. All we have are imputations that deny the actual content of political struggle and ascribe a stock motive best known only to Bettelheim through a process of discovery he does not reveal.

While these kinds of psychological explanations tend to depoliticize political reality, they do so in a politically selective way. For example, Bettelheim has never thought it necessary to sift through the psyches of those who ordered and conducted the B-52 carpet bombing of Indochina. Nor did the anti-Communist Feuer ever consider searching for hidden motives among dissident students in Communist countries — whose rebellions he supported and deemed free of psychopathology.

Similarly, Arnold Rogow seems to equate political deviancy with psychological abnormality when he writes: "While most political leaders neither require nor merit a psychobiography, the form is particularly appropriate when we are dealing with odd or deviant political careers . . . right and left extremists."[15] A political judgment is being made here. The leaders referred to by Rogow are "odd and deviant" *politically* speaking, not psychologically. That political deviance is in special need of psychological investigation is what needs to be demonstrated rather than assumed. Whether a leader is acting with admirable "firmness" or "aggressive rigidity" in a situation will often depend on the political values and views of the observer.[16] In a word, what is or is not a "psychological displacement" may be determined less by the psychology of the political actor than by the politics of the psychologist.

Discovering a hidden psychological need in political personages tells us very little about the *political* significance of what they are doing. Nevertheless, the psychopathological explanation does cast a pale on political things. Once convinced that revolutionaries are impelled by unresolved feelings about their fathers, for instance, we cannot help but wonder about the value of the revolution itself—even though nothing is established about the revolution's substantive issues. When Bettelheim or others reduce the student protest movement to a collective guilt trip or to some infantile or adolescent disorder, the inevitable impact is to devalue the protest, making the protestors the issue rather than the thing they are protesting.

This kind of *argumentum ad hominem* tells us very little, if anything, about the political worth of an issue or action. We might decide that people opposed the Vietnam War because they (a) had an irrational, displaced hatred of authority or (b) a sense of justice and a love of peace. And we might conclude that people supported the war out of (a) love of country and a desire to stop Communism or (b) a taste for violent activity. But none of this brings us to an informed position regarding the war itself, for the question of whether to support or oppose armed intervention as a *policy* rests on a body of data that extends beyond the private motives of particular individuals.

Individuals involved in public protests are often accused of merely seeking to escape boredom or vent their anger. Indeed, politically active people do sometimes feel more engaged with life. Communists, revolutionaries, radicals, liberals, centrists, conservatives, reactionaries, and fascists have all testified to the personal invigoration experienced in active political engagement, especially when the effort brought results. But, again, this tells us nothing about the political significance of their particular actions and ideologies. In sum, personal motivations—as opposed to political ones—are, if not irrelevant, then certainly of marginal importance for evaluating public policy.

Society's view of who is psychologically disturbed rests to a great extent on existing standards of normality. By definition, rebels are people who do not accept some of society's conventional beliefs and dominant interests. Not surprisingly, such rebels are more likely to be diagnosed as driven by aberrant private motives. Rycroft observes that many "world-shakers" and other exceptional people have been "manhandled by psychiatrists and [psycho]analysts. . . . Jesus Christ has been diagnosed schizophrenic, Beethoven paranoid, the Old Testament prophets (collectively) schizophrenoid, Leonardo da Vinci schizoid-obsessional, etc. etc."[17]

Some of us believe that people usually rebel because all is not well in the world. In contrast, the psychopolitical belief is that people rebel because *they* are not well. Rebels are diagnosed as troubled because they are troublesome. Because they see a particular authority as unjust, it is concluded they oppose all established authority—which is not the case with most political reformers or revolutionaries. For the political psychologist, rebellion against authority becomes prima facie evidence of rebellion against parental authority once removed. There is no need to demonstrate the linkage; it has been established by a reference to "clinical evidence" that itself has no command over political data unless one imagines it does.

The psychological explanation, then, harbors the fallacy of "affirming the consequent": the political rebel is really rebelling against parental authority. Proof? the rebel is rebelling. This problem obtains in all "innate drive" theories that purport to explain observable behavior. Thus we are told that people are impelled by an inborn drive for power or love or wealth. Evidence for such claims is then found in instances of people pursuing power, love, and wealth. The theory uses as evidence the very phenomenon it is trying to explain.

Dubious Clinical Data

Aside from how "depth" psychology has been applied to politics, we might question its reliability as a science. In so doing, we share the company of none other than Harold Lasswell, who admits that his formulations are asserted in "rather dogmatic fashion" and that they rest on "the highly unsatisfactory nature of the materials and methods of contemporary psychopathology."[18] After thirty years of psychoanalytic labor, he noted, there still did not exist a body of documents that might be consulted by specialists who could resolve their differences over what goes on in a treatment session.

Fifty-nine years after Lasswell made this observation, the American Psychiatric Press published a four-volume reference work intended as a manual for treatment. It contains contributions by more than four hundred experts, mostly psychiatrists, and seems close to being the body of documents Lasswell thought specialists should have available for consultation. But the work evoked heated controversy, including complaints from psychologists who felt that certain theories were slighted and new approaches would be discouraged. The manual was published with a disclaimer saying that it was not an official publication of the American Psychiatric Association.[19] Even many psychiatrists doubted that the categories of disorder listed in the manual represented real and distinct conditions.[20]

Notes taken of therapy sessions are often inaccessible and woefully inadequate for systematic study. Nobody knows "the value of the published scraps" or what processes distort the reporting practices of different clinical investigators, remarks Lasswell. And there is no follow-up data on posttreatment conditions of clients.[21] As Lasswell was not the first to observe, patients tend to produce the kind of material the analyst is looking for. Hence, they dreamed of anima figures if analyzed by Jung, relived birth traumas when treated by Rank, talked of their inferiority feelings for Adler, and dealt with their Oedipal anxieties and castration fears under Freud's supervision. Thus, different investigators, ostensibly using the same methods, produce different data or arrive at widely varying conclusions when looking at the same data.

The rules for attributing meaning to data remain obscure, as Lasswell admits. Thus, when someone reports he was warned during childhood that his nose would be cut off if he persisted in "handling himself," Lasswell asks: "How do we know what importance to assign to this alleged reminiscence?" Are we to accept this as a historical statement or are we to construe it as a fabrication that shows what he supposed would happen if he disobeyed orders? Is the recollection just a sign of the patient's fear of the therapist couched in the memory of the past? Or maybe a self-inflicted fantasy to punish himself for hostile feelings toward the therapist? Or an attempt to win approval by producing what he thinks the therapist finds important? Or an original trauma which once uncovered will ease the patient's anxiety?[22]

Regarding the clinical discovery process, I would raise other questions. Consider the concept of "reaction-formation," one of the "defense mechanisms of the ego" to which political psychologists refer; it might be singled out as emblematic of the dubious nature of much clinical data. Through reaction-formation a person, who might be expected to show one form of behavior, may react away from that form even to the point of showing the very opposite behavior. For instance, one might be expected to manifest hostility and jealousy toward a sibling but through reaction-formation will show friendliness and loyalty — supposedly a compensatory psychological cover-up for unconscious negative feelings. Thus the clinician can assume that an underlying motive exists, and then can find evidence for it in contrary behavior patterns.[23] Both A and the opposite of A stand as evidence of the same thing. Diametrically opposite patterns can be treated as supporting a theoretical claim, making the theory nonfalsifiable.

But how do we know when actions and attitudes harbor unconscious motives that relate to earlier experiences? When are they, if ever, what they seem to be? (It is said that even

Freud, a heavy cigar smoker, noted that sometimes a cigar is just a cigar.) Behind such questions looms the problem of validation: how do we know we are observing the thing we say we are observing—especially in regard to submerged psychic forces which by their nature are not observable?

Furthermore, can we ever think of individual action and attitude as existing apart from the larger configuration of social relations? If a given behavior is a response to both the imperatives of social reality and interior psychic motives, how much weight do we ascribe to larger social forces and how much to family relations? For instance, how much to oppressive class conditions and how much to filial conflicts?

And what are we to make of psychological pronouncements about long-past presidents, prophets, and revolutionary leaders, about whom the psychological data is fragmentary and the possibilities of clinical investigation are nonexistent, since such leaders have taken their dreams and fantasies and hidden conflicts to the grave with them?[24]

Since almost anything about a person can be endowed with psychopathological significance, what decides the process of selectivity and embellishment? What role do such things as ideology, a desire for justice, economic self-interest, and religious and ethical teachings play? Can we make a reliable interpretation of pathology by treating the individual as someone relatively untouched by these wider forces?

If psychology "is behind everything," we might wonder whether the psychological has any boundaries. Seeming to permeate everything, it loses much of its defining value and explanatory power. But psychological characteristics are no substitute for social ones. Thus people often perceive reality and act upon it in accordance with the position they occupy within the social structure, frequently because there is no other way they can act, even if they are endowed with exceptional personalities. And there is no reason to assume that individuals who act in extraordinary ways do so because of rationalized emotions displaced from early life rather than because of a host of other things relating to talent, intelligence, family advantage, class interest, or resistance against racial or gender oppression. In other words, when acting with exceptional courage, skill, and insight—or for that matter, exceptional stupidity, timidity, recklessness, or blindness—they are *acting,* not *acting out.*

Lenin as Oedipus

By way of illustrating some of the problems already touched upon, let us consider Victor Wolfenstein's psychobiography of Lenin, from his book on Lenin, Trotsky, and Gandhi, three leaders who "came to have revolutionary identities as a result of essentially interminable conflicts with parental authority."[25]

Lenin was raised in a family "not bothered by unusual stress or disruption," with a "considerable brood of children" who got along well together.[26] Lenin's father is described by Wolfenstein as a warm, patient, loving parent, "who devoted substantial time to gently teaching his children how to behave. He taught them to play chess, and played other games with them as well."[27] Lenin's mother is described as being of steady disposition, relatively well educated, and "devoted to the well-being and advancement of her children." She too spent a good deal of time with the children, teaching them to read, play the piano, leading them in family singing, and helping them compose a weekly handwritten family magazine.[28]

Wolfenstein's picture of Lenin is also generally positive. As a child Lenin appears to have been jovial, humorous, loud, a practical joker, "given somewhat to boasting and bullying, but on the whole well liked and likeable." He easily performed well in school work and was esteemed by teachers. In all, Lenin, was "a bright assertive but not unusual lad."[29] Whence the pathological revolutionary?

The problem, it turns out, was that Lenin's father occasionally was kept away from his family for long periods of time by his official duties. This pattern of a loving, attentive parent suddenly absenting himself "must have had a strange effect on young Lenin's mind."[30] Wolfenstein offers no supporting evidence for this conjecture. He does not consider the likelihood that while Lenin and the other children may have missed their father during his job-related travels, they seemed securely enough placed in his affections not to have reacted with deep feelings of abandonment and betrayal.

Another "problem": Lenin's father never used corporal punishment on him but resorted to "firm moral suasion" which "left little room for anti-paternal rebellion with a clear conscience." Apparently Lenin would have been better off had his father beat him occasionally. The gentle father's "high moral rectitude undoubtedly resulted in an unusually demanding superego for the son." So young Lenin probably was unable to express the resentment he felt about his father "without experiencing guilt as a consequence."[31]

Even before all this, when Lenin was but eighteen to twenty months old he "had already developed a basically mistrustful nature." He was a late walker out of a need to emulate the behavior of a newly born sister in order to get the maternal attention she received. This slow walking demonstrated an early mistrust for his environment and shows that "Lenin's adult behavior, above all his mistrustfulness and the aggressiveness which grows out of mistrust . . . had deep roots indeed in his life experiences. A predisposition would exist towards viewing the world in kill-or-be-killed terms."[32] Wolfenstein does not reveal how he arrived at these breathtaking conclusions.

Lenin's loving identification with his older brother and father—frequently expressed both verbally and in the way he emulated each—becomes yet another source of pathology in Wolfenstein's hands. The death of both father and brother, it seems, evoked intense guilt feelings in Lenin who, according to

Wolfenstein, harbored a love-hate ambivalence for both older men that was "the central problem of his life." Wolfenstein eventually lowers the Freudian boom: "Lenin, it must be remembered, felt he bore the double responsibility for the deaths of his father and brother — whom he had wished dead in order that he might possess his mother."[33]

What is missing is any evidence that Lenin nursed such compelling feelings of guilt, aggression, ambivalence, hate, and murder toward his brother and father, or an incestuous love for his mother.[34] Nor, for Wolfenstein, is any evidence needed since the Oedipus complex has been declared a universal phenomenon, part of every son's psychic heritage. Thus a common affliction is used to explain a most uncommon man. One wonders why Wolfenstein bothered to construct the other interpretations when all along he could apply, as if by fiat, the prefabricated Oedipal judgment.

Wolfenstein suggests that revolutionary Marxism was the therapeutic cure for the psychopathology Lenin suffered. Lenin found "a benevolent, omniscient father" in Marx, and a "vengeful Oedipal father in the Czar," over whom, however, "Marx promised victory."[35]

This treatment of Lenin invites the criticism offered earlier that almost anything about a person can be endowed with psychopathological significance and then woven into his or her political life. Both A and the opposite of A can be treated as evidence of pathology: both a loving, gentle father and a harsh unloving one; both a positive identification with familial figures and a negative one. And at times no data at all will do quite well as when we invoke the universal curse of Oedipus. Behavior in later life is presumed not to result from a quest for justice or a desire for a better world, but from acting out earlier unresolved scenarios. Even if an individual like Lenin creates a new and greater drama in his engagement with life, in the pyschopathological view, he is still bound to an old script, a hapless victim of an interior demonology that needs a lifetime—and sometimes a whole revolution—for its proper exorcism. History becomes little more than unconscious family enmities writ large.

The Compulsive Hoover

Psychopolitics is not just a matter of mainstream investigators psychologizing about rebels. Conservative leaders also have come under scrutiny. The results are hardly any more encouraging.[36] Let us consider political psychologist James David Barber's treatment of Herbert Hoover, a man he categorizes as an "active-negative president." The active-negative president is one who experiences severe deprivation in childhood and who subsequently tries to wring from his environment a sense of self-worth through achievement and a search for power over others.[37] According to Barber, Hoover suffered from a fatal flaw of character that caused him to discard an earlier flexibility and replace it with a latter-day self-defeating rigidity and compulsion.[38] Who would have anticipated, Barber asks, "that Herbert Hoover, the pragmatic miracle worker who negotiated relief for war-torn Europe in the midst of World War I, would freeze in opposition to relief for jobless Americans?"[39]

In a chapter entitled "The Origins of the Presidential Compulsion," Barber informs us that Hoover was orphaned by the age of eight, lived with relatives, liked the outdoors, and had an upbringing that stressed "a close restraint of emotions." As a child Hoover presumably was scarred by the loss of his parents and experienced "a sense of powerlessness, an inability to guide his own fate, a vulnerability to sudden externally imposed radical changes in his life." To overcome these feelings he strove to establish control over the world around him, a pattern that persisted into college, where he also supposedly manifested an "extreme individualism."[40]

Actually, based on the data Barber presents, one could conclude that Hoover worked in close unison with schoolmates, had a normal number of friendships, displayed exceptional skills as a student organizer, and exercised effective campus leadership. If anything, at Stanford, Hoover developed his exceptional gifts in seemingly creative and self-rewarding ways.

Barber believes the fatal flaws in Hoover's character surfaced most pronouncedly when he was in the White House. As a president, Hoover appeared to be trying "to make up for something, to salvage through leadership some lost or damaged part of himself" and to struggle "against an inner sense of inadequacy." "His power-seeking reflected a strong compensatory need for power"[41] Like other active-negative presidents such as Woodrow Wilson and Lyndon Johnson, Hoover harbored "a felt necessity for the denial of self-gratification" (a trait I find hard to imagine in Lyndon Johnson). According to Barber, Hoover "struggled to control aggressive impulses" and was a perfectionist who was "supposed to be good at everything all the time."

Drawing from the limited data provided by Barber himself, we might conclude to the contrary that Hoover had a realistic, nonperfectionist view of his own limitations. Thus he refused to try to excel in the presidency's every role. For instance, he made no attempt to fulfill the dramatic needs of the office, remarking on one occasion: "You can't make a Teddy Roosevelt out of me."[42]

Barber tells us Hoover was an emotionally blocked man, taciturn, humorless, reserved, and seldom capable of crying. But what little evidence he offers seems to contradict this picture. Hoover could express anger, as on the occasion he threatened to fight a heckler in the 1932 campaign. And Barber cites two instances when Hoover was moved to tears in public.[43] How often might a less emotively blocked president be expected to cry in public?

Furthermore, Hoover was profoundly moved, both emotionally and to action, when visited in the White House by three children who were pleading to have their unemployed father released from jail. Curiously, the one contemporary testimony Barber offers is that of Eugene Lyons, who said that Hoover was not cold, but "a sensitive, soft-hearted person who craves affection, enjoys congenial company, and suffers under the slings of malice."[44]

In sum, the data Barber offers on Hoover's life are not only selective but lend themselves to contrary interpretation. He fails to make a convincing case that the character traits he ascribes to Hoover are as dominant and significant as he claims. Consequently, one comes away with the feeling that Barber *tells* rather than *shows* us. And we are left asking: how does he know that?

The Political Hoover

Barber's question remains: How could Hoover, the man who administered relief to the children of war-torn Europe, refuse to allocate relief funds to alleviate the hunger of millions of Americans during the Great Depression, thus helping to bring down his own presidency? Before proposing some psychological compulsion, let us investigate the political Hoover, for therein may rest the clues to his political behavior.

When Hoover was president he once said: "The sole function of government is to bring about a condition of affairs favorable to the beneficial development of private enterprise."[45] Indeed, a look at Hoover's career reveals a consistent lifelong dedication to the private enterprise system at home and abroad. As head of the Belgian Relief Commission, a private organization, and later as director of the American Relief Administration, Hoover allotted aid in a highly opportunistic way. His commission did not *give* food to the Belgians, it *sold* food for cash at wartime prices, as though the supplies had been bought on the open market. Belgium was drained of funds in exchange for food. Among the Belgians who could not pay, drastic shortages arose by 1916, followed by hunger riots among the poorer classes.[46]

257

As early as November 1918, Hoover made it clear that food was to be used as a political weapon "to stem the tide of Bolshevism."[47] Hoover's American Relief Administration sent aid to Russia for a purpose never intended by Congress, to areas occupied by General Yudenich's counterrevolutionary White Guard army. In the Baltics aid went to areas held by General von der Goltz's German expeditionary corps. Both these armies were dedicated to overthrowing the Soviet government, and both engaged in widespread pillaging and execution of prisoners and civilians. By 1919 Yudenich's army subsisted totally on Hoover's aid.[48] In a report to Congress in January 1921, Hoover admitted using U.S. relief funds to supply the reactionary White armies.[49] His manner of distributing relief moved the *Nation* to criticize him for refusing to deliver tons of food to starving inhabitants of Russia until "they surrender to the ideas and armies" of the Western powers.[50]

Similarly Hoover withheld financial aid and food intended for Hungary until the short-lived revolutionary Bela Kun government was overthrown—even though the supplies had been purchased with funds advanced by that government. Aid was forthcoming only after the reactionary Admiral Horthy was installed, backed by the bayonets of the Romanian army, which instituted a "White terror," executing hundreds of Hungarian revolutionaries and Jews.[51]

In similar spirit, Hoover characterized his relief efforts in support of the Allied-sponsored government in Austria as "a race against both death and Communism." He had posters plastered all over Vienna announcing that food shipments would cease should an uprising occur. He also placed large sums at the disposal of the rightist Polish militarists during their invasion of Soviet Russia in April 1920. Senator James Reed of Missouri charged on the Senate floor that $40 million of relief funds voted by Congress to feed the hungry "was spent to keep the Polish army in the field."[52] The political psychologist

Alexander George describes Hoover as a "sincere humanitarian."[53] He might better be described as a "selective humanitarian," using food as a weapon, ruthlessly expending or withholding funds as political ideology dictated.

As secretary of commerce in 1927, at the time of the great Mississippi flood, Hoover coldheartedly supervised relief efforts and manipulated local leaders as a means of bolstering his chances of winning the Republican nomination for president.[54] As commerce secretary, he also ruled that corporate-sponsored commercial radio served the general public but noncommercial broadcasters represented special interests.[55]

While hailed as someone who did good, Herbert Hoover did well. Frequently described as an "engineer," he was in fact a multimillionaire with business ventures in Burma, Nigeria, Australia, South Africa, Nicaragua, the United States, and Czarist Russia. Prior to World War I he had secured a major interest in no less than eleven Russian oil corporations, along with major concessions in Russian timberlands, mines, railroads, factories, refineries, and gold, copper, silver and zinc reserves.[56] Had the October Revolution not happened and the Bolshevik government not canceled the vast concessions, Hoover would have been one of the world's top billionaires.

Whether motivated by concern for his personal investments, a more generalized class interest, or an ideological conservatism or some blend of these—there is no reason to assume they are mutually exclusive—Hoover manifested an unswervingly militant opposition to communism and to any reforms that might limit the prerogatives of private enterprise. During the period after the Russian Revolution, he remained a persistent supporter of the military campaigns against Soviet Russia.

Hoover eventually did offer relief to Soviet Russia during the famine of 1921, a move designed to undermine the Bolshevik government in a manner more devious than openly counterrevolutionary, according to Peter Filene.[57] Hoover believed that the

Bolsheviks were about to lose their grip on the reins of power. The hope was that some large international relief body would be able to take over economic control in Soviet Russia, in what became known as a "bread intervention."[58] In a memorandum to President Wilson that seems remarkably contemporary in its counterinsurgency approach, Hoover demonstrated that the containment of communism was uppermost in his mind. He mapped out how aid might serve to moderate the militancy of a new revolutionary government, especially after "bitter experience has taught the economic and social follies of present [revolutionary] obsessions."[59] Within two years after the food program began, when it became evident that the Soviets were not about to collapse or be subverted, Hoover abruptly canceled all aid to Russia while continuing to assist conservative regimes in Austria, Poland, and Czechoslovakia.

During his tenure as president, Hoover repeatedly voiced his opposition to public ownership and government regulation of the economy. At the time of the Great Depression, political and corporate leaders were divided as to what strategy to pursue in the face of economic collapse and growing public unrest.[60] There were those who advocated reforms in the hope that by giving a little they could keep a lot. Others feared that such concessions would not stem the tide but only open the floodgates and inundate them. They believed the private enterprise system should not be tampered with, that reports of popular suffering were greatly exaggerated, and that the economy was basically sound and would soon right itself.

Hoover was firmly in this latter camp. What Barber considers to be his "inflexibility" and "compulsion" were attitudes not unique to him. In his refusal to spend the billions needed to ease the plight of the destitute, Hoover shared an opinion that prevailed within most of the business community right up to 1932 and beyond. Indeed, at least until mid-1932, even the American Federation of Labor, "consistent with its historic emphasis on voluntarism," opposed government assistance to the unemployed.[61]

Like so many other conservatives then and now, Hoover preached the virtues of self-reliance, opposed the taxation of overseas corporate earnings, sought to reduce income taxes for the higher brackets, and was against both a veteran's bonus and aid to drought sufferers. He refused federal funds for the jobless and opposed unemployment insurance and federal retirement benefits. He repeatedly warned that public assistance programs were the beginning of "state socialism."[62] Toward business, however, he suffered from no such "inflexibility" and could spend generously. He supported multimillion-dollar federal subsidies to shipping interests and agribusiness, and his Reconstruction Finance Corporation doled out $2 billion to banks and corporations.

The above information, all a matter of public record, provides us with a portrait different from the one sketched by Barber. Rather than moving from flexibility to rigidity because of some psychological flaw, Hoover maintained a position that was consistently in line with the ideology shared by most of his class. As an administrator of emergency relief he used aid to buttress autocratic capitalist governments and armies, while undermining revolutionary governments and movements, yielding very little even in the face of repeated criticisms from Congress and the press.

The man who, for political reasons, could withhold funds from starving populations in eastern Europe and Soviet Russia, could, for political reasons, deny relief to American workers. The man who could assist mass murderers like General von der Glotz and General Yudenitch would have no trouble ordering General MacArthur to drive out the unarmed Bonus March veterans, in an action that left two dead and many wounded. Having fought but a decade before against socialist revolutions in Austria, Hungary, the Baltics, and Russia, President Hoover was not about to introduce what he and many of his supporters considered to be insidious forms of socialism at home. (Even here, Hoover's "characterological rigidity" gave way to political expediency when, faced with a national election, he belatedly moved in the direction of federal relief in the summer of 1932.)

In sum, the mystery about Hoover's character appears to be no mystery at all. Herbert Hoover was very much a political animal. Unyielding and uncompromising he could be, but in a politically self-serving manner. The "pragmatic miracle worker," who supposedly was suddenly beset by a compulsion when in the White House, was all along a hardline, anti-communist, multimillionaire conservative. He operated in an ideologically consistent way, taking class positions that even today are standard ones in conservative circles. On behalf of the things he believed in and cherished, Hoover knew what he was doing.

That he acted rationally does not mean he acted infallibly. It certainly can be argued that subsequent events demonstrated how wrong he and his supporters were about both economic conditions and the popular mood. Once again we see that the psychological explanation achieves plausibility only by slighting—rather than explaining—important political realities.

When the Political Becomes Personal

The Lasswellian model assumes that since childhood antedates adulthood it creates a more compelling and enduring nexus than the experiences of adult life. This presumed progression from apolitical-formative childhood to political-reactive adulthood treats the individual as a generic entity. The notion is compatible with the liberal model of the market society as an aggregation of individuals acting out their desires and demands, shaping the larger reality in accordance with their private desires.

But what is primary in time sequence is not necessarily primary in formative power. Chronological primacy may not be a sure indication of affective impact. For many important political phenomena one could argue that the causal progression goes both ways. Thus there are numerous studies indicating that the anxieties generated during times of nuclear escalation and cold-war confrontations penetrate the unconscious minds of American children, investing many youngsters with unnervingly pessimistic prognoses about humanity's survival.[63] Other political developments like recession, unemployment, poverty, loss of family income, police repression, political assassination, and war have a discernible impact on the psychic dispositions of whole populations of adults and children.[64]

To posit an apolitical childhood as the crucial antecedent to political adulthood is to ignore the fact that childhood is likely to be no more apolitical than the rest of life. That American children are not usually active in political life does not mean they are insulated from its formative effects. In fact, they undergo an early political and ideological socialization from television, movies, grade school, community, and from the social experiences and prejudices to which they are exposed in the family itself. Much of the political socialization literature indicates that the family is far from apolitical and that it has an important impact on political loyalties — not through the circuitous route of a psychopathological ontology but more directly as a socializing mediator of political opinions, social images, gender roles, racial attitudes, and class values.

All this suggests that *socialization* and *internalization* may be more crucial than displacement and rationalization for linking the private and public worlds. Lasswell's "political man" model: $p \} d \} r = P$ might be modified and put in reverse to read as follows: $P \} s \} i \} = p$. Political forces *(P)* have a socializing effect *(s)* on individuals, who through a process of internalization *(i)* embrace particular images and interests of political life so that these become compelling components of their private motives *(p)*. I submit that the explanatory power of this alternate model

263

is greater and less mysterious than the Lasswellian one. It requires fewer and less embellished assumptions. It is supported by more readily available evidence and by interpretations devoid of the overextended extrapolations found in psychopolitics and psychohistory. It recognizes that individuals and families do not antedate the social reality into which they are born. They do not exist in a prepolitical vacuum. However, like all models, this alternate one is incomplete because it does not take into account individual differences in processing social experience.

My intent has not been to call for the elimination of political psychology. Fred Greenstein notes areas in which personality can have relevance for the study of politics. He asserts, for instance, following Alex Inkles, that there is a great deal of evidence suggesting that particular institutional statuses attract or recruit particular kinds of personalities.[65] But there is also evidence suggesting that institutionally defined roles and statuses and other institutional imperatives will prefigure individual behavior, causing persons of different personalities to act in roughly similar ways.[66] Thus, it should be noted that U.S. presidents of different backgrounds, family histories, and personalities have all been fairly consistent in their devotion to making the world safe for corporate America, opposing competing systems, and extending U.S. military power in the service of multinational investors.[67] Likewise, the various personalities of capitalists do not change their predominant need to invest for profit, compete, exploit, expand, and accumulate. Individuals at the pinnacle of political and economic power must abide by the imperatives of the system they serve and are served by, perhaps more than anyone else.

Focusing too closely on personality causes us to overlook the wider institutional imperatives of power and interest that shape our options and our performance. But a purely structuralist view leaves out the crucial role that individual personalities or group psychology might play. In other words, we should have no argument with those who assert that differing personalities may under certain circumstances effect different outcomes.

But it is one thing to say that personality may affect political reality—who can deny the impact of a Lenin or a Gandhi?—and quite something else to argue that political actors, both leaders and masses, are really displacing upon the manifest content of political life their unresolved hidden psychological agendas. It is this latter assertion that I take to task without wishing to dismiss in toto the role of psychological factors in the timing, formulation, and expression of political actions.

After doing correlations of political, social, and psychological attitudes, Sutherland and Tannenbaum conclude:

> Political scientists [and historians, it might be added] who study mass political preferences in relation to "basic" personality dimensions . . . are mining an area of negligible potential. . . . Political preferences will more likely be shown to arise from rationally held "cognitions" about how society itself functions, than from deep seated personality needs. . . . It seems obvious that "personologists" in political science have been hasty in focusing on supposed universal effects of "personality" variables like political efficacy and authoritarianism, which have turned out on reflection to be class-based.[68]

In sum, psychopolitics tends to reduce large social phenomena to simple personal causalities. It is reductionist, although in a tortuously circuitous manner. Psychopolitics takes an elaborately convoluted path, preferring explanations that are far removed from the actual events. Psychopolitics tends to underplay manifest content. It is simplistic in its interpretation yet highly esoteric and rarified in the nature of the evidence (or nonevidence) upon which it rests. At the heart of all psychologistic explanations is the denial of Occam's razor. The direct cut is never made.

In reversing Lasswell's formula I am not claiming that the formative causality goes only from the political to the private but am insisting that we give a new definition to the private, recognizing its social dimensions. Certainly people are not passive absorbents of politico-economic forces. They synthesize, challenge, and even create anew their social experience. But the existing literature on psychopolitics and psychohistory is too deeply flawed to be of much help in understanding historical realities.

Early psychohistorians like Harry Elmer Barnes and H. Stuart Hughes saw psychology (and psychoanalysis in particular) as providing the historian with new insights into human motivation.[69] With the use of personal biographical data, psychohistory introduced a fresh view of historic figures ranging from Jesus and Jefferson to Luther and Lenin. But is it a more *important* view? Eric Erickson's personality study of Luther is interesting but does it help us better understand the Reformation, or even Luther's impact upon the Reformation? As Hamerow reluctantly concludes, "The theoretical justifications of psychohistory sounded very persuasive, but its practical achievements have remained disappointingly small."[70]

Having taken note of the inaccessibility of reliable data and the plentitude of questionable interpretations, both in the science of depth psychology and its political applications, and having noted the tenuous and seemingly arbitrary linkage of causalities, the way sweeping conclusions might rest on frail suppositions and sketchy psychologisms, and the way readily observable political data are slighted, we might be forgiven if we choose not to tread the path opened by the practitioners of psychopolitics and psychohistory. They promised us a secret garden and instead gave us a swamp.

Afterword

In 1969, Nobel Prize–winning economist Sir John Hicks noted that Karl Marx seems to be the only one with a theory of history. It is, Hicks wrote, "extraordinary that one hundred years after *Das Kapital* . . . so little else should have emerged."[71] Nor has much changed since Hicks made that observation. To be sure, there are theories aplenty: folk-blood theories, great-men theories, psychohistory theories, socio-biological theories, and the like. But they tend to go nowhere. They lack explanatory power for those of us who seek to understand the forces that have shaped politico-economic reality through the ages.

This might explain why even many non-Marxist historians refer to classes when dealing with historic epochs. They see antiquity as the age of slavery, the Middle Ages as the age of feudalism, and the modern industrial era as the age of capitalism. Though it makes some of them uncomfortable to say it, slavery, feudalism, and capitalism are *class* systems. Mainstream historians also passingly acknowledge the class-based nature of competing political interests within any epoch. So they will speak of patricians and plebeians in ancient Rome, the rising bourgeoisie of the eighteenth and nineteenth centuries, and aristocrats and commoners in the French Revolution. But rarely are these competing class interests recognized as motor forces in history. And rarely, if ever, do these historians make an explicit acknowledgment of the debt they owe Marx. Instead, they avoid dealing candidly with class power and class struggle. Along with their political leaders, major media, and textbook producers, they look everywhere but at the brute political-economic realities of past and present. They seek anything that might divert us from a class theory of history, anything that helps them to dismiss Marxism as irrelevant and moribund. Established elders and young acolytes alike search not for theory but for ideological legitimacy and professional acceptance.

So they continue to pour out their nuanced complexities and evasive simplifications. This book was intended as a relief from that kind of mystification. History has many unanswered questions, but it is no mystery as such — except for those who make it so.

NOTES:

1. C. Wright Mills, *The Sociological Imagination* (New York: Oxford Univeristy Press, 1959), 12.
2. Both psychopolitics and psychohistory are treated as one field herein, the major difference between them is that the political psychologists concentrate on more recent events and personalities than do the psychohistorians, though even that is not always the case. In this chapter the examples chosen are representative, not exhaustive, of this type of literature.
3. Harold Lasswell, *Psychopathology and Politics* (Chicago: University of Chicago Press, 1930), 74.
4. Lasswell, *Psychopathology and Politics*, 75–76.
5. Lasswell, *Psychopathology and Politics*, 173.
6. Bruno Bettelheim, Testimony before Special House Education Subcommittee, reported in *New York Daily News*, March 21, 1969.
7. Lewis Feuer, *The Conflict of Generations* (New York: Basic Books, 1969), 250.
8. Feuer, *The Conflict of Generations*, 311.
9. Ernest Van den Haag (ed.), *Capitalism, Sources of Hostility* (New Rochelle, N.Y.: Epoch Books, 1979).
10. Friedrich Engels, *The Condition of the Working Class in England,* translated and edited by W. O. Henderson and W. H. Chaloner (Stanford, California: Stanford University Press, 1958), xxv–xxviii.
11. Quoted in *About Face!* (Newsletter of the U.S. Servicemen's Fund), December 1972: 2.
12. Michael Ratner and Michael Steven Smith, *Che Guevara and the FBI: The U.S. Political Police Dossier on the Latin American Revolutionary* (Melbourne and New York: Ocean Press, 1997), 20–25, 89, 115, and passim. The file consists mostly of CIA reports relayed to the FBI.
13. Philip Agee, *On the Run* (Secaucus N.J.: Lyle Stuart, 1987), 43ff.
14. After looking at survey data, along with Rorschach tests and Thematic Apperception Tests, two politically conservative political psychologizers discover to their satisfaction that the New Left was inhabited by many who exhibited a psychological syndrome which they term "inverse authoritarianism," stemming from psychological pathologies relating to child-rearing practices and other family problems: Stanley Rothman and S. Robert Lichter, *The Roots of Radicalism: Jews, Christians, and the New Left* (New York: Oxford University Press, 1982).
15. Arnold Rogow, review of E. Victor Wolfenstein, *The Revolutionary Personality,* in *American Political Science Review* 62 (1968): 605.
16. Alexander George, "Assessing Presidential Character," *World Politics* 26 (1974): 235–236.
17. Charles Ryroft, *Wilhelm Reich* (New York: Viking Press, 1972), 8.

18. Lasswell, *Psychopathology and Politics,* xxv.
19. Task Force on Treatments and Psychiatric Disorders, *Treatments of Psychiatric Disorders,* 4 vols. (Washington, D.C.: American Psychiatric Press, 1989).
20. Keith Russell Ablow, "A Murky Link: Character and Mental Illness" *Washington Post Health,* June 18, 1991: 9.
21. Lasswell, *Psychopathology and Politics,* 205.
22. Lasswell, *Psychopathology and Politics,* 206–207.
23. See H. J. Eysenck, *Uses and Abuses of Psychology* (Baltimore: Penguin Books, 1953).
24. Rogow, review in *American Political Science Review,* 605. Two editors of a volume on psychohistory offer a cogent and telling listing of "the inherent evidentiary problems of psychohistory: the difficulty of gathering data on childhood; the resultant danger of circular reasoning in hypothesizing antecedents from adult words and actions; the absence of personal contact enjoyed by the psychoanalyst, the misuse of subjectivity; the danger of reductionism; the question of whether psychoanalytic theory is valid for other times and places (and, indeed, whether the application of any contemporary model can illuminate the special mentalities of earlier periods)": Geoffrey Cocks and Travis Crosby (eds.), *Psycho/History: Readings in the Method of Psychology, Psychoanalysis, and History* (New Haven: Yale University Press, 1987), x.
25. Victor Wolfenstein, *The Revolutionary Personality: Lenin, Trotsky, Gandhi* (Princeton, N.J.: Princeton University Press, 1967), 49.
26. Wolfenstien, *The Revolutionary Personality,* 36–37.
27. Wolfenstein, *The Revolutionary Personality,* 34.
28. Wolfenstein, *The Revolutionary Personality,* 35.
29. Wolfenstein, *The Revolutionary Personality,* 37–38.
30. Wolfenstein, *The Revolutionary Personality,* 39.
31. Wolfenstein, *The Revolutionary Personality,* 39.
32. Wolfenstein, *The Revolutionary Personality,* 40–41.
33. Wolfenstein, *The Revolutionary Personality,* 113.
34. For a much different view of Lenin's adult personality see the contemporary portraits by N. K. Krupskaya, *Reminiscences of Lenin* (New York: International Publishers, 1960) and Leon Trotsky, *Lenin, Notes for a Biographer* (New York: G. P. Putnam, 1971).
35. Wolfenstein, *The Revolutionary Personality,* 117.
36. See for instance, Eli Chesen, *President Nixon's Psychological Profile* (New York: Wyden, 1973); David Abrahamsen, *Nixon vs. Nixon: An Emotional Tragedy* (New York: Farrar, Straus & Giroux, 1977); Bruce Mazlish, *In Search of Nixon: A Psychohistorical Inquiry* (Baltimore: Penguin Books, 1972). For a critique of Clinch and Mazlish see Robert Cole, "On Psychohistory," in Cocks and Crosby (eds.), *Psycho/History,* 96–99, 102–104. A work worthy of respectful atten-

tion but deserving of some of the same criticisms made herein is Alexander George and Juliette George, *Woodrow Wilson and Colonel House: A Personality Study* (New York: Dover, 1964); see the critiques of George and George by Robert C. Tucker, "The Georges' Wilson Reexamined," *American Political Science Review* 71 (1977): 606–618; and Edwin Weinstein et al., "Woodrow Wilson's Political Personality: A Reappraisal," *Political Science Quarterly* 93 (1978–1979): 585–598, and the response by George and George, *Political Science Quarterly* 96 (1981–1982): 641–665, all reprinted in Cocks and Crosby, *Psycho/History*. For some especially crude instances of psychologizing, see Fawn Brodie, *Thomas Jefferson: An Intimate History* (New York: Norton, 1973); Nancy Clinch, *The Kennedy Neurosis* (New York: Gosset & Dunlap, 1973); and of course Wolfenstein, *The Revolutionary Personality*.

37. James David Barber, *The Presidential Character* (Englewood Cliffs, N.J.: Prentice-Hall, 1972), 99–100.

38. In a *New York Times* op-ed piece (November 8, 1973) Barber asserts that presidents as ostensibly different in personality as Wilson, Nixon, Johnson, and Hoover are "strikingly similar in character." This raises a question about the use of "character" as a psychological construct and its relation to personality. If we think of "personality" in the lay sense to mean the observable expressions of temperament and attitude, and "character" in the more clinical sense — as does Wilhelm Reich — of "the form of the typical reaction" used by individuals to mediate reality and psychic conflict, or, as does Barber, the enduring and early developed structured "stance toward life," then the claim that these four rather different presidential personalities are of similar character is not an impossible one: Wilhelm Reich, *Character Analysis*, 3rd ed. (New York: Noonday Press, 1969); and Barber, *The Presidential Character*, 10. But the claim could be established only by an in-depth clinical character analysis of all four presidents, something that of course cannot be done. Barber's character typology deals not only with surface manifestations of activity-passivity and positive-negative expressions but deeper psychodynamic patterns. As George points out, "the data are not always good" supporting Barber's contention that a particular presidential style also contains the deeper psychodynamics that Barber associates with it: Alexander George, "Assessing Presidential Character," *World Politics* 26 (1974): 251. Both Lasswell and Barber sometimes emphasize the biographical specificity of some displaced and rationalized childhood sentiment or experience, and other times refer to the habituated, structured modes of response that are what Reich called the individual's "characterological" way of mediating between outer life and inner self. In a word, the political psychologists are dealing with both developmental psychology and ego adap-

tive psychology, relying sometimes on the idiosyncratic features of the individual's psychic history and sometimes on the generalizable forms of character defenses. These are interrelated but conceptually and presumably empirically separate approaches. As applied to political psychobiographies, it is not always clear why and when it should be one or the other.

39. James David Barber, "The Things We Might Have Seen," Op-Ed, *New York Times,* November 8, 1973.

40. Barber, *The Presidential Character,* 128–129.

41. Barber, *The Presidential Character,* 78.

42. Barber, *The Presidential Character,* 69.

43. Barber, *The Presidential Character,* 77.

44. Barber, *The Presidential Character,* 77–78.

45. Barber, *The Presidential Character,* 74.

46. John Knox, *The Great Mistake: Can Herbert Hoover Explain His Past?* rev. ed. (Baltimore: Grace Press, 1932), 115; John Hamill, *The Strange Career of Mr. Hoover Under Two Flags* (New York: William Faro, 1931), 327–328.

47. Benjamin Weissman, *Herbert Hoover and Famine Relief to Soviet Russia, 1921–1923* (Palo Alto, Calif.: Hoover Institution Press, 1974), 29.

48. Weissman, *Herbert Hoover and Famine Relief,* pp. 36–37; Michael Sayers and Albert Kahn, *The Great Conspiracy* (San Francisco: Proletarian Publishers, 1946), 106.

49. Walter Liggett, *The Rise of Herbert Hoover* (New York: H. K. Fly, 1932), 260–267.

50. *Nation,* editorial, June 7, 1919.

51. Liggett, *The Rise of Herbert Hoover,* 255; Weissman, *Herbert Hoover and Famine Relief,* 215.

52. Sayers and Kahn, *The Great Conspiracy,* 93; Weissman, *Herbert Hoover and Famine Relief,* 37.

53. George, "Assessing Presidential Character," 257.

54. John M. Barry, *Rising Tide: The Great Mississippi Flood of 1927 and How It Changed America* (New York: Simon & Schuster, 1997).

55. Ralph Engelman, *Public Radio and Television in America: A Political History* (Beverly Hills, Calif.: Sage Publications, 1996).

56. Hamill, *The Strange Career of Mr. Hoover,* 298–300; Knox, *The Great Mistake,* 97–99.

57. Peter Filene, *Americans and the Soviet Experiment 1917–1933* (Cambridge, Mass.: Harvard University Press, 1967), 78.

58. Weissman, *Herbert Hoover and Famine Relief,* 44–45, 49–51.

59. Harold Fisher, *The Famine in Soviet Russia 1919–1923: The Operations of the American Relief Administration* (Palo Alto, Calif.: Stanford University Press, 1927), 11–14.

60. Frances F. Piven and Richard A. Cloward, *Poor People's Movements:*

Why They Succeed, How They Fail (New York: Vintage, 1979), 44–45.

61. Piven and Cloward, *Poor People's Movements,* 72.

62. Liggett, *The Rise of Herbert Hoover;* Harris Warren, *Herbert Hoover and the Great Depression* (New York: Norton, 1959).

63. W. Beardslee and John E. Mack, "The Impact on Children and Adolescents of Nuclear Developments," *Psychological Aspects of Nuclear Developments,* American Psychiatric Association, Task Force Report #20, Washington, D.C.: spring 1982; and Beardslee and Mack, "Adolescents and the Threat of Nuclear War," *Yale Journal of Biology and Medicine* 56 (1983): 79–91; Marcia Yudkin, "When Kids Think the Unthinkable," *Psychology Today,* April 1984: 18–25; S. Escalona, "Children and the Threat of Nuclear War," in M. Schweble (ed.), *Behavioral Science and Human Survival* (Palo Alto, Calif.: Science and Behavioral Books, 1965).

64. Harvey Brenner, *Mental Illness and the Economy* (Cambridge, Mass.: Harvard University Press, 1973): Irving Bernstein, *The Lean Years* (Baltimore: Penguin Books, 1970); George Brown and Tirril Harris, *The Social Origins of Depression* (New York: Free Press, 1978); David Caplovitz, *Making Ends Meet: How Families Cope with Inflation and Recession* (Beverly Hills, Calif.: Sage Publications, 1979).

65. Fred I. Greenstein, "The Impact of Personality on Politics: An Attempt to Clear Away Underbrush," *American Political Science Review* 61 (1967): 629–641; see also Alex Inkeles, "Sociology and Psychology," in Sigmond Koch, *Psychology: A Study of a Science* (New York: McGraw-Hill, 1963).

66. See my *Power and the Powerless* (New York: St. Martin's Press, 1978), 114–123 and passim.

67. See my *Against Empire* (San Francisco: City Lights Books, 1995).

68. S. Sutherland and E. Tannenbaum, "Irrational Versus Rational Bases of Political Preference," *Political Psychology* 5 (1984): 177, 194.

69. See Harry Elmer Barnes, "Psychology and History: Some Reasons for Predicting Their Active Cooperation in the Future," *American Journal of Psychology* 30 (1919): 362–376.

70. Theodore S. Hamerow, *Reflections on History and Historians* (Madison, Wisc.: University of Wisconsin Press, 1987), 194.

71. See John Cassidy, "The Return of Karl Marx," *New Yorker,* October 20 and 27, 1997: 248–259.

ABOUT THE AUTHOR

Michael Parenti is considered one of the nation's leading progressive thinkers. He received his Ph.D. in political science from Yale University in 1962, and has taught at a number of colleges and universities. His writings have been featured in scholarly journals, popular periodicals, and newspapers, and have been translated into Spanish, Chinese, Japanese, Polish, Portuguese, German, Turkish, and Bangla.

Dr. Parenti lectures around the country on college campuses and before religious, labor, community, peace, and public interest groups. He has appeared on radio and television talk shows to discuss current issues or ideas from his published works. Tapes of his talks have played on numerous radio stations to enthusiastic audiences. Audio and video tapes of his talks are sold on a not-for-profit basis; for a listing, contact People's Video, P.O. Box 99514, Seattle WA 98100; tel. 206-789-5371. Dr. Parenti lives in Berkeley, California. You can visit his web site: http://www.vida.com/parenti.

CITY LIGHTS PUBLICATIONS
Acosta, Juvenal, ed. LIGHT FROM A NEARBY WINDOW: Contemporary Mexican Poetry
Alberti, Rafael. CONCERNING THE ANGELS
Alcalay, Ammiel, ed. KEYS TO THE GARDEN: New Israeli Writing
Alcalay, Ammiel. MEMORIES OF OUR FUTURE: Selected Essays 1982-1999
Allen, Roberta. AMAZON DREAM
Angulo de, G. & J. JAIME IN TAOS
Angulo, Jaime de. INDIANS IN OVERALLS
Artaud, Antonin. ARTAUD ANTHOLOGY
Barker, Molly. SECRET LANGUAGE
Bataille, Georges. EROTISM: Death and Sensuality
Bataille, Georges. THE IMPOSSIBLE
Bataille, Georges. STORY OF THE EYE
Bataille, Georges. THE TEARS OF EROS
Baudelaire, Charles. TWENTY PROSE POEMS
Blanco, Alberto. DAWN OF THE SENSES: Selected Poems
Blechman, Max. REVOLUTIONARY ROMANTICISM
Bowles, Paul. A HUNDRED CAMELS IN THE COURTYARD
Bramly, Serge. MACUMBA: The Teachings of Maria-José, Mother of the Gods
Brecht, Bertolt. STORIES OF MR. KEUNER
Breton, André. ANTHOLOGY OF BLACK HUMOR
Brook, James, Chris Carlsson, Nancy J. Peters eds. RECLAIMING SAN FRANCISCO: History
Politics Culture
Brook, James & Iain A. Boal. RESISTING THE VIRTUAL LIFE: Culture and Politics of Information
Broughton, James. COMING UNBUTTONED
Brown, Rebecca. ANNIE OAKLEY'S GIRL
Brown, Rebecca. THE DOGS
Brown, Rebecca. THE TERRIBLE GIRLS
Bukowski, Charles. THE MOST BEAUTIFUL WOMAN IN TOWN
Bukowski, Charles. NOTES OF A DIRTY OLD MAN
Bukowski, Charles. TALES OF ORDINARY MADNESS
Burroughs, William S. THE BURROUGHS FILE
Burroughs, William S. THE YAGE LETTERS
Campana, Dino. ORPHIC SONGS
Cassady, Neal. THE FIRST THIRD
Chin, Sara. BELOW THE LINE
Churchill, Ward. FANTASIES OF THE MASTER RACE: Literature, Cinema and the Colonization
of American Indians
Churchill, Ward. A LITTLE MATTER OF GENOCIDE: Holocaust and Denial in America, 1492 to
the Present
Cocteau, Jean. THE WHITE BOOK (LE LIVRE BLANC)
Cohen, Jonathan. APART FROM FREUD: Notes for a Rational Psychoanalysis
Cornford, Adam. ANIMATIONS
Corso, Gregory. GASOLINE
Cortázar, Julio. SAVE TWILIGHT
Cuadros, Gil. CITY OF GOD
Daumal, René. THE POWERS OF THE WORD
David-Neel, Alexandra. SECRET ORAL TEACHINGS IN TIBETAN BUDDHIST SECTS
Deleuze, Gilles. SPINOZA: Practical Philosophy
Dick, Leslie. KICKING
Dick, Leslie. WITHOUT FALLING
di Prima, Diane. PIECES OF A SONG: Selected Poems
Doolittle, Hilda (H.D.). NOTES ON THOUGHT & VISION
Ducornet, Rikki. ENTERING FIRE
Ducornet, Rikki. THE MONSTROUS AND THE MARVELOUS
Dunbar-Ortiz, Roxanne. OUTLAW WOMAN: A Memoir of the War Years, 1960–1975
Eberhardt, Isabelle. DEPARTURES: Selected Writings
Eberhardt, Isabelle. THE OBLIVION SEEKERS
Eidus, Janice. THE CELIBACY CLUB
Eidus, Janice. URBAN BLISS
Eidus, Janice. VITO LOVES GERALDINE
Ferlinghetti, L. ed. CITY LIGHTS POCKET POETS ANTHOLOGY

Ferlinghetti, L., ed. ENDS & BEGINNINGS (City Lights Review #6)
Ferlinghetti, L. PICTURES OF THE GONE WORLD
Finley, Karen. SHOCK TREATMENT
Ford, Charles Henri. OUT OF THE LABYRINTH: Selected Poems
Franzen, Cola, transl. POEMS OF ARAB ANDALUSIA
Frym, Gloria. DISTANCE NO OBJECT
García Lorca, Federico. BARBAROUS NIGHTS: Legends & Plays
García Lorca, Federico. ODE TO WALT WHITMAN & OTHER POEMS
García Lorca, Federico. POEM OF THE DEEP SONG
Garon, Paul. BLUES & THE POETIC SPIRIT
Gil de Biedma, Jaime. LONGING: SELECTED POEMS
Ginsberg, Allen. THE FALL OF AMERICA
Ginsberg, Allen. HOWL & OTHER POEMS
Ginsberg, Allen. KADDISH & OTHER POEMS
Ginsberg, Allen. MIND BREATHS
Ginsberg, Allen. PLANET NEWS
Ginsberg, Allen. PLUTONIAN ODE
Ginsberg, Allen. REALITY SANDWICHES
Glave, Thomas. WHOSE SONG? And Other Stories
Goethe, J. W. von. TALES FOR TRANSFORMATION
Gómez-Peña, Guillermo. THE NEW WORLD BORDER
Gómez-Peña, Guillermo, Enrique Chagoya, Felicia Rice. CODEX ESPANGLIENSIS
Goytisolo, Juan. LANDSCAPES OF WAR
Goytisolo. Juan. THE MARX FAMILY SAGA
Guillén, Jorge. HORSES IN THE AIR AND OTHER POEMS
Hagedorn, Jessica. DANGER & BEAUTY
Hammond, Paul. CONSTELLATIONS OF MIRÓ, BRETON
Hammond, Paul. THE SHADOW AND ITS SHADOW: Surrealist Writings on Cinema
Harryman, Carla. THERE NEVER WAS A ROSE WITHOUT A THORN
Herron, Don. THE DASHIELL HAMMETT TOUR: A Guidebook
Higman, Perry, tr. LOVE POEMS FROM SPAIN AND SPANISH AMERICA
Hinojosa, Francisco. HECTIC ETHICS
Jaffe, Harold. EROS: ANTI-EROS
Jenkins, Edith. AGAINST A FIELD SINISTER
Katzenberger, Elaine, ed. FIRST WORLD, HA HA HA!: The Zapatista Challenge
Keenan, Larry. POSTCARDS FROM THE UNDERGROUND: Portraits of the Beat Generation
Kerouac, Jack. BOOK OF DREAMS
Kerouac, Jack. POMES ALL SIZES
Kerouac, Jack. SCATTERED POEMS
Kerouac, Jack. SCRIPTURE OF THE GOLDEN ETERNITY
Kirkland, Will. GYPSY CANTE: Deep Song of the Caves
Lacarrière, Jacques. THE GNOSTICS
La Duke, Betty. COMPAÑERAS
La Loca. ADVENTURES ON THE ISLE OF ADOLESCENCE
Lamantia, Philip. BED OF SPHINXES: SELECTED POEMS
Lavín, Mónica, ed. POINTS OF DEPARTURE: New Stories from Mexico
Laure. THE COLLECTED WRITINGS
Le Brun, Annie. SADE: On the Brink of the Abyss
Lucarelli, Carlo. ALMOST BLUE
Mackey, Nathaniel. ATET A.D.
Mackey, Nathaniel. SCHOOL OF UDHRA
Mackey, Nathaniel. WHATSAID SERIF
Manchette, Jean-Patrick. THREE TO KILL
Maraini, Toni. SEALED IN STONE
Martín Gaite, Carmen. THE BACK ROOM
Masereel, Frans. PASSIONATE JOURNEY
Mayakovsky, Vladimir. LISTEN! EARLY POEMS
Mehmedinovic, Semezdin. SARAJEVO BLUES
Meltzer, David. SAN FRANCISCO BEAT: Talking with the Poets
Mension, Jean-Michel. THE TRIBE
Minghelli, Marina. MEDUSA: The Fourth Kingdom
Morgan, William. BEAT GENERATION IN NEW YORK

Mrabet, Mohammed. THE BOY WHO SET THE FIRE
Mrabet, Mohammed. THE LEMON
Mrabet, Mohammed. LOVE WITH A FEW HAIRS
Mrabet, Mohammed. M'HASHISH
Murguía, A. & B. Paschke, eds. VOLCAN: Poems from Central America
Nadir, Shams. THE ASTROLABE OF THE SEA
O'Hara, Frank. LUNCH POEMS
Pacheco, José Emilio. CITY OF MEMORY AND OTHER POEMS
Parenti, Michael. AGAINST EMPIRE
Parenti, Michael. AMERICA BESIEGED
Parenti, Michael. BLACKSHIRTS & REDS
Parenti, Michael. DIRTY TRUTHS
Parenti, Michael. HISTORY AS MYSTERY
Pasolini, Pier Paolo. ROMAN POEMS
Pessoa, Fernando. ALWAYS ASTONISHED
Pessoa, Fernando. POEMS OF FERNANDO PESSOA
Poe, Edgar Allan. THE UNKNOWN POE
Ponte, Antonio José. IN THE COLD OF THE MALECÓN
Porta, Antonio. KISSES FROM ANOTHER DREAM
Prévert, Jacques. PAROLES
Purdy, James. THE CANDLES OF YOUR EYES
Purdy, James. GARMENTS THE LIVING WEAR
Purdy, James. IN A SHALLOW GRAVE
Purdy, James. OUT WITH THE STARS
Rachlin, Nahid. THE HEART'S DESIRE
Rachlin, Nahid. MARRIED TO A STRANGER
Rachlin, Nahid. VEILS: SHORT STORIES
Reed, Jeremy. DELIRIUM: An Interpretation of Arthur Rimbaud
Reed, Jeremy. RED-HAIRED ANDROID
Rey Rosa, Rodrigo. THE BEGGAR'S KNIFE
Rey Rosa, Rodrigo. DUST ON HER TONGUE
Rigaud, Milo. SECRETS OF VOODOO
Rodríguez, Artemio and Herrera, Juan Felipe. LOTERIA CARDS AND FORTUNE POEMS
Ross, Dorien. RETURNING TO A
Ruy Sánchez, Alberto. MOGADOR
Saadawi, Nawal El. MEMOIRS OF A WOMAN DOCTOR
Sawyer-Lauçanno, Christopher. THE CONTINUAL PILGRIMAGE: American Writers in Paris
Sawyer-Lauçanno, Christopher, transl. THE DESTRUCTION OF THE JAGUAR
Scholder, Amy, ed. CRITICAL CONDITION: Women on the Edge of Violence
Schelling, Andrew, tr. CANE GROVES OF NARMADA RIVER: Erotic Poems from Old India
Serge, Victor. RESISTANCE
Shepard, Sam. MOTEL CHRONICLES
Shepard, Sam. FOOL FOR LOVE & THE SAD LAMENT OF PECOS BILL
Solnit, Rebecca. SECRET EXHIBITION: Six California Artists
Tabucchi, Antonio. DREAMS OF DREAMS & THE LAST THREE DAYS OF FERNANDO PESSOA
Takahashi, Mutsuo. SLEEPING SINNING FALLING
Turyn, Anne, ed. TOP TOP STORIES
Tutuola, Amos. SIMBI & THE SATYR OF THE DARK JUNGLE
Ulin, David. ANOTHER CITY: Writing from Los Angeles
Ullman, Ellen. CLOSE TO THE MACHINE: Technophilia and Its Discontents
Valaoritis, Nanos. MY AFTERLIFE GUARANTEED
VandenBroeck, André. BREAKING TH ROUGH
Vega, Janine Pommy. TRACKING THE SERPENT
Veltri, George. NICE BOY
Waldman, Anne. FAST SPEAKING WOMAN
Wilson, Colin. POETRY AND MYSTICISM
Wilson, John. INK ON PAPER: Poems on Chinese and Japanese Paintings
Wilson, Peter Lamborn. PLOUGHING THE CLOUDS
Wilson, Peter Lamborn. SACRED DRIFT
Wynne, John. THE OTHER WORLD
Zamora, Daisy. RIVERBED OF MEMORY